Contents

Preface   vii
> The author's motivation for improving the understanding of
> monetary theory and creditary structures. Appreciations of help.

1   **Suppositions and Truths**   1
> The principal truths of monetary theory. A summary of the history of
> money and credit.

2   **Modern Monetarism**   24
> The 1979 General Election brings monetarism to the fore. The effects
> of the attempts to control the money supply.

3   **The Theory of Monetarism**   36
> A summary of the beliefs of mainstream monetarists.

4   **Credit Control by Interest Rates**   47
> The traditional view of the effect of interest rates is challenged.

5   **Credit Control by Reserve Assets**   71
> Why has the intermediated credit supply not been limited by the
> imposition of reserve requirements?

6   **Credit Control by Special Deposits**   88
> An analysis of the accountancy of special deposits shows they merely
> transfer borrowings to the Central Bank.

7   **Credit Control by Overfunding**   94
> Why overfunding can have the opposite effect of that intended. Some
> comments on under-funding.

8   **The Basel Capital Accord**   101
> The importance of capital adequacy ratios. The terrible effect of the
> Accord on Japanese banks.

9   **The Currency Principle**   114
> The folly of revaluing depreciated currencies.

v

10   **Irving Fisher's Equation**   142
       The famous equation of Professor Irving Fisher, MV=PT is
       questioned and amended. A better version is proposed.

11   **The Unintended Consequences of Taxes**   159
       How the introduction of Corporation Tax caused inflation and
       distorted the capital market.

12   **Savings, Investment and Debt**   174
       The belief that savings equal investment is challenged and corrected.

13   **Eruptions of Credit**   195
       The genesis of the huge rises in the credit supply, and the lessons to be
       learnt therefrom.

14   **Planning or the Market**   210
       The failings of both the unplanned and the planned economy are
       studied, and a compromise is suggested.

15   **Creditary Economics**   220
       The study and control of the total credit supply, not the money
       supply, is advocated.

16   **101 Principles of Creditary Economics**   235
       A summary of the principles which are derived from the earlier
       chapters.

Appendix A   243
       Henry Tooke's illustration of the importance as money of bills of
       exchange backed by trade credit.

Appendix B   250
       Graphs of the short-term interest rate (Libor) and inflation.
       A. H. Gibson's Graph covering 107 years.

Notes   260

Bibliography   266

Index   269

Preface

Credit and credit alone is money.
ALFRED MITCHELL INNES

IT IS UNLIKELY that a day goes by without some new development in the credit systems of the world, and therefore a full analysis of all known creditary structures would be a very big project indeed. The guise and disguise of credit is affected by differing legal systems, and at times by the intervention of those with some religious objective. There is therefore an environment of law and religion to be taken into account with relation to what might otherwise be a straightforward matter of accountancy. We can touch upon only some of the issues which arise from the differing environmental backgrounds.

The 'Evolution' part of the present project is a summary of work done by associates and myself and published in other publications, the titles of which will be found in the bibliography. A key figure in these studies has been Professor Michael Hudson because of his expertise, not only in economics, but also in philology, anthropology and archaeology. Professor Hudson's *Institute for the Study of Long-term Economic Trends* (ISLET) has done exemplary work, and I am very grateful to him for allowing me to take a part in it since we first made contact in 1996.

The 'Controls' part of the project is simpler but very controversial, as my analysis of the accountancy upon which much of the theory of the control of credit rests shows it to be of challengeable quality, including much in the category of just plain wrong.

The background

A total involvement in the wide world of financial services, plus practical experience in all industries, including farming, commerce and manufacturing, is the best qualification for a writer who is attempting to describe the evolution and use of creditary structures, and for analysing the effectiveness of proposed controls on the creation of credit. Such experience and knowledge I have either sought to acquire, or it has come unbidden into my life through a remarkably fortunate concatenation of circumstances. Not least of these fortunate events was being born 50 metres from a factory employing 6,000 people at its peak, and all my large extended family and their friends worked at some time for the company that owned it at every level from factory cleaner to work's manager. From my earliest moments in life, the talk around me was of industry. I learned about the differentiation of labour not from the first chapter of Adam Smith's *The Wealth of Nations*, but from being shown, at the age of only seven, how motor cycles were made on a slowly moving conveyor belt. In the 18th century Adam Smith himself studied the principles of mass production in a pin factory in the centre of Birmingham. My introduction to the advanced version, pioneered by Henry Ford, took place 3½ kilometres to the south west, in the 1,077,000 square foot factory of the Birmingham Small Arms Company Ltd (BSA) in Armoury Road, Birmingham.

In the age before television and with radio in its infancy, people who worked together also lived near each other, and were constantly socialising in each other's houses. The talk, inevitably in such small houses with only one room normally heated, was always before the children, and if one was thought to be showing an intelligent interest, one was included. It was possible for a mere child to learn everything about what was going on in the factories around us in the veritable birthplace of the Industrial Revolution. Opportunities for reading were also easily available. Not only did we own several sets of encyclopaedias, but we also had superb local libraries, such as are unknown today. I could study any subject I fancied, and did, but when I first looked at a book on economics it seemed far too elementary compared with the reality around me. I therefore put that subject aside until I had to study it for a professional examination, and in the meantime I concentrated on law, history, archaeology, anthropology, taxation, accountancy, and the organisation and administration of industry, all of which are relevant to a thorough understanding of the present economic process.

In the long run, perhaps the most significant of the learning opportunities which fortune put my way was being allowed to spend three months in the Cost Office of BSA's largest factory and other satellite plants. The Cost Office is the brain of an industrial empire and contains its cleverest staff. I was shown every detail of the processes of time and motion study, the calculations of the costs of every component and the difference between piece work and day work. Adam Smith saw 18 stages of production; I saw thousands, every one costed to a thousandth of a penny. As I had many relatives in the employ of the company, the workers treated me as one of their own who had to be given all possible help in getting to know the functioning of the company, one which had employed 30,000 people at its wartime peak.

More profound experience

While at university I took a holiday job with the newly set up Ministry of National Insurance. It provided a wonderful opportunity to see how the Civil Service functioned, and functioned at a time of maximum stress, for the system of National Insurance came into being on one single day, the 5th July 1948. Every system was new. While I was there it was decided that we needed to know exactly what firms we had to deal with, and the manager of my office asked me to do a study of all the businesses in his patch, which included six of Birmingham's postal districts, and covered the famous Jewellery Quarter, and the Gun Trade (shotguns, not military weapons). I found that there were 891 firms employing more than ten persons, and thousands more employing fewer people. The commonest industry in the zone was brassfounding.

Cost accounting was at that time unknown in the financial services industry, and when I joined the staff of Barclays Bank's Trustee Department I came to the conclusion that I was the only one of the Bank's staff who knew the principles of costing. Yet I found myself in an activity through which I could learn about every kind of business, besides everything about the tax system. Although solicitors do much probate work, they are not equipped to supervise businesses, so estates containing businesses are more likely to find themselves in the hands of professional executors, usually trust corporations like ours. If someone owning a business died, we had to take charge of it, and one could not confine oneself to just one business at a time. One person who trusted us to deal with his estate was himself a probate solicitor, and for a while, until I sold it, I had a solicitor's practice on my hands. The biggest headache of all the businesses I had to look after was a glasshouse manufacturing company. We were in charge for over five years. It was difficult not only because it was under-capitalised, as is often true with private business, but the state wanted 40 per cent of what capital it did have in Estate Duty. Eventually a take-over fight by two major companies took the problem off our hands at a very favourable price.

I had a ringside seat for over 30 years at the destruction of British private industry by badly focused taxation, the slaughter being actively encouraged by academic economists whose inspiration was no longer Adam Smith, but the philosophers of National Socialism and Communism.

One feature of our work which for a while worried me was having to get to grips with agriculture, something which had not been a major part of my family's experience for a couple of generations. My first big farming case was the estate of the tenant of a 200 hectare farm belonging to a member of a very famous landed family. Luckily for me I discovered that the adviser to the owner had misunderstood the advice of Counsel on the interpretation of the Agricultural Holdings Act of 1948, and we got a very good deal for the widow. Never again did I wholly trust the advice of any professional without satisfying myself that the advice was right.

When my employers moved me to the Cambridge office of the Trustee Department in 1964, the Fellows of Christ's College welcomed me to their lunch table, along with other former members of the College who were businessmen in Cambridge. A small after-lunch discussion group formed, consisting of those with an interest in economics. Brian Tennet, a contemporary as a student, was a bank manager who had read economics. Charles Phillips, a barrister who had spent five years with the Public Trustee, had been deputy treasurer of the University, and was the bursar of the College. His business skills were superb. Of the academic economists in the group, the famous one was Professor James Meade, an Oxford graduate in Classics who had turned to economics, had been a close ally of Lord Keynes during the late war. A decade later he was awarded the Nobel Prize for Economics. The group discussed mainly two topics, firstly the controls the government was operating to fight inflation, and secondly the changes it was making in taxation. The first enabled me to expound the bookkeeping principles which the controls flouted, and the second enabled me to analyse in depth the unintended knock-on effects of the new taxes introduced. I like to think that the latter developed Meade's interest in taxation and that he found them useful when he later chaired the Meade Committee appointed by the Institute of Fiscal Studies in the late nineteen-seventies to study the system of direct taxation in Britain. By that time we had lost touch, but it seemed to me that in many important details the report of his Committee reflected my analyses of some technicalities.

Residence in Cambridge made it easy to attend such events as Professor Nicholas Kaldor's inaugural lecture, and when I was asked in 1971 to write on an economic topic for the Journal of the Institute of Chartered Secretaries and Administrators, I chose as my subject the errors in Kaldor's lecture, the least of which was an error in applying a principle of elementary arithmetic. Two years later I was chosen by members of the Institute to represent them on its governing body, and my workload henceforward included the study of every discussion paper on matters concerning financial services which came from either the British Government or the European Commission. Probably the most technically difficult thing we had to do was to advise on the technique of inflation accounting, following the release of the Sandilands Report.

By then my seniors in Barclays had come the conclusion that I was a good economist, and I was occasionally asked to represent the Bank at conferences which involved economics as well as law, the field in which I had more obvious qualifications. The most interesting was a week-long conference at the Civil Service College, Sunningdale, on *The Problem of the Control of Inflation*. Barclays put no restrictions upon me, merely requiring me to report back to the General Managers. The discussion sessions were led by the most important economists in Britain at that time (1973).

Origins of this study

Because of time constraints I have had to construct this book from existing writings which were not composed originally to illustrate the title I have now given it. The conversion process may not have been as seamless as one would wish. Some chapters stem from articles written for fellow members of the Institute of Chartered Secretaries and Administrators. Some owe their origin to an unpublished book entitled *How to Wreck the Economy*. The arguments about interest rates and inflation first appeared in a long report to the Forum of Private Business. I was urged to publish that report, and with massive help from Christopher Meakin, it was adapted to appear as *Towards True Monetarism*, and published by his Dulwich Press in 1993. The target readership was businessmen, not academics, in the hope that those who employed economists could be persuaded to display some concern about the errors in monetary theory which were emanating from universities. Three professors of economics, Hudson, Wray, and Arestis, recently insisted that the book be revised and published properly. At the instigation of Professor Arestis I submitted a proposal to Palgrave, and this book is the result.

Towards True Monetarism was based on the credit theory of money. It provoked research into the possibility of other earlier work on the credit basis of money. Professor L. Randall Wray found that there had been serious discussion of the nature of money in the years just before the outbreak of the 1914–18 war, and that John Maynard Keynes had been involved. Sadly the advent of war seems to have brought the discussions to a premature end. They had been precipitated by two articles which appeared in 1913 and 1914 in the *Bankers Law Journal* of New York, of

xii   *The Evolution of Creditary Structures and Controls*

which the author was a British diplomat named Alfred Mitchell Innes. Mitchell Innes appears to have been a polymath, though how he acquired his education is a mystery as he is described as 'privately educated'. Whatever that meant, there is no doubt that Mitchell Innes' scholarship was of the very highest quality and breadth, and Professor Wray saw that it was important that the two papers should be made available to modern scholars. They were therefore re-published in 2004 in a book edited by Professor Wray and entitled *The Credit and State Theories of Money*. Professor Wray and four other authors provided chapters which discussed the relevance of Mitchell Innes' views. Your present author contributed one of the chapters under the heading *The Primacy of Trade Debts in the Development of Money*. In this present book I acknowledge that I am making use of Mitchell Innes' research and also of the contents of two more of the chapters in the book, *The Archaeology of Money: Debt Versus Barter Theories of Money's Origins*, by Professor Michael Hudson, and *The Emergence of Capitalist Credit Money* by Dr. Geoffrey Ingham. Dr. Ingham has also published an excellent book of his own, *The Nature of Money*.

There had been cross-fertilisation of ideas between these published authors and myself. Another leading participant in the discussions is Christopher Meakin, the editor and publisher of *Towards True Monetarism*. He has lectured about the credit theory of money to great acclaim, but the book version of his lecture is still awaited. Indeed it was his first lecture at a conference at the British Museum in 1996 which led to the formation of an international Internet discussion group on what he decided should be called '*Creditary Economics.*' He and I had made contact in 1988 as a result of letters by both of us in the Financial Times, and we had been joined by an American resident, IMF staffer Gunnar Tómasson, an Icelander by origin and possessor of outstanding intellectual gifts. A regular correspondence, initially by 'snail-mail' commenced.

Christopher studied Politics, Philosophy and Economics at Oxford, and then became a financial journalist, commencing on the Financial Times. In the mid 1990s he became interested in the extensive accounting records which survive from ancient Babylonia, and his thought processes followed the same course that had been pioneered, unknown to him, by Mitchell Innes in 1913. Christopher saw their great significance for the understanding of money and credit. The result was an interdisciplinary conference at the British Museum in September 1996 for lawyers, accountants, economists, and assyriologists. My Internet report on the conference (which was not formally reported) came to the notice of Professor Michael Hudson within 24 hours of being issued, and he wrote to me. We immediately discovered that we had similar views on topics of great controversy, and we formed a discussion group consisting of his associates and mine. As there were originally eight members it was called *Gang 8*, and it was moderated by the Norwegian economist, Arno Mong Daastøl. The Group is a closed one, but non-members can be permitted to access the Group's Internet discussions, and its archive is public. The membership of the group has changed with time, and there was an influx of new members from the Post-Keynesian Thought group run from Colorado University. I acknowledge with enthusiasm and gratitude the great help I have received from all the members of the Group. To be able to hone one's ideas by discussion with scholars of such high ability is a priceless privilege.

I must also express my deepest thanks for the guidance and help I have received during 38 years from one who is not an economist but an internationally respected physical-chemist, Dr. Jitendra N. Mehrishi. He was the first to insist that I should publish my ideas, and his latest help has been to show me the solution of the problem of finding a title for this book.

Support has been generous from the committee of the Economic Research Council, including Chairman Damon de Laszlo, John Mills, and James Bourlet. Finally there has been invaluable support from Dr. Michael Moore without whose insistence I might never have read Maynard Keynes' *The Economic Consequences of Mr. Churchill*, Keynes' greatest polemic.

I should like to express my appreciation of the fine work of the members of the International Scholars Conference on Ancient Near Eastern Economies. The membership has varied from time to time, but the participants who have been of particular help in improving my understanding of the history of finance are as follows:– Robert Englund, William Hallo, Michael Jursa, Carl Lamberg-Karlovsky, Marc Van De Mieroop, Thomas Palaima, Johannes Renger, Eleanor Robson, Piotr Steinkeller, Christopher Walker, Cornelia Wunsch, Carlo Zaccagnini.

The Institute of Financial Services has been very helpful, and as owner of the former *Bankers' Magazine* provided copies of A. H. Gibson's papers and permission to make use of them.

The earlier version of this book was dedicated *'with deepest sympathy to all those people throughout the world who have suffered from the folly of high interest rates. Their suffering was quite needless. Sadly they may be the largest group of people ever to receive a dedication.'* This time I should like to commemorate a single individual, one of the most important scientists of the 20th century, Professor Sir Frank Engledow CMG FRS (1890–1985), onetime Drapers Professor of Agriculture in the University of Cambridge. Sir Frank's name is known now to few, yet in the years 1912–14, he improved the yield of wheat so much that the present population of the world can more than survive. He also masterminded the food policy of Britain from 1940. For that he made use of the research into nutrition done by two other great Cambridge scientists, Professor Robert McCance and Dr. Elsie Widdowson. It is now known that as a result of their decisions the British nation has never been fitter than it was during the Second World War. The significance of Sir Frank Engledow for economists is that the sophisticated statistical techniques created by Professor Ronald Aylmer Fisher for him to use in plant breeding are the ones which econometricians now abuse so freely. I quote Sir Frank: *'Economists use multi-linear regressions every parameter in which is an assumption.'* The written word cannot convey the passion and contempt with which those words were spoken.

Geoffrey W. Gardiner,
November 2005
geoffrey.gardiner@btinternet.com

1

Suppositions and Truths

> *Money is like a sixth sense without which you*
> *cannot make complete use of the other five.*
> W. SOMERSET MAUGHAN

WE DO NOT KNOW when or how credit was first used, as it happened long before there were written records. It might be assumed that there is some very primitive society somewhere in the world which is about to make the big step into the modern era of financial services and that we could observe how its members make the change, but there is no society which is not contaminated by influences from more advanced societies, and therefore the evidence would not be totally reliable. Nevertheless social scientists, including anthropologists, archaeologists and economists are happy to make suppositions and assumptions, and write them up in their academic papers as if they were established facts. In this book we shall try to avoid this error, and will make clear what is a supposition and what is a fact.

The older a supposition is, the more likely it is to be believed, and especially if it has the ancient Greek philosopher Aristotle as its parent. It is unfortunate, therefore, that Aristotle was the first economist, and the first to deduce the way in which money came into use. Aristotle assumed that the exchange of goods was first effected by barter, and commented that many foreigners still practised barter. What he should have said was that trade with foreigners usually takes the form of barter, an acceptable fact, not that barter was the only form of exchange some foreigners knew, a statement not likely to have been true, and certainly not true of the civilisation to the east of the Ancient Greeks, for it had had, for at least two millennia before Aristotle, a sophisticated exchange system, little different in kind from that of the modern era.

Differentiation of labour

A little less of supposing, unsupported by facts, and a little more thought, would have made Aristotle state that the need to exchange

1

goods and services first arose when mankind adopted the practice of differentiation of labour, a major step on the path to economic improvement. Specialisation of function started so many tens of thousands of years ago that we have no written record of its invention. Its importance was not commonly understood, so Adam Smith found it necessary to explain its virtues at great length in the very first chapter of *The Wealth of Nations*,[1] where he uses as a case study the sequence of 18 processes for making pins. Professor George Selgin has stated in a draft book that Smith saw pin-making in Phipson's Pin Manufactory in Little Cannon Street, Birmingham, though an editor of Smith's book suggests that the example is taken from Volume One of the French *Encyclopédie* of 1755. All those 18 processes took place in the same manufactory, but the raw materials, such as iron, had to be bought in, and had probably changed hands many times between the mining of the iron ore and delivery to the pin factory. The chain of deliveries and processes from mining of ore to the consumer of pins must have required trade credit at every stage. Those early in the chain of production would have had a long wait for their contractual reward, and they would therefore have loaded the price to include an element of interest to compensate them for the wait.

Aristotle's assumption that early trade took only the form of physical exchange of goods shows lack of clear thinking. How can a hunter exchange haunches of venison for a supply of a bow and arrows when he has no venison until he has the weapons with which to hunt? Nor could he keep a store of haunches pending his need to exchange them for something he needed, for they are perishable. From the very earliest era of differentiation of labour people must have exchanged *promises* to supply goods, not bartered physical goods themselves. In the very many stages of production, from primary producer to consumer, credit is given to the next person in the line of production.

Nowadays we call it trade credit. The monetisation of the resulting trade debts was the most important invention of ancient mankind, and it is commonly believed to have taken place at the beginning of the Mesolithic Age. Perhaps the hunter gave to the fletcher markers which evidenced his promise to supply haunches of venison in return for an immediate supply of arrows. If a custom were established that those markers could change ownership by mere delivery, that is were negotiable, they could be used as a form of commodity money. The fletcher might hand a marker to the woodsman in return for a supply of wood. The enforcement of the agreements would have been the task of the headman of the village, and he would have been entitled to a cut of the meat as his reward, for all commercial activity in ancient societies appears to have been closely controlled by their elites, and therefore one must not assume that a fully free market economy existed anywhere. It is also likely that relative prices were administered by the elite, and were not wholly the result of individual bargaining.

Accountancy commences

As the economy became more developed, and the differentiation of labour more marked, the task of keeping track of the network of debts could be a big task. The community may have met regularly to recount and verify their mutual obligations. Archaeologists may have mistaken the evidence of ceremonies to remember debts as religious rituals, though one must also remember that ancient societies turned many important economic activities, such as the making of iron weapons, into religious ceremonies, so there may have been no true difference. Was the clan chief a priest or a remembrancer or both? The temples made the process easier by inventing writing and number systems sometime in the third millennium BC. They also developed calendrical systems, partly to keep track of the agricultural year, but also, we hope we are right to suppose, for the accurate calculation of the date on which an obligation became due for fulfilment. Even before the invention of writing, clay tokens seem to have been used to evidence transactions during at least 5,000 years, and over a very wide area. They are described in *Before Writing: from Counting to Cuneiform*, Volume One, by Professor Denise Schmandt-Bessarat.[2] In his amazing work of scholarship, *The Universal History of Numbers*, George Ifrah asserts that the technology of the wooden tally sticks which were used as markers of debt from a very early period, and were used by the British Government until 1826, is the second oldest of mankind's innovations.[3] On page 65 he adds:–

> *The tally stick, therefore, served not just as a curious form of bill and receipt, but also as a wooden credit card, almost as efficient and reliable as the plastic ones with magnetic strips that we use nowadays.*

How it began, we cannot know for sure, as no records go back the necessary 40,000 years. The oldest written records of commercial transactions are those found in Mesopotamia, preserved on almost indestructible baked clay for 4,000 years or more, and they reveal a commercial system already very advanced, very little different from the modern system, which has indeed adopted its legal framework. There may have been equally advanced commercial systems in use in regions of the world where baked clay was not used, and no record survives. The asymmetry of archaeological evidence inevitably gives us a very unbalanced record of what happened in the ancient world.

The Ancient Greeks develop coinage

The palaces and temples of Mesopotamia had already adopted silver as the basis of currency before the time when the earliest surviving written records were made, but it was not coined, nor was it measured by a modern value system. It was measured by weight. The two weights in use were the mina and the shekel. The mina was defined as the weight of 7,200 grains of plump barley, and the shekel was 120 grains of barley, that is one sixtieth of a mina. Modern readers will assume that the people of the fourth millennium BC were already using silver as a measure of value, and that this supports the commodity theory of money. This might be true if silver had a value and a constant one, but silver probably obtained most of its value from the demand for it for use as a means of exchange. It is even likely that before silver could be used to measure value, silver itself must be given a value, and that was done by an edict equating it to a more useful product, barley. It was decreed that a shekel of silver should be worth one gur (a volume, about 300 litres) of barley.[4] The modern reader, indoctrinated from childhood with the concept of precious metals as stores of value does not realise that this decree was probably not valuing barley in terms of silver, but the other way around. By this decree silver was thus given a value, a constant value in terms of a useful but bulkier substance, and that made silver usable as a means of exchange. Otherwise the value of silver would have been very erratic, as supplies varied. Indeed, as it was not locally produced, the value of silver as a mere commodity must have been wildly variable in Mesopotamia. Modern readers are very mystified that cowrie shells were used as money for millennia, rather than precious metals, not realising that the two cases are similar. Both are tokens, given their values by custom or decree. Writing in 1914, Alfred Mitchell Innes is adamant in his paper, *The Credit theory of Money,* that precious metals are not a standard of value.[5]

In the later Babylonian era the market was freer, probably because it was no longer possible to regulate prices strictly. The prices in terms of silver of several basic foods, including barley, were recorded daily by temple officials over a 400 year period. The records show a variation in the price of barley of 45:1. Did this enormous variation reflect variable supplies of silver, or of food?

Silver can be impure, and the weight has to be checked. Both problems can be completely and easily overcome by using documents which represent silver. As the silver is notional, there is no need to check its weight or purity. Thus people had every incentive to move from using silver as a symbol of credit to the use of a documentary credit for silver. the documents were made of baked clay, paper not yet being available. The 'case tablet', *shubati* in the original language, was the result. This was a clay tablet inscribed on the outside with a receipt by a temple for a quantity (weight) of silver. If one breaks open the tablet, one finds it contains a direction to the temple to hand the silver to the bearer. It requires no imagination whatsoever to see that this document is identical in legal concept and use to a modern banknote. The only difference is that it is no longer possible to get any silver from the Bank of England or the Federal Reserve Bank in respect of their notes. As hundreds of case tablets survive unbroken, it may be that no-one saw any point in getting the silver returned, the tablet was so much more useful as money than the physical silver.

When the Greeks under Alexander conquered the region, they found vast quantities of hoarded gold and silver, 180,000 talents of silver, according to Arrian, Alexander's biographer.[6] Did the temples therefore hold enough silver to redeem all the case tablets? We shall never know, but as there is no surviving record of a temple keeping an account of the number of case tablets it had issued, one suspects that they did not need to bother to keep track of how much silver they owed.

Receipts for silver issued by foreign temples of strange religions were of no use for the payment of Alexander's Macedonian and Greek soldiers. It is for the payment of troops that precious metals were necessary, and for foreign trade. Alexander's coins and those of his successors, the Seleucids, proved useful for expanding foreign trade to the east of his empire, and were so well known that the archaeologist and explorer, Sir Aurel Stein,[7] found forgeries still on offer in central Asia in 1907 AD. It is strongly suspected that the first coins, those of Gyges of Lydia, were made solely for the payment of troops. Sixteen hundred years after Gyges, the Saxon kings of England were coining silver pennies, 40 million a year, not primarily for use as a means of exchange in England, but to bribe the Vikings to go away. Consequently more of the coins have been found in Scandinavia than in England. There they were needed as money, perhaps, whereas the Saxons in their own well-governed land were probably doing what had been done for thousands of years in settled communities, using wooden tallies as currency.

Besides case tablets, bills of exchange, sometimes in the form of promissory notes to bearer, were also used by the Babylonians. Some clay bills of exchange declare the name of the payee as *tamkarum*, literally 'the merchant.' One can guess that in the carefully regulated Mesopotamian societies a 'tamkarum' was an officially authorised merchant, not just any dealer. Thus the silver could be claimed by the bearer of the tablet provided he was an authorised tamkarum.

The right legal system

The Babylonian system of 'virtual' money required the backing of a legal system which allowed two things: one, it had to allow debts to be transferred without the consent or knowledge of the debtor, and two, there must be specific performance of the debtor's promise. English Common Law allowed the assignment of a debt, but only if the assignment was notified to the debtor. The Common Law would not, however, give specific performance of a promise, only damages for breach of contract. It took a very long time to cure these defects in English Law, and until they were cured England was not equipped with a legal system suitable for a great trading nation. There was some recognition of something called *International Commercial Law,* which was based on Babylonian principles, but the position was not at all satisfactory. It was not until 1707 AD that legislation was passed in Britain which made bills of exchange fully negotiable, though they had been in use for a very long time. It was not until 1882 that the law on bills of exchange, and similar documentary credits like promissory notes and cheques, was codified by statute.[8] In the meantime bills of exchange had become the most frequently used instrument for the settlement of debts. Scarcely known by today's public, they were for a long time the best kind of money to hold. Amazingly, modern calculations of 'the money supply' ignore them completely.

The currency for day-to-day use

In modern times people are so used to the state providing the currency for money transactions that they find it difficult to understand that this was not always so. As Adam Smith makes clear, in his day no bronze coins were issued by the government, nor gold, and it was very reluctant to issue silver coins. The supplying of currency to the public was almost wholly privatised. A sudden need for silver coins during the reign of King George III, occasioned by war, was met by over-stamping 2,000,000 Spanish coins as British. At that time the Birmingham button-makers supplied the small change of society in the form of copper tokens, mostly issued by the Parys Mountain Company, operator of what was then the largest copper mine in the world. Each Parys Mountain coin had inscribed upon it a promise to pay 'one penny', whatever that might mean, at its offices in London, Liverpool or Amlwch. When the Government finally entered into a contract with Matthew Boulton, the largest of the Birmingham manufacturers, to produce copper coins of the realm, Boulton was left to put them into circulation himself. So great was the unsatisfied need for small change, he was often able to sell them at a premium to their face value.[9]

Mitchell Innes' principles

Alfred Mitchell Innes[10] finished his 1914 essay on the credit theory of money by setting out a number of principles. All are important for the understanding of the nature of money, but the critical one is the third. *'Credit and credit alone is money.'* Another is *'The value of a credit does not depend on the existence of gold behind it, but on the solvency of the debtor.'* That makes state issued credit a bad risk, as the solvency of the government is dependent on its ability to tax, and consequently one of Mitchell Innes' other principles is, *'Government money is redeemed by taxation'.* One could widen that to say that all government debt can be redeemed only by taxation. If the government defaults, there are no assets to attach, and indeed the King could not be sued for debt in his own courts. On the other hand a merchant who has borrowed to buy a herd of cows may still have the cows and they can be attached as security for the debt, or even sold.

Another of his principles is, quite rightly, that the redemption of paper money in gold coin is not redemption at all, but merely the exchange of one obligation for another of an identical nature. He asserts that the governments of the world have cornered the market for gold and forced its price above its intrinsic value.

His penultimate assertion later became the foundation principle of monetarism. *'The inflation of government money induces a still greater inflation of credit throughout the country, and a consequent general depreciation of money.'* One can see readily the historical precedents which caused him to say this, but this is one principle of his which is questionable, for when we look closely at the modern money supply, we shall find that very little of it consists of government debt; indeed most of the huge government debt has been sterilised by long-term funding. There is ample evidence to show that currently inflation is fuelled by new credit creation which is issued to inflate asset values, assets which are bought by private buyers with credit of private origin.

For the purposes of this book, the definition of *'money'* is *'Negotiable claims on value'*. Jurists assert, quite rightly, that no claim can exist without a corresponding liability also existing. So all money is debt, and is created only by the act of going into debt. Thus control of the money supply must entail control of the credit supply and the credit creation process by which the credit supply is increased. 'Money' which is in the form of banknotes, coins and bank balances is only a small part of the credit supply.

For many decades governments, on the advice of economists, have ignored most of the credit supply, and concerned themselves only with the control of whatever they happen to define as the money supply at any one time. We shall later look more carefully at the principles and practices of monetarism, and expose its many mistakes.

LETS

Just as the best way to learn a subject thoroughly is to teach it, the best way to understand a technology is to reinvent it. The technology of early money has been revealed to observers by reinventing it in the form of Local Exchange Trading Schemes (LETS). For a full discussion of the place of LETS in the money system the reader is referred to Dr. Geoffrey Ingham's book, *The Nature of Money*.[11] The avowed purpose of LETS is to make credit available to people who are outside the regular credit system. Members of the scheme perform services for each other, and the intention is that the services provided and the services received by each member shall, in the long term, balance. A credit balance – more provided than received – is signified by receipt of tokens in which each service is priced. The tokens have no intrinsic value. They are given a name, sometimes with a local significance. Dr. Ingham tells us that the Manchester LETS uses the name 'Bobbins', and the Canterbury LETS uses the name 'Tales'. The tokens can be linked to the national currency, as were the tokens issued in the 18th century by the Parys Mountain Company, but it is not necessary that they should be.

LETS are promoted by enthusiasts with great fervour, not only for their economic value, but also for promoting 'social solidarity'. Social solidarity has however always been a necessary concomitant of any trading and credit system.

One thing is not mentioned in the propaganda for LETS; it is a marvellous way of avoiding taxation. Although LETS are a way of creating a credit system among the poor, those who are beyond the margin of the regular credit granting system, they are also popular with wealthier people who are not marginalised by the banking system, but know a good thing when they see it. As taxes are usually now around 40 per cent of GDP, a participant in a LETS scheme can get two-fifths more for his or her contribution than would be the case in a taxed system. Credit Unions can serve the same purpose. Like all tax-evading schemes they are also the happy hunting ground of the fraudster.

To get a LETS scheme functioning, the members need to have an initial allocation of credits, just as at the beginning of a game of '*Monopoly*' there is an initial handout of cash. The system has to be primed by credit.

It may surprise the modern promoters of LETS, but surely the schemes reflect exactly the earliest exchange system. Although one must admit that one could probably not prove it to the satisfaction of all anthropologists, it is clear that the LETS model must be the original model of primitive trade and exchange. The medium of exchange which is used in a community with social solidarity does not have to have any intrinsic value. It can be, and most commonly is, a token currency, and almost always has been. It is when there are transactions between those who have no close social nexus that currencies with an intrinsic value come in to use. They are used to pay soldiers, for armies to buy supplies in foreign countries, and for trade between peaceful nations until more sophisticated systems of international finance are developed.

Say's Law

Studying a LETS also shows the importance of another truth of economics. With the proceeds of the sales of my production of goods and services, I buy yours, and with the proceeds of sale of your production, you buy mine. In the aggregate the expenditure of sellers and buyers is equal. This principle is often put in the form '*Supply creates its own demand*', and the statement of the principle is attributed to the French economist Jean Baptiste Say, who called it 'La loi des debouchées', *The Law of Outlets*. (Some prefer to translate debouchées as 'Markets'.)[12]

When words in popular use are also used as technical terms in economics, confusion is caused, as popular words have several meanings. Some writers have interpreted Say's Law as meaning that one will automatically find a market for whatever supply of goods one produces. That is obvious nonsense, and Say made it absolutely clear that there must be a need for whatever one produces in order to find a market for it. In his law 'supply' means an actual sale of goods or services, not merely having a stock ready to supply, and 'demand' means an actual purchase, not just asking for something. Put the law as '*Aggregate expenditure from sales and aggregate income from sales are equal'* and what he means becomes crystal clear. It is also axiomatic.

But how does the process gets going? Until I have sold my produce, I cannot buy yours, and until you have sold yours, you cannot buy mine. We stand there willing and able to supply one another but are unable to do so as neither of us has any money. In a barter system we would just swap our produce, but as we have seen earlier the process of barter has very limited usefulness, and despite what the great philosopher Aristotle said, barter was never the correct model for the exchange of services within a community with social solidarity, though it might serve the purpose of foreign trade. Therefore the problem of getting the buying and selling going is solved by the granting of credit, and the monetising of the resultant debt. This why a LETS scheme needs priming by an initial allocation of vouchers.

But the percipient reader will say, *'But surely once credit is granted, the equilibrium of supply and demand breaks down. Aggregate income and expenditure from sales are no longer equal in value. Someone has obtained goods or services who has done nothing in return. The economy is not in equilibrium. And what if the debtor cannot pay? He has had a supply for nothing.'*

The answer to the first part of the question seems to be that credit has introduced a time lag, but the equilibrium has not broken down.[13] As regards the credit which is not repaid, the supply bought with it has become of zero value, though the loss may be carried by someone other than the person who made the supply. The credit may have come from a third party. Overall, however, the income of the community remains equal to its expenditure.

Truths about Money

It is a truth less than universally acknowledged that there are but two final limits on the creation of money: they are the willingness of people, businesses and other institutions to borrow or lend, and the amount they are willing to borrow or lend. Indeed most people do not even understand that all money is debt, debt which has been made assignable.

The above truth is the basic premise of the arguments put forward in this book, but there are other truths to be considered. Among them, a third and vital truth, almost universally rejected, is that interest is a cost like any other, and must be reflected in prices. A fourth truth, universally ignored by generations of the economists, is that the major determinant of the intermediated credit supply, also known as the money supply, is the capital base of the lending institutions. Although the Basel Capital

Accords have at last brought capital adequacy ratios to the notice of economists, few, if any, have noticed that they could be made part of an apparatus of control of bank credit.

There are a surprising number of other truths which excite little attention among academic economists, though they are of concern to more practical professionals. A fifth example is the influence of the tax system on the level of interest rates. As will be seen in Chapter Eleven, the introduction of a system of Corporation Tax had an effect in raising interest rates in the UK, and perhaps in the US too, and therefore had a knock-on effect on inflation. There is also a sixth truth which conflicts sharply with accepted economic wisdom, and that is that real investment is deflationary, because, if viable, it lowers costs. Our seventh truth is that there cannot be a multiplier effect from investment unless there is additional new credit creation. An eighth truth, on the other hand, is that new credit creation *does* have a multiplier effect, because primary lending creates a claim on value ('money') which can circulate, and can be lent again, and again. We can call the latter process secondary lending, the onward lending of the credit balances (deposits) created by new lending. That leads to additional demand which creates an environment for a demand for further real investment. This point will be discussed in Chapter Twelve. We will also look at the contention that final demand inflation, effected by new credit creation, is the sole source of profit.

A ninth truth which one would have expected to be universally understood is that the debits must equal the credits, yet one finds that there are people, calling themselves monetary reformers, who believe strongly that there is a form of money which is not debt. One example is the 'Greenbacker' movement in America, led presently by the American Monetary Institute, and another example is the British based Christian Council for Monetary Justice. The pronouncements of some professional economists occasionally seem to show that they too have not grasped the fundamental principles behind double entry bookkeeping. They seem to lack the perception that money is a claim on value, and, as any jurist will confirm, that no legal claim can exist unless there also exists a legal liability to match it. So for every creditor there has to be a debtor. From that it follows that a form of money which is not debt is a juridical, as well as a logical, impossibility.

A tenth truth about money is that money earned by exporting to foreign countries must either be spent in that country, or sold to someone who will spend it there. But if there is a constant net trade surplus with the rest of the world, the proceeds of that surplus cannot be spent in the home country as they represent claims on foreign value, not on the production of the creditor nation. This is a particular problem for the Norwegians, who have a huge surplus on current account from their oil revenues and would like to spend it on paying pensions to the retired members of the population.

There are two truths, our eleventh and twelfth, totally ignored by the supporters of market economics. The first is that the Free Market has no fourth dimension; it cannot plan forward. Secondly it cannot create a successful policy for industries where either the demand or the supply is not under the control of humans but of nature.

The two schools, real or imaginary

Although the truths of economics must be universal, there are inevitably schools of thought about what factors are the most important. Sometimes the differences are more assumed than real. Twentieth century economists thought that the world of economists was divided sharply between Keynesians and Monetarists, the prophet of the first being John Maynard Keynes, (Lord Keynes), and of the latter Professor Milton Friedman. But those who have studied the writings of Lord Keynes in detail will know that the roots of monetarism are in them. The difference between the two schools of thought concerns only the effect of interest rates.

The myriad schools of economic thought will not be discussed here as there are excellent modern summaries which cover the important ground. *A Critical History of Economics* by John Mills,[14] and *A New Paradigm in Macroeconomics* by Richard A. Werner[15] are excellent sources of comment and criticism. With these books available, and others mentioned in the bibliography, all we need to look at in this volume are those points which affect modern policy. That does not mean there will be no history. On the contrary, history gives us understanding so we shall look at the archaeology of finance from the earliest times. For that we have made good use of the reports of the proceedings of the International Scholars Conference on Ancient Near Eastern Economies which take place under the aegis of the Institute for the Study of Long-term Economics Trends (ISLET).

With the help of such historical evidence we shall see that the monetarist trend of the late 20th century was not soundly based. It was not TRUE monetarism, for that would study the whole credit supply, and not just that small part of the credit supply which the monetarists have focused upon. For fifty years or more the study of creditary structures was obscured by a miasma of simplistic monetarism.

The state theory of money

Our first chapter rests upon the truth of what is known as the *Credit Theory of Money,* and it is the basis for a school of economics called *Creditary Economics.* Some might think that the *State Theory Of Money* is a rival to the credit theory of money, but it is not; it is an adjunct of it. The state theory was publicised at the same time, for G. F. Knapp, the proposer of the theory, wrote his book about it in 1905, though it was not translated from German into English until 1924.[16]

Knapp uses themes similar to ours, but he adds a theory that a currency is acceptable as money because one can pay one's taxes to the state with that currency. This does not at all contradict the credit theory, but supplements it, for it shows why state debt is acceptable as a negotiable claim on value. As Mitchell Innes showed in the papers he wrote for the *Bankers Law Journal of New York* in 1913 and 1914, in earlier times people preferred a currency which was based on the debts of reputable merchants, as merchants had assets which could be attached in payment of their debts, whereas the state had no assets other than what it could extract in taxes. Moreover the state could not be sued for debt. State debts, he correctly avers, can be redeemed only by taxation. Mitchell Innes explains that as a result merchants' debts were 'monnaie forte' and state debts were 'monnaie faible'.

Knapp's state theory may have fallen on ground which was fertile at the time, as the early part of the 20th century was the time when the virtues of state control were being lauded as a contrast to Adam Smith's belief in free enterprise. One might even see the theory as a precursor to national socialism which became, under various names, the dominant theme in political economy during most of the century. Richard Werner showed in his book *Princes of the Yen* how the principles of national socialism were at the heart of Japan's wartime and post-war economic success. State control was successful in other countries, even though in Britain it was much less successful. Of course all the countries which applied national socialist policies would deny hotly that there was any connection with or inspiration from the Nazism of Adolf Hitler. They prefer to call themselves democratic socialists and declare total opposition to Nazism, but in practice the social and industrial policies were similar. Post-war Britain was even more controlled than Nazi Germany had been, probably for the very reason that the controls had the consent of the people, whereas in Germany they had been imposed by an authoritarian regime.

Monnaie faible

The concept of state money as 'monnaie faible' must surprise many modern students of monetary theory, yet the examples of failed state debts are legion. Popular examples are the bankrupting of two Florentine banking houses, the Bardi and the Peruzzi, as a result of the failure of King Edward III to repay the debts he incurred to finance his wars in France in the 14th century, despite having the largest income of any mediaeval English king. The bankers should have known better than to make loans to a king whose foreign income consisted of the proceeds of the wool staple, and whose campaigns in France were likely to interrupt the flow of wool from Calais to the textile mills in Florence. A third Florentine banking house, the Mannini, suffered a similar fate later in the century as a result of lending to King Richard II.

The last British king to default was Charles II, who in 1672 dishonoured the tallies he had issued by postponing their maturity. Tallies were replaced by paper money in less conservative societies, like those of the British North American Colonies, where state and city debts, in the form of paper promissory notes, began to be used as money though with mixed results. Some overdid the issues and they became valueless, but others were successful. Benjamin Franklin, at the age of twenty, went into business as a printer of paper money, and published an essay in praise of them in 1729. In *The Wealth of Nations*,[17] published in March 1776, Adam Smith expresses his disapproval of the system. There were bonds in use as money which were expressed to be repayable in 15 years and bore no interest. Smith claimed that one should value such paper money by discounting it to redemption at an interest rate of 6 per cent, similar to the way bills of exchange were valued. He was unable to understand a system which 150 years later was to become the norm throughout the world, with the sole difference that in the modern world paper money has no final redemption date at all, yet still bears no interest.

Smith may have conveyed his doubts to his influential friends, such as Charles Townshend, at some date before his book was published, for in 1764 the British Government banned the use of such bonds as currency. The effect of having its credit system destroyed must have been catastrophic for the North American colonies, and Franklin later told the British Government that the Currency Act of 1764 was the real cause of the American Revolution. Townshend was Chancellor of the Exchequer in 1767, and Prime Minister in all but name. His relationship with Smith was a close one, for it was he who persuaded Smith to abandon his £200 a year post as professor in the University of Glasgow to become tutor to

Townshend's young stepson, the Duke of Buccleugh, a very large landowner in Scotland. The young Duke covenanted to give Smith an annuity of £300 a year for life. In 1764 Smith and Buccleugh, Buccleugh's younger brother, and Sir Alexander Macdonald of Skye departed on the Grand Tour. In France they met the physiocrats and learned about market economics, among other things.

Victims of Adam Smith

Economics becomes a more exciting subject if one studies it with reference to real people and how they reacted to popular economic theories. Sir Alexander MacDonald is ideal for this purpose, for he seems to have absorbed Smith's free market theories and applied them on his own estates, to the great discomfort of his tenants.

Sir Alexander's father appears to have been at the side of the Duke of Cumberland, not with the Highland rebels, during Bonny Prince Charles' campaign of 1745–46 to regain the throne for the Stuarts, but the policy which the British Government introduced after the defeat of the rebels, of having the sons of the great Highland landlords educated in England, was applied to his son. Sir Alexander MacDonald therefore became a scholar at Eton. Whether the use of the word 'scholar' means that he was a King's Scholar, and therefore one of the intellectual elite at Eton, is not quite clear, but he seems to have been bright enough to be one. James Boswell published in his life of Dr. Samuel Johnson[18] very competently written Latin verses composed by Sir Alexander in praise of Dr. Johnson. Johnson and Boswell knew Sir Alexander in London, and were impressed by him. They were his guests on Skye during their tour to the Western isles in 1773, but seeing Sir Alexander among his own people changed their feelings about him. Sir Alexander applied Smith's principles by rack-renting his tenants. When that did not produce the results he hoped for, presumably a more rigorous exploitation of the land, he got rid of them. Boswell and Johnson, in their separate accounts of the journey, mention the emigration to North America which was already taking place. Boswell's account describes poignantly the feelings of those remaining behind at parting from friends and relatives they knew they would never see again. Boswell wrote, 'Someone observed that Sir Alexander MacDonald was always frightened at sea.—*Johnson*, "He is frightened at sea; and his tenants are frightened when he comes to land."'

MacDonald may have originated the Highland Clearances, a long episode in Scottish history which still causes virulent feelings today, and yet Sir Alexander was right in his economic assessment. There was no future for the extremely marginal farming of the area because monetary policy, which made sterling the strongest currency in the wold, condemned all the farmers of Britain to poverty, and condemned to death many of the native inhabitants of lands which were developed to produce food for England's exploding population.

The population removed from Highland estates were helped to go to Canada and America. They were the lucky ones. Some of the surplus workers in the Lowlands of Scotland found work in the lead mines belonging to the Duke of Buccleugh, a deadly occupation.

Paper currencies

But why was Smith wrong about the valuation of paper currencies? What he did not see is that people need some currency for their day-to-day transactions, and that because of the convenience of the medium used, they are prepared to forgo interest upon it. So long as the demand for physical currency and the supply are in balance, no interest is necessary. In the modern British system, the balance of supply and demand for banknotes and coin is always in balance at the point on the supply and demand curve where no nominal interest is required. Sometimes inflation causes the real interest rate to be negative.

The same principle applies to balances on checking (current) accounts.

Having gone to war as a result of having their paper currencies banned, the American revolutionaries then proceeded to pay for the war in the same way. $200 million of Continental Currency was issued by the Revolutionary administration in order to pay its way. This currency went the same way as King Edward III's borrowings from the Florentine bankers. As government debt is redeemed only by taxation, a nation which used high taxation as a pretext for revolt was not likely to be a good credit risk. Not only did the new nation's citizens lend disastrously to their government, the French did too. The French Government loaned $7,900,000. Presumably that figure is in addition to debts incurred to French arms dealers. One of the dealers was named Pierre-Augustin Caron, to whom 5 million French livres were owed for arms supplied. The debt was not paid. In 1793 a delegate of the Congress of the United States fixed the liability at FF2,280,000, but nothing of that was paid until 1835, when the family of Caron received US$800,000. By then he had been dead for 35 years. Caron, better known under the name with which he had been ennobled, Beaumarchais, wrote plays. Bankruptcy obviously did not deprive him of his sense of humour for he wrote *The Barber of Seville* and *The Marriage of Figaro*.[19]

The need for a trade surplus

It is difficult to see how the United States could have repaid its foreign debts as it does not appear to have had a trade surplus with its creditors, an essential prerequisite for external payments in foreign currencies. In this context one would, of course, regard a transfer of bullion as a commodity export, but at the time of the Revolution the US was not yet a bullion producer on the vast scale of a later age when it acquired the rich mineral resources of the American West. The lack of precious metals may have been the reason its citizens had preferred to develop the use of paper money, rather than waste exports to acquire useless bullion. This factor is pertinent today when the US is importing vast amounts it cannot requite with exports, with the result that its suppliers are lending it the money to purchase their goods and services. There is nothing the US can do about the deficit so long as the world prefers to hold its savings in the form of US Government debts. If they ceased to do that, the deficit would vanish. In the meantime the policy advocated by leading US economists is to ensure that the growth in GDP is greater than the interest rate paid on the borrowings. One would expect that the advantage to living standards of large capital imports –the natural effect of the deficit – to be only short term. The facts of American history suggest that the short term has already been about 400 years, for surely the United States had always been a net importer of capital except for brief periods around the two world wars of the twentieth century.

The economic consequences of George Washington.

It is remarkable how events originating in the United States have directly or indirectly had the effect of developing credit markets in favourable environments, or of wrecking them in unfavourable ones.

It started when a young lieutenant-colonel of militia named George Washington lost control of his troops on the Ohio river and they killed ten French soldiers. There was no state of war at the time, but there soon was one, for the French took the incident seriously, and one historian called it *'the spark which set the world alight'*. The first ever world war began. When it ended in 1763, the British tax-payers were £75,000,000 the poorer. Having directly caused one world war, Washington then played a large part in indirectly causing a second. The cost to the French of supporting his military campaigns during the American Revolution proved to be such a burden on the French economy that it may have precipitated the French Revolution. That revolution led to the

Napoleonic Wars, the second world war. By the end of the conflicts in 1815 the British national debt had risen to £845,000,000.

The French financial system had not been able to cope with the financing of the wars, but the British system had amazing success. That was despite the fact that the American War of Independence was twice as costly to the British as it was to the French. How had the British financial system managed so well? One reason may have been the development of a market in interest-bearing long-dated government debt. A large part of the principal of the debts incurred in those wars, and indeed of earlier wars, is still outstanding. Far from being a burden on the nation, the government debt became the assets of the wealthy. One of the greatest ironies of economics is that an indebted nation is also *ipso facto* a wealthy nation. A proviso is that the indebtedness should be to its own citizens.

Monetary heretics

There are those who claim that governments can issue notes in infinite quantity. In the United States the group which maintains this heretical belief are often referred to as 'Greenbackers', a term which confuses foreigners who refer to modern American notes as 'Greenbacks', not understanding that the 'Greenbackers' are referring only to the notes issued in great quantity by the Federal Government during the American Civil War. There is a delusion among the 'Greenbackers' that these notes were not government debt, could be unlimited in supply and yet remained acceptable as currency at full value. Of course they were government debt, and were convertible at the option of the holder into five-year bonds carrying six per cent interest. The Federal Government had learned the secret of Britain's financial system, long-term interest-bearing debt, though it appears to have been promptly forgotten by populist politicians.

The British Government also backs its issue of banknotes with interest-bearing assets, creating the illusion of making a useful annual profit from the note issue, over a billion pounds a year in the right conditions. The assets may consist of government stocks or commercial bills of exchange, but since the British government allowed a market in repos to be established, the backing has been largely repos.

During the 18th century the British Government succeeded in making state debt acceptable as a form of wealth. Some would like to think the secret was the gold backing of the currency, but that was absent during the crucial years in which the debt grew fastest, that is from 1797 to 1821. The extreme caution of the Bank of England was probably more significant, a caution which was often a serious drag on the economy. As we shall see later, the public found a way around it. A sound income tax system, introduced at the same time as the abandonment of the gold backing for the currency, will, in many eyes, be proof of the importance of the State Theory of Money, and the fact that state debts can only be redeemed by taxation as the state rarely has enough other income-producing assets.

The Credit Theory of Money

The essential principle of Mitchell Innes' *Credit Theory of Money* is that all money is debt, of one form or another, but the debts have to be assignable. So when, later in this book, it is stated that a debt is 'monetised', it will mean that the debt is assignable by the bearer, and preferably assignable in a very simple way. Another term for describing debts which are freely assignable without the consent of the debtor is to say they are *negotiable*.

The most readily negotiable money is coins, but most readers will have difficulty in perceiving coins as a form of debt. Adam Smith had the necessary perception for he remarked that if a man had a golden guinea it was as if he had a bill on every trader in his neighbourhood.[20] By 'bill' Smith meant a bill of exchange, an instrument of debt, and of course the commonest form of money in his time. Why should the holder of a coin have the effective status of a creditor of society at large? Because the reason he has the coin is that he has provided goods and services to someone, and he has had nothing in return except the debt token which we call a coin. He has a moral right to some recompense. A coin is an 'anonymous debt token', an expression of which Christopher Meakin, a protagonist of the modern revival of the credit theory of money, was the author. It might be even more illuminating to call it *a credit token*. Both names are valid.

That the holder of a coin is a creditor of society is effectively recognised by anyone who supplies him with goods or services in return for the coin. The coin itself will normally be intrinsically valueless, and its acceptance as a negotiable claim on value is due to convention. Mitchell Innes maintained that all coins, whatever their bullion content, were tokens. Numismatists have another way of saying this: coins have a large fiduciary component in their value.

People are conditioned from childhood to accept coins as being valuable, and it does not even occur to them to question that belief. As already mentioned, supporters of the state theory of money give an additional reason why state minted coins are acceptable; they say it is because the state will take them in payment of taxes. One can agree that was a very valid reason in olden times, but in the present age it is only partly true. In practice the British tax authorities, the Inland Revenue, will not accept coins, but one can pay coins into a bank for the credit of the Inland Revenue. The bank is unable to hand the coins to the Inland Revenue, so it makes the payment by a switch from its credit balance at the Bank of England to the Inland Revenue's account at the Bank of England. The bank has to retain the coins, hoping that someone else will want them.

When coins are a useless asset

If that does not happen the bank has a problem, as can be proved by an example of banking error.

In the 1950s Barclays Bank had a poor share of the market for business banking in the City of Bristol, and to remedy the weakness it made what proved to be a foolish bid for the banking business of the local bus company. What the bank's management did not realise was that bus companies have an embarrassingly strong positive flow of notes and coin. Notes and coins poured into Barclays Bank. The surplus notes could be paid by Barclays into the local branch of the Bank of England, but the coins could not. Nor was there sufficient demand for the coins from other users, so bags of coin accumulated in the safe. Soon the area of the bank's vault which was set aside for coins was full and the surplus had to be laid on the floor of the whole vault, at least two bags deep, so that the staff had to walk on bags of coins.

But the bank was making another mistake. It was allowing interest to the bus company on the balance on its account, even though the asset held as counter-party for part of that balance, the bags of coin, could not earn interest for the bank. After some years inflation raised the demand for coins, but another factor played a part in getting them out of the bank's vaults, the fact that those coins which had a silver content, the ones minted before 1947, became worth more than their face value as money as a result of inflation. Some bank staff are keen numismatists, and aware of what was happening, they swapped their own money for the coins which had become worth more than face value. Melting down coins for their bullion content was probably illegal, but no doubt it was often done.

The ancient Greek philosopher Aristotle had stated in *The Politics* that it was wrong to pay interest on a loan of money as money produced no *tokos*, no offspring. That is correct if one borrows coins and continues to hold them, which was exactly what Barclays Bank in Bristol was unwillingly doing, but of course it is totally wrong if one can spend the borrowed money on a productive asset, which Barclays could not do. Aristotle's mistaken comprehension has coloured opinion ever since, and is the probable basis of the Islamic ban on charging interest. Even though Aristotle's works were not translated into Arabic until the 'House of Knowledge' in Baghdad was set up by the Khalif Mamoun around 850 AD, his ideas may have been known. The translator was a Persian Christian.21 Aristotle's remark was as foolish as it is to hold bullion as an asset, and one wonders if he really wrote the passage. It sits uncomfortably in the text, and may be a comment by a later and less clever scholar which has been incorporated in the text by a lazy copyist.

Bank money

If state debt was feeble money and merchants' debts were strong money, what was the rating of banks' debts? For a long time, not very high, and bankers had to have huge reserves. Eventually, one assumes, the convenience of bank deposits and cheques swung sentiment towards the use of banks' debts. They are currently by far the commonest form of money, and the bill of exchange is now unknown to the general public. In Britain the public's holdings of bank debts may now exceed its holdings of banknotes by a factor of at least thirty times.

Banking was the second great invention in the evolution of creditary structures, if we assume it came after the invention of documentary credits such as tallies and bills of exchange, and before coins. The exact date when true banking, that is the acceptance of deposits and the granting of loans, developed from simple moneylending is not clear. A moneylender lends his or her own money (women financiers were known in ancient times), not the money of depositors, and it not clear when bankers are referred to in ancient literature whether they were just moneylenders. The Babylonian Egibi Archive from 800 to 400 BC shows that the Egibi family were accepting deposits, but Professor Cornelia Wunsch, who has done much work on the archive, has pointed out that they appeared to be allowing the same interest rate as they were charging.

That is not obviously a profitable exercise. But there is a very ancient practice among moneylenders, and that is to get the debtor to acknowledge he owes more than he has received as a loan. In later times this was the way of disguising the fact that one was practising usury, but that has not been the only reason. Besides charging interest a banker may charge an arrangement fee. When a bank lent me money for a bridging loan, they not only charged an interest rate of 6.95 per cent, but also a one and a half per cent arrangement fee which was added to the amount loaned. As the loan was outstanding only for a few days, instead of the six months I had thought possible, the arrangement fee was several times the interest charged and treating both as interest gave an effective interest rate of 37 per cent.

The lesson is that what one reads in ancient or modern documents does not necessarily show an accurate account of what truly happened.

European banking is supposed by historians and the Goldsmiths Company of London to have developed out of dealing in precious metals. The goldsmiths and silversmiths, we are assured, accepted deposits of precious metals, and then discovered they could lend them out. Nice story, but is it true that the dealers broke the law of bailment? It was probably a more complicated matter than the way it is usually described. Given the large part dealers in precious metals are said to have played in the development of banking, one would expect the great banks of today to bear the names of the ancient goldsmiths and silversmiths who founded them, but they do not. Two of the big four British banks bear the names of Quaker businessmen. Moreover we are told by historians of banking that some bankers refused to accept deposits of precious metals. Why? Because it was unprofitable. Governments wanted bullion to pay their soldiers, but businessmen did not need it.

While the Goldsmiths Company cannot be accused of propagating an untruth, it is detailing a sideshow of banking which has been over-emphasised because of the popular obsession with gold. Banking in essence is about accountancy, not bullion dealing. The latter could be left to the Bank of England which incompetently tied up its whole capital in a substance, which, as Aristotle had pointed out, produced no 'offspring'. Bullion is idle capital. When a bank holds gold, silver, or government debt as permanent counterparts to its liabilities to depositors, it is restricting the supply of credit to those other activities which develop an economy.

Accounting

Accountancy is the basis of financial systems, not bullion. Alfred Mitchell Innes brought that fact to the notice of the world in 1913, and it was promptly forgotten. Archaeologists ignored the evidence which came into their possession, and preferred to interest themselves in religion, sex, weapons, art, and culture, while the millions of financial documents from the ancient world lay hidden in the vaults of museums. The first full conference of the international scholars on the specific subject of ancient accounting took place at the British Museum in November 2000, at the suggestion of Professor Michael Hudson and myself.

Throughout the vast literature relating to economics one finds time and time again that authors have a very poor grasp of the principles of accounting, and often get their debits and credits mixed up. An example of the confusion occurs on page 11 of Arie Arnon's book about Thomas Tooke, the great monetary theorist. He describes the wooden tallies which the government issued as *'receipts for tax payments'*, and then asserts, *'When the King needed a loan he gave tallies which were used for paying taxes in exchange for gold.'* What the King really gave was tallies acknowledging that he owed money. These tallies could be used for paying taxes, following the principle that government debts are redeemed by taxation. The principles of this system had been well publicised as early as the twelfth century AD in the *Dialogus De Scaccario*, written by the Treasurer of King Henry II, and widely read in Europe. 22

Acceptances

The final piece of structure to be added to the overall system of credit was making it possible to effect foreign payments without transfers of coin and bullion across national boundaries. This was done by the development of Acceptance Houses, which made it possible to use documentary credits over long distances. Acceptances seem to have been used in the ancient world's great empires, but their fullest development had to wait until the 18th century.

2
Modern Monetarism

There have been three great inventions since the beginning
of time: fire, the wheel, and central banking.
WILL ROGERS

A HISTORIC GENERAL ELECTION was held in the United Kingdom on Thursday, 3rd of May 1979. Future historians may even conclude that it was a turning point in the economic history of the world as well as in the history of the United Kingdom, for much of what was done by the new government elected that day was later imitated in many other countries.

The election removed from power a government which reflected an uneasy compromise between intellectual middle-class socialists, and leaders of the working class, mostly trade union barons. More importantly, a left-wing tradition which had been dominant throughout the twentieth century and absorbed even by nominally right-wing parties, was put into slow retreat. That tradition had become too destructive, despite its very good intentions.

By one of the greatest ironies of all political history, the radical policies of the incoming Conservative government were strongly reminiscent of those which the nineteenth century architect of the party, Benjamin Disraeli, had contested forcefully. In his day unrestricted capitalism, free trade, the market economy, and non-intervention by government were all left-wing causes espoused by the Liberal party. Even the new government's views on social welfare tended towards the Malthusian principles of the Poor Law of the 1830s, rather than the mutual insurance format adopted in 1946. It seems unlikely that many of the new leaders had read with much enthusiasm Disraeli's memorable political and social novel *Sybil: or The Two Nations.*[1] That novel had highlighted the grim realities of the new industrial society, and preached the responsibilities of the rich and the government towards the poor. Three decades after writing the novel, Disraeli as Prime Minister led a government which ameliorated the evils of an unplanned economy by great public works.

The new Conservative government of May 1979 favoured the economic principles of Adam Smith, reasoning with considerable justification that intervention by the state in industry had proved to have the opposite effect of what was intended. Naturally the new policies came to be known as '*Thatcherism,*' after the new Prime Minister without whose support the changes would not have been effected. The election therefore precipitated a chain of events which led to the toppling of communist and socialist dominance of political and economic theory worldwide. Although the term 'national socialism' was avoided by all, the previous consensus on state control and state planning had been inspired by the success of the national socialism of Italy and Germany in the era before 1939, and especially the latter which had experienced a 65 per cent growth in GDP in five years.[2]

Many will see that decline in state socialism as wholly good for the world. It also triggered important changes in the structure of the economy and the industry of the United Kingdom. The consequences of those changes were to be partly very good, and partly very damaging. The evaluation of whether the good outweighed the bad must be left to future economic historians, but what can now be proved is that many of the bad effects were wholly unnecessary.

A chilly start

General Election Day 1979 was very cold for early May. A long and severe winter seemed most reluctant to end. It had been made especially uncomfortable by a succession of strikes precipitated by leaders of public-sector trade unions who were angry at the effect of inflation on the purchasing power of their members' wages. Journalists named it *The Winter of Discontent*. The considerable and longstanding ability of the trade unions to disrupt the economy had been strengthened by the minority Labour Government, which was unprepared to do anything to reduce the powers of trade union leaders.

Many who voted that day had not supported the existing Labour Government, for they hoped that there could be some change in the post-war socialist consensus which had hampered British industrial growth, and had considerably damaged the private business sector. The success of numerous private companies, small and large, was very important to those whose professional experience had included a long and deep involvement either as principal or adviser with private business. My colleagues and I could detail at great length the damage governments could do, and had done, to industry. Indeed, for the previous 26 years I had watched the destruction of British private industry by taxation measures inspired by aggressive egalitarianism, and which also had the secondary objective of making private businesses dependent on the state for capital. It seemed good sense to wish to see the destructive process brought to an end. For many years some of us had campaigned for sensible economic and taxation policies which would both ensure the survival of small private businesses, and encourage them to grow. I had contributed comment to the government on economic and legal topics through membership of committees and conferences, and had conducted economic research of my own, including, in 1971, an inflation accounting appraisal of the whole of the industrial sector of the British economy. For that I had to invent my own methodology as inflation accounting was not yet a settled technique. My calculations convinced me that conventional historic cost accounting was disguising the fact that the capital assets of British industry were reducing.

In 1973 I took part, as the representative of Barclays Bank, in a conference of economists at the Civil Service College, Sunningdale, on the problem of the control of inflation. Primarily the conference was for Civil Service economists, but a few outsiders had been invited, two from clearing banks, one from the Bank of England, one from the American Embassy, and the French Département de la Prévision sent a representative. He was especially impressive for his knowledge and understanding of short-term international capital flows. Discussion leaders at the conference included the well-known economists Francis Cripps, Professor Geoffrey Maynard, and Professor Alan Walters. The College's own staff at the time included Alec Chrystal, who later became a professor.

Professor Alan Walters advanced the monetarist viewpoint, which was still something of a novelty even though it had been strongly advocated for some years by Harold Wincott, leading columnist of *The Financial Times* until his death in 1969, and by John Enoch Powell MP. Among the general public the latter was the ardent proselytiser of the new doctrine, his outstanding rhetorical skill being allied to passionate advocacy. Monetarism, the control of the money supply, was advocated as superior to credit controls and incomes policies.

My contribution to the discussion at the conference was, I thought, original and constructive, but it found no favour, and not even understanding. I suggested that since the capital base of the banks determines the amount of intermediated credit which can be created, we should consider whether the money supply could be controlled by restricting the banks' access to new capital, whether from the market or from accumulation of profits. The tool for effecting the restriction would be the control of borrowing legislation, supplemented by a new power to prevent banks from capitalising profits rather than distributing them to their shareholders as dividends.

There was plenty of discussion of monetarism and so my report on the conference included the following comment:–

> *At the end of the seminar everyone present was agreed that an incomes policy was necessary. Although the monetarist view was appreciated there was no-one who agreed with Enoch Powell that the problem could be resolved by purely monetarist measures. The importance of the money supply was not under-rated but it was felt that a monetarist solution must in the present circumstances and given the present attitude of trade unionists result in high unemployment.*

Nevertheless the note went on to express the unhappiness of the members of the conference with the idea of long-term physical controls of incomes and prices. Certainly we did not have in mind the sort of incomes policy then generally advocated, and later developments made it unnecessary. The last sentence of the quotation later proved to be a very accurate prediction.

Three years later, I was invited to take part in *The Cambridge Policy Conference on the Future of British Agriculture* which met in late 1976. Although officially organised by Professor Sir Joseph Hutchinson, an emeritus Professor of Agriculture of Cambridge University, and Dunstan Skilbeck, former principal of Wye College, the driving force was undoubtedly Professor Sir Frank Engledow, also an emeritus Professor of Agriculture, and one of the most important scientists of the twentieth century. My part in the conference was a dual role of taxation expert and economist. Shortly before the 1979 election a working party of the Conference, consisting of Dr. Michael C. Thompson, of the Cambridge University Department of Land Economy, F. Roger Goodenough, a director of Barclays Bank and a farmer, and myself, had at the request of Sir Frank, published a paper called *Tax and British Agriculture*. In it we had included the comment that the advent of North Sea oil raised a strong possibility that sterling would become overvalued. We therefore suggested a taxation regime which might counteract the detrimental effect of the over-valuation of Sterling on the competitiveness of British industry. Our fears proved all too true, but despite some publicity in the farming press for our paper, no official action was taken to ameliorate the effect of the appreciation of Sterling. Our views were repeated in a book, *Britain's Future in Farming*, edited by Sir Frank Engledow and Leonard Amey, a former agricultural correspondent of *The Times* newspaper.

Commencing in 1973 I served on the Council of the Institute of Chartered Secretaries and Administrators. My duties included membership of the Law and Technical Services Committee which formulated the Council's responses to all government and European Commission discussion documents, and commented on draft legislation. Inflation accounting and company law reform were two lively topics then under consideration. I also became chairman of a working party which considered a new legal structure for small businesses, and I served on a working party which advised on the reform of the bankruptcy laws. The views of both these working parties were later reflected in legislative changes, but only many years later.

On 4th May 1979 there was naturally a question in my mind: *'Will any of the policies and theories which I have instigated or campaigned for find favour with the new government?'* I had long been an advocate of a more market-oriented economy at a time when that was an unpopular stance, and of neutral taxation when that too seemed a lost cause. On those two topics the answer to my questions proved to be a qualified *'Yes!'* Between 1964 and 1971, stimulated by lunchtime conversations with Professor James Meade and by discussions with another well-known economist, Dr. Malcolm R. Fisher (later to be the first professor of economics at a new business school in Sydney, Australia), I had evolved my own analysis of monetary theory and policy, but the new government's conclusions were totally different from mine.

I wrongly assumed that the deep flaws in monetary theory which I thought I had detected, would also be noted by the government's advisers. I did not therefore expect high interest rates to be imposed for a long period because high rates cause a revaluation of the currency, and I regarded a permanently overvalued sterling to be the most damaging eventuality for the economy. I assumed that perhaps only a brief bout of severity would take place, just enough to frighten the unions into acquiescence. However, I underestimated both the crusading zeal of the new government and the intransigence of the trade unions.

The United States had also adopted a monetarist regime of interest rates, with total disregard of the effects on the competitiveness of its export industry.

On the other hand, I overestimated the government's ability to be tough towards organised labour. Margaret Thatcher's first Minister of Labour, though highly respected for his knowledge and business experience, seemed to prefer persuasion to tough action. Effective action to deal with the irresponsible trade union barons was badly delayed. All but a very few people underestimated the importance of the need for privatisation of Britain's loss-making public sector industries. Now it is the norm to acknowledge that detecting the importance of privatisation was Margaret Thatcher's greatest contribution to industrial efficiency. Across the world, even socialist parties have decided that the principle is valid. The person who probably turned the tide of Conservative opinion in favour of privatisation, by pushing the idea with more influential political leaders, was Christopher Meakin. It had little support at first. But once she was convinced, Margaret Thatcher, by her determined action on privatisation helped Britain; and Britain's example helped the world. Overall, though, her gamut of economic policies was reminiscent of the legendary curate's egg – good and bad by parts. Indeed one must go further and say that it was very good, and very bad by parts.

The Chancellor of the Exchequer acts

Sir Geoffrey Howe, (Lord Howe), a lawyer by profession, was appointed Chancellor of the Exchequer in the new Cabinet in May 1979. He put into effect a tough policy for the control of the British economy. It was a policy that would lay waste much of British industry, and especially manufacturing industry, though the Prime Minister and the Chancellor believed that the purpose and achievement were to revive the British economy. Great things were indeed done, which were vitally necessary for industry and the economy, but the aggregate net effect of all the measures taken was long-term damage.

That damage need not have happened.

Although the policies of the post-1979 Conservative Governments are the main objects of criticism in the following chapters, the criticism is in no way party political. Indeed one of the continuing threats to the British economy is that the doctrines which Chancellor Howe accepted and applied from 1979 are accepted by opposing politicians and their advisers. All parties seem to have accepted the same basic monetarist teaching. The subsequent Labour Government, which was elected in 1997, not only continued the Conservative policies, but strengthened them. Because the Conservative Party could not bring itself to acknowledge that an error had taken place, it lost all ability to attack the Labour Government of Tony Blair. Blair was Margaret Thatcher's greatest disciple, but equally devout in accepting her creed was his finance minister, Gordon Brown. Other countries of the European Community also accepted monetarism as their economic philosophy, as have many countries elsewhere in the world. But the latest tendency seems to be for the large stalwarts of the European Union, like Germany and France, to retreat from some Thatcherite policies, while continuing with the *Monetary Consensus* that resulted from her example. The *Monetary Consensus* is also very strongly supported by the International Monetary Fund.

The new economic policy

The keystone of Chancellor Howe's policy was control of the money supply. There are however substantial differences among monetary theorists as to what are the correct measures to be applied in order to control the money supply. Chancellor Howe adopted the variant of monetarism which relies on the level of interest rates to control credit creation, and he supported it by the technique of overfunding government debt. The principles behind these and other techniques will be described and discussed in Chapters Three to Seven. In adopting interest rates as the main weapon for the control of credit, the new government departed from the teaching of Professor Milton Friedman, who was accepted as the leading authority on monetarism. Friedman favoured more direct forms of control. Howe's policy has been continued by all subsequent UK governments.

Shortly after taking office Chancellor Howe introduced a Budget. At the same time he raised the Minimum Lending Rate to 14 per cent. The clearing banks responded to the rise in Minimum Lending Rate by raising their base rates to 14 per cent on 15th June 1979, an increase of two per cent. On November 16th 1979 base rates rose by three per cent to 17 per cent, a record level, and almost a record rise too. Although the level of Minimum Lending Rate set in June 1979 was not the highest ever known, the level of short-term nominal interest rates in 1979 was a record for the century. It was soon to be broken. The average annual return on Treasury Bills for 1978 was 8.06 per cent, for 1979 13.45 per cent, and for 1980 17.17 per cent, 34 times higher than the return in the period 1946 to 1948, a period which had included a grave crisis for sterling.

Market economics

The new government was of course also committed to the principle of a market-oriented economy. The markets were to be left to decide what might be best for the economy, and the government intended not to intervene. In practice governments can never resist the temptation to intervene, and even though the Prime Minister appeared to be strongly committed in principle to the philosophy of non-intervention, not all her ministers were so adamant. Did they perhaps recognise the weakness in market economics, which is that it cannot plan forward in time? Probably not.

Those who are sceptical about fancy economic nostrums accept that an economy is a complex living organism with its own natural balance, and that interference by government is usually based on too poor an understanding of the way the organism works for it to do anything but harm. There can be very good reasons for interfering, but one must accept that in 1979 there was a very strong argument in favour of allowing market forces to have greater influence than had been permitted by any government since the end of the 1939–45 War.

Paradoxically Chancellor Howe's action in arbitrarily raising interest rates was an immediate contravention of the principles of market economics. There are those who think that in a free market for money, market forces will set interest rates, and should be encouraged to do so. The Chancellor's action had the effect of confirming that a Central Bank can, within quite wide limits, fix the interest rate without regard to market forces. In economic jargon interest rates can be *administered*.

Economic vandalism

From 1979 the British government sought to limit its interference in the economy to the determination of interest rates, leaving the rest to market forces. Its action, however, in raising interest rates was crucial. The effects were far-reaching, and turned out to be different from what were intended. Many in British industry have since concluded that the raising of interest rates in 1979 was nothing less than an act of economic vandalism.

There have been other acts of economic vandalism in Britain. Perhaps the most famous was the repeal of the Corn Laws by Sir Robert Peel in the 1840s. That was done in response to famine, and in order to make food cheaper for urban industrial workers. The international competitiveness of Britain's manufacturing industry was thereby improved, but its farming industry was wrecked, causing very great suffering for farm-workers, suffering which was ignored by those who benefited from the policy. Two world wars taught the British people the lesson that to leave agriculture unprotected was strategic suicide, and the policy on agriculture was changed. Paradoxically the effect of the earlier ill-treatment of the farming industry was to make what was left of it very efficient. Chancellor Howe's punitive interest rates had the same effect on whatever manufacturing industry survived his bitter remedy, but the cost in both cases was horrifying.

Productivity certainly, increased. It became clear that the era of full employment after the 1939–45 War had been something of an illusion, and that Britain had almost certainly had much disguised under-employment, an experience, it has since been learned, which often pertains in countries where socialist principles inspire government policy towards industry. Unfortunately the very high nominal interest rates of 1979 and after inhibited the provision of sufficient new productive employment to absorb the labour shaken out of over-manned industries.

If it was high interest rates and not their intrinsic inefficiency which killed businesses, then their demise was an unnecessary calamity. Those businesses which relied on borrowed capital were more vulnerable than those whose capital was mainly equity. The death of a business could therefore be the fortuitous result of its capital structure, rather than of any operational weakness.

If the government hoped that manufacturing industry might somehow imitate the example of the farming industry and become efficient in response to adversity, it failed to appreciate that agriculture had not been brought to efficiency and high productivity by market forces on their own, but had received much outside help. A cleverly executed campaign to restore farming had involved government, the universities, the chemical industry, and many others. Even the British Broadcasting Corporation played a significant teaching role through its daily radio programme, *The Archers*. No such campaign was put into effect to help manufacturing industry in 1979, though various ad hoc policies gradually emerged in the later years of the crisis. The resuscitation of the farming industry should have been a model for the restoration of other industries.

Local government helped weaken industry

The agriculture industry had been given one useful competitive advantage in 1925: it had been freed from local taxation (the rating system). At the same time all other industry was given an abatement of three-quarters of its rate liability. Local rates are a non-wage cost of production, but most of the expenditure financed by the rates has no bearing whatsoever on the production of goods and services. Local rates therefore inflate production costs, and thereby damage competitiveness with foreign produced goods. This point was fully argued by the Confederation of British Industry in its paper, *Tax – Time for Change*, published in 1985, possibly influenced by the earlier paper on taxation prepared for the Cambridge Policy Conference on the Future of British Agriculture in 1978.

The concession on rates made in the 1920s had been withdrawn more than thirty years earlier. Manufacturing industry in the 1980s not only suffered the full burden of local taxation, but local taxes grew faster than general inflation. It was a classic case of taxation without representation. In the United States local taxes were an even greater burden. The votes once exercised by businessmen in local elections in the United Kingdom had been removed by the 1945–50 government. There was no democratic voice to explain directly in local council chambers the drastic consequences of high rate burdens on local prosperity. Many councillors responsible for increasing the rate burden had been elected by inner city residents, themselves exonerated from some or all local taxation. Some were employed in local government. Some were the tenants of housing subsidised by local taxation.

Following an ill-conceived campaign of political pressure, the exemption of unused buildings from local taxation was abolished. Local authorities were given discretion to charge half rates on them, the purpose being to discourage owners from leaving buildings idle. The change in the rating law owed its origin to the vacancy of one property, Centre Point, in Oxford Street, London, a new building which had remained unlet for many years after its completion. The owners, Oldham Estates Ltd, were suspected of deliberately leaving it vacant in pursuit of some future profit. The notion that one could make a profit by foregoing rent made sense only to populist politicians who were eager to run a hate campaign against commercial property developers. The truth seems to have been that Centre Point was not easy to let profitably. By a curious irony, when a tenant was at last found, it was the Confederation of British Industry, whose members were to suffer terribly from the aftermath of that campaign.

They suffered because local authorities in old manufacturing districts tended to be under the control of old-fashioned Labour Party members, brain-washed from an early age about the supposed sins of property owners. These politicians were prepared to exploit their discretionary powers to devastating effect. One real life example of this problem is no doubt typical of many. It concerned a fairly modern 800 square metre factory in an old district of Sheffield which was a mixture of factories and 19th century terrace housing. Because it was partly residential, the planners, under pressure from residents, who included many university students, insisted that the property be used for warehousing only, not noisy manufacturing. There were many potential purchasers or tenants wanting it for light industrial use, but there was no immediate demand for warehousing. After a four year search a prospective user was at last found, and planning permission for warehouse use was granted. In order to tempt the purchaser a price 95 per cent below building cost had to be conceded. The planning consent was then appealed against by the Public Transport Authority which claimed that warehousing would lead to increased heavy traffic in a residential area, and suggested that the correct use would be light industrial, exactly what had always been wanted. By this time the local taxes had bankrupted the trust to which the property belonged. With the next rate demand came a circular letter from the Lord Mayor of Sheffield boasting of all that the City was doing to help small businesses!

Because of the government-induced recession, many owners of factories were unable to sell or let them, however strong the financial incentive to do so. To avoid paying rates, they took the roofs off the buildings, after selling the machinery and equipment contained in them. In many districts it was financially impossible to mothball an unused factory and await better times. It was rumoured that the machinery, much of it out-of-date and therefore labour intensive, found a ready market in countries like South Africa, which had ample cheap labour.

A growing surplus of sites with industrial planning permission brought their value down below that of housing sites, and therefore many of the vacant sites were sold for housing. A knock-on effect of this was the gradual segregation of housing and industry, which, though appealing to many, was inconvenient for the lower paid, and extra strains were added to the transport system, to the detriment of the environment. With no outlet for investment in industry, lenders used their funds to finance the purchase of houses, thereby creating a house-price boom. In driving up the price of houses (unadjusted for inflation) they increased the price of building plots by anything up to one hundred times. The planning system introduced in 1947 had already pushed up house prices by creating an artificial scarcity of building plots. This effect was enhanced by the easy availability of mortgage finance for house purchase in an unregulated market for credit. The planning authorities were doubtless much more willing to grant planning permission for the conversion of old industrial sites to housing than to allow green field sites to be used. To them the dereliction of industry was a heaven-sent solution to the problem of vigorous protests against housing developments on green field sites.

The planning controls on new industrial building, though very necessary in an over-populated country, had the effect of raising capital cost in British industry, and Britain's competitiveness was injured.

Inflation uncured

For sixty years before 1979, despite the best of intentions, a succession of governments took actions which had the effect of weakening the British economy, and Chancellor Howe continued the process. The efficiency which he encouraged was most necessary, but it was matched by the destructiveness of his measures. He failed in his primary objective, the defeat of inflation, and his failure resulted from defects in the monetary theory on which his policies were based.

From the beginning of 1979 to the end of 1983 inflation as measured by the Retail Prices Index was 67.87 per cent. This was less than the 108.17 per cent inflation of the preceding five years, but it still ranked as the second highest inflation of any other five year period. After 1983 inflation fell, but that was a result of the recession and unemployment which had been caused by high interest rates. The unemployment would have been even greater if the war in the South Atlantic had not precipitated the government into sanctioning some additional public expenditure which it might not otherwise have allowed. The war also secured the government's re-election, setting a bad example for future governments.

In this chapter we have set out how ideologies of right and left were synchronised to wreck an economy, and how bad monetary theory and bad taxation decisions were the tools of the destruction. The subsequent chapters contain detailed analyses which reveal the technical reasons why the policies and theories were wrong.

3

The Theory of Monetarism

Money should circulate like rainwater.
THORNTON WILDER

MONETARY THEORISTS believe that inflation will more readily take place if there is an excessive creation of credit (money). Professor Sir Alan Walters put the point cogently in the Eighth Wincott Memorial Lecture.[1]

> *The essence is very simple: if the quantity of money is increased by a substantial amount, the 'Price' of money (in terms of goods exchanged per unit of money) is likely eventually to fall. In other words, the general level of prices must rise.*
>
> *It is, of course merely an illustration, but a very famous one, of the laws of supply and demand.*

Sir Alan may have gone a little too far in saying that an increase in credit causes inflation. This is not necessarily true. It would be more accurate to say that the creation of credit provides the *fodder* for inflation, which may have another primary cause or other causes. Moreover, inflation cannot take full hold unless there is an increase in money incomes. An increase in the credit supply facilitates such an increase, but it is perhaps not merely a quibble to query whether it actually causes it. More fuel in the tank of the car will enable it to go further, but will not cause it to do so.

Money is debt

It has already been asserted that all money is debt. If one holds money, it means that one has claims on value, redeemable in goods and services to the customary value of that money. Money should be defined, as suggested earlier, as assignable or negotiable debt. As all money is debt, additional money can be created only by the creation of additional debt, and debt is created by the granting of credit.

Of course, debt, or credit, if one prefers the complementary terminology, is readily created by a lending institution such as a bank simply by granting a loan to someone. The ordinary person assumes that money cannot be lent until it has already been created (and 'saved'), but that cannot be true as money itself is debt and therefore cannot exist until a loan has been taken up. A bank allows a customer to make a payment which will result in an overdraft on his bank account. The credit balance which is needed to match the eventual debit on the borrower's account is provided by the payment to a depositor by the borrower. The clearing of the cheque which was used to create the deposit will cause the debit to the borrower's account. An additional lending therefore creates the deposit which supplies the borrowed money. One can call the deposit a 'saving' if one wishes, but to do so confuses the common understanding of the credit creation process. The time gap between the two creations – deposit and lending – can be momentary or even non-existent, but the one creation is dependent on the other, and it is the **deposit** which is the dependent creation, not the **lending**. Only a lending which is as yet unmatched by an existing deposit can create new money.

To the ordinary person this statement may appear to be contrary to commonsense, but it is impossible to understand monetary theory until this basic principle is grasped. A bank's balance sheet can be increased by the dual process of making loans, and then borrowing back the money it has itself thus helped to create. In this way the bank establishes a liability upon itself (that is a deposit) to balance the loan. A loan is an asset: a deposit is a liability, a debt. Thus the assets and liabilities sides of the bank's balance sheet are kept equal. It is of course a formal requirement for all banks that they should always be equal, in accordance with the normal principles of bookkeeping.

Monetary reformers get it wrong

In the 1930s there were many very active groups of people who regarded themselves as monetary reformers, and they included some very eminent persons. Many are listed on page 42 of Edward Holloway's book, *Money Matters*.[2] Holloway was the main moving force in the monetary reform movement for fifty years. He was co-founder and secretary of the Economic Reform Club, now known as the Economic Research Council (ERC). The ERC still exists and is very active, being a forum for many economists who are interested in monetary theory, but its origins were more polemical and less scientific. Holloway's purpose was to unite all the disparate groups who were agreed on one point, that the banks had the power to create money, created it entirely for themselves, and earned interest for themselves on what they created. The financing of the 1939–45 War gave campaigners a chance to publicise their views, and a lot of pamphleteering took place. The purpose was to make the banks create the money needed for the war effort, and lend it free of interest to the government. All bank deposits would have to be backed by government debt. It did not occur to the campaigners that that meant that industry would not be able to borrow at all from the banks.

The President of the Institute of Bankers in Scotland, Mr. J. Mackenzie, challenged Holloway and his allies, describing their activities as *'misdirected, misconceived and mischievous'*. He claimed, rightly, that *'It is not the Banks but the borrower — any borrower — who "creates" credit.'* [3]

Mackenzie, not Holloway, was correct. Banks create money for their depositors, not themselves. Their reward is the difference between the rate of interest allowed on a deposit and the rate charged on a loan, but they also take the risk of loss. If a borrower fails to repay, the loss is born by the bank up to the limit of the whole of the bank's shareholders' funds and deferred loan capital, the two together being referred to as the 'capital base' of the bank.

More bank bookkeeping

When a bank accepts new deposits (that is money created by some other bank) which bring its deposits above the level of its existing lendings, naturally it must lend the new deposit immediately, even if all it does is lend it to the Central Bank by paying the cheque into its account with the Central Bank. The totals of both the debit and credit sides of its balance sheet are thus increased. If the deposit originates from a drawing down of a loan granted by another bank, the balance sheet totals of *both* banks are increased. The true origin, however, of both balance sheet increases is the first of the two loans.

A loan granted by one bank can thus cause the indirect credit supply to increase by more than the amount first lent. If two banks are involved, the 'money supply' rises twice as much as would be the case when the new deposit resulting from the granting of the loan is at the same bank as the loan account. Monetarists totally fail to see the innocence of the multiplier illusion we have just described.

An increase in the money supply can arise only from an increase in the level of debt. Of course this statement becomes obvious – even a tautology – if for the word money we substitute credit. In the study of monetary theory we should do so. It also follows that the indirect credit (money) supply can be reduced **only** by a payment which reduces both the deposits and the lendings of the same bank.

The money supply

One customary definition of the money supply is that it is the total of all the debts (deposits and other borrowings) of the lending institutions. Money in this definition is confined to debt which is intermediated by lending institutions.

Money which is to be used solely for transactions could be differently defined as *assignable debt* or *negotiable debt*. The money supply would then include some direct (non-intermediated) debts, such as bills of exchange and Treasury Bills, but would exclude non-assignable intermediated debts, such as fixed term deposits. But the inclusion of some direct debts in the definition does not affect the argument that money is created by the lending of money. What we have called *the money supply* in the last paragraph, we should, in the interests of clarity, call *the intermediated money supply* when we want to distinguish it from assignable but non-intermediated debt which may sometimes be used as money.

The process of creating intermediated debt can be more readily seen if the loan agreement between banker and customer is immediately put into effect by debiting a loan account in the customer's name, and then crediting the money to the same customer's current account. At this stage the two accounts, one with an increased credit balance, and one overdrawn by the same amount, are still in the same person's name at the same bank. The credit creation process has taken place nevertheless. The indirect money supply, and the indirect credit supply, its counterpart, has already been increased. When the customer draws a cheque to draw down the balance on his current account he is not destroying the money, for the cheque will have to be paid into another account, owned by the recipient of the cheque. As a result, the total of debit balances and the total of credit balances within the banking system remain in balance.

In the aggregate all the debit balances of the whole banking system will exactly balance all the credit balances. This is a natural law, even though the rules of double-entry bookkeeping are the creation of man, not of nature. Though it looks like a conjuring trick, money is created in the very simple way described above, but there are still very many people who cannot accept that it is true. Some of them are bankers! The argument ought to have been settled by the evidence of the Bank of England and The Treasury to the Radcliffe Committee on Credit and Currency which reported in 1959. The Bank of England summed the matter up as follows:-4

Because an entry in the books of a bank has come to be generally accepted in place of cash it is possible for the banks to create the equivalent of cash [i.e. credit]. Thus a bank may pay for a security purchased from a customer merely by making an entry in its books to the credit of the customer's account; or it may make an advance by means of a similar entry. In either case, an increase in its deposits will occur.

How to create money electronically

It is easy to overlook an example which clearly shows the money creation process, and which happens at regular, fixed intervals. It is initiated by the touch of a button on the computer. What happens is that every quarter most clearing banks charge and allow interest. Those customers who owe money have their accounts debited with the interest which has accrued. Thus an additional debt may be created if there is no credit account against which the interest due can be charged. At the same time the owners of interest-bearing deposits are credited with the interest which has accrued on their behalf. The difference between the amounts charged and allowed will be transferred to the bank's profit and loss account. If the bank has run its business profitably the amount transferred to profit and loss will be a credit.

This operation initiates credits and debits which will, as is the rule in double-entry bookkeeping, be equal. If the debiting of interest increases the debit balances of some overdrawn accounts, the bank's balance sheet total will increase. The two sides of the bank's balance sheet will rise by identical amounts, and when the Bank of England collates the figures for the total deposits in the banking system for the month, it will be able to announce that there has been an increase in the money supply. Some of those who regularly watch the monthly figures of M4, and comment in the press about the rate of increase in the money supply, seem to be quite unaware of the fact that the crediting and debiting of interest can put spikes in the graphs which illustrate the growth or growth rate of the money supply, or of its complement, the credit supply.

Inflation

It is axiomatic that if a large quantity of money is created (by encouraging borrowing), the public's demand for goods and services is stimulated, though the relationship can be the reverse, demand for goods leading to demand for credit. The demand may be stimulated beyond the ability of industry to provide them immediately. In that case the excess money will tend to bid up prices, and inflation will be triggered. But a permanent increase in retail price inflation is unlikely unless at some stage the increase in the money/credit supply is used to pay higher wages or to make higher profits. The possibility of permanent inflation of prices must therefore rest on whether the struggle for increased wages or profits is favoured by the existence of appropriate environmental factors.

If nominal profits and wages do not increase, then there has to be a downturn in demand until the level of debt has reduced. Thus a cycle of boom and recession is initiated unless wage and profit inflation continues. A higher money/credit supply enables it to continue. But we also know from experience that wage and price inflation can take place without a higher credit/money supply. When that happens inflation leads to high unemployment, because there is no longer enough money to sustain the previous quantity of production of goods and services; the recession therefore deepens.

Attempts to control wage inflation directly have tended to fail since 1945. Margaret Thatcher's government preferred to believe that the control of the money supply would indirectly control inflation of wages, profits, and prices. They believed this despite warnings that the pressure for wage increases was too strong, and that the trade unions would continue to demand and get wage increases at a rate always greater than the increase in production. Therefore high unemployment would result from an exclusively monetarist policy as there would be insufficient money to finance the same physical volume, but higher nominal value, of production and sales.

Monetarists having decided that the increase in the money supply is the cause of inflation, and having also decided that inflation must be controlled, are faced with the problem of how to control the growth of the money supply. They have recommended and used a number of methods. It is now our task to examine the effectiveness of the methods and the validity of those recommendations. The examination leads to results which may surprise readers who are conversant with current dogma. See Chapters Four to Seven.

The flow of money

Let us summarise. A bank may lend money it does not yet possess in the certain knowledge that the laws of double-entry bookkeeping will ensure that the money must also exist as a credit balance somewhere around the banking system. It can therefore be retrieved as a deposit to provide the bank with the liability which will balance the asset resulting from its new lending. If one bank has fewer deposits than lendings, it is a logical and arithmetical certainty that some other bank will have fewer lendings than deposits. In a real time accounting system this would be immediately apparent.

If the money transfer system could operate electronically in real time, a simple banking system which had no Central Bank might be operable. The problem of ironing out surpluses and deficits in the balances of individual banks would be solved by loans made direct from the one with a surplus of deposits to the one with excess lendings. The interbank money market would deal with the problem. But such a direct answer is not always the preferred solution. The final source of funds when a bank is desperate for deposits is the Bank of England. If the required funds cannot be found anywhere else in the money market, by elimination, they must be in the books of the Bank of England. The Bank of England can set any price it likes for its emergency lending, and the price it chooses, in the form of the rate of interest it charges, influences, or, most would say, determines interest rates throughout the banking system. That is the theory, though some may prefer to argue that the Central Bank only appears to control interest rates, and that the real force at work is the consensual instincts of the banks; it could be convention which rules, not *force majeure*. Nothing is gained by arguing the point; it does not matter. What does matter is whether the attempt to administer interest rates is wise, or based on a true understanding of how the economy works.

The money transfer system does not operate entirely in real time. So there may also be time lags which could aggravate the problem of shortages of funds.

The Central Bank's power to influence interest rates is certainly not dependent only on the effect of time lags in the flow of money through bank accounts: it has the support of another important factor. The Bank of England also relieves banks' shortages of banknotes by swapping them for investments. The price which it elects to pay for investments, usually repos, gilts, Treasury Bills or bills of exchange, will tend to establish the rate of interest on those investments also.

Shortages of funds

Conventional textbook theory needs a slight clarification. Popular textbooks imply that banks can suffer shortages of funds which the Bank of England can supply only by creating new money. They have failed to see that all money is debt, and that if debt has been created by a bank, then money for a balancing deposit has inevitably been created too. Any funds needed to eliminate a shortage must already be on their way to the Bank of England, because any surplus must show up in its books once the system's brief time lag has been overcome. A permanent creation of new money should therefore never be necessary. Judging by their private statements, Bank treasurers well understand this principle. A bank can run short of money on its account at the Bank of England, *High Power Money,* as some like to call it, but that shortage is a different matter, to be solved only by the sale of an asset to the Bank of England, but which may be temporarily relieved by a repo transaction. A repo could be categorised as a loan which creates new money, but the semantics are not important.

Another factor in the British system is the Discount Houses. These once stood between the Bank of England and the commercial banks, and they ran what amounted to an interbank money market. Their presence in the market appears to have one enormous defect: surely it blunts the efforts of the Bank of England to exert direct pressure on individual banks. There can be little of the *'Window Guidance'* which is such an important influence in the Japanese financial system. The Bank of England could not discipline individual banks, but only the money market as a whole. The European Union has insisted that banks shall have direct access to the Bank of England, if they wish, and not be dependent on the Discount Houses, but that is only a small step towards the Japanese or United States systems.

The Treasury Bill market

There was another curious custom. When the government wished to borrow short-term money it offered a quantity of Treasury Bills for sale, usually at regular weekly sales. The custom was that the Discount Houses were obliged to acquire any unwanted bills to ensure that the whole issue was sold. If the Discount Houses had insufficient money to complete the purchase, the shortage was covered by a loan from the Bank of England. This practice can only be described as farcical. On page 460 of his book *Money and Banking in the UK: A History,* Michael Collins, a sober historian, records the view that the bill tender contained an element of financial masquerade, and that it was a procedure akin to printing money. The Bank of England, however, was satisfied there was a need for such a masquerade.

Category one money

The Bank of England's power to manage short-term interest rates rests also on its control of the supply of two special forms of money – (a) the common currency (banknotes), and (b) Bank of England deposits.

Professor Charles Goodhart[5] tells us that there is a natural tendency for the national stock of banknotes to flow towards the Bank of England.

Although the balance sheets of the clearing banks show that they hold what appear to be gigantic sums in notes and coin, it is their practice to keep their stocks of banknotes as low as possible, as they earn no interest and cost a lot to store. Consequently, when banks' customers need to top up their own supplies of banknotes, the banks have to buy them from the Bank of England. The banknotes have to be paid for with the second special variety of money – Bank of England deposits. Perhaps for the immediate purpose of this discussion we need a distinctive name for this special variety of money, and a simple yet flattering appellation would be *Category One Money*. Most modern economists refer to these deposits as bank reserves, but they may also call them *High Power Money* (HPM), but the latter term is appropriate only if one accepts an associated doctrine, that of fractional reserve banking, which assumes that by controlling the issue of HPM the Central Bank can determine the money supply.

The British clearing banks could pay for banknotes by running down their own balances on deposit at the Bank of England, but there is a limit to how far they can do this: each bank is obliged to keep a minimum amount on its account with the Bank of England, the amount being agreed with the Financial Services Authority (FSA). The FSA bases its decision about a particular bank's liquidity on stress factors, related to one week and one month expectations. The matter is complex and full details can be found in the FSA Handbook which is available on its website. In other countries the amount to be held is determined in different ways. In the United States it has to be at least ten per cent of the total of checking account balances held by a bank.

One would expect banks to wish to keep no more than a working minimum credit balance on the account as deposits at the Bank of England are not remunerative. If the banks in the aggregate do not have enough category one money to satisfy the reserve requirement, they can acquire more only by selling investments, directly or indirectly, to the Bank of England. The Bank of England has the whip hand in dealing with these shortages.

The factor over which it has total discretion is the price it will pay for investments. If it buys them at a low price, it causes interest rates to rise. In the past it has been reluctant to do that because one of its policy objectives has been to support the price of gilts.

There are other special moneys

When one looks closely at the nature of money one discovers that there are many different varieties of money. Each could be given a different label: there is HSBC money, Barclays Bank money, Lloyds Bank money, and so on. Each bank's money is a special variety, because it represents its own debts. If a customer of the HSBC bank makes a payment to a customer of Barclays Bank, the HSBC then owes money to Barclays. Barclays, however, may not want to hold HSBC money – that is a debt from HSBC – as an asset, perhaps because it can get a better return elsewhere. The alternative is for HSBC to pay over to Barclays in settlement of its debt some of the *category one money* on its account with the Bank of England. If the HSBC has insufficient money on that account, it can be sure that the Bank of England will be unwilling to hold HSBC money in return for supplies of *category one money*. That would make the two banks creditors of each other! So HSBC must acquire some *category one money* by selling an investment to the Bank of England, or to some other institution or bank which holds *category one money*. Or it may borrow from an institution which holds its money on an account at the Bank of England.

Formalised interest rates

At one time interest rates throughout Britain' banking system had a formal structure. This began in 1917, presumably to ensure stability in wartime. The justification for the formalisation, if there was any, must have been that since the Bank of England could determine rates of interest by market operations, everything could be simplified by relating all interest rates automatically to an announced Bank Rate, as the Bank of England's lending rate was then called. From 1917 to 1971, therefore, there existed a full cartel of clearing bank interest rates, and every clearing bank would set its interest rate on its lending in the form 'Bank Rate plus '*x* per cent (usually one per cent), minimum five per cent', or four per cent. Interest allowed on deposits was usually 'Bank Rate less two per cent, minimum a half of one per cent'. Building society rates of interest were also subject to a cartel, being set for both borrowings and deposits by the Building Societies Association. A very few societies were not members of the Association and were therefore free to set their own rates. During the 1930s the banking cartel's lending rate was above the market rate of interest on bonds traded on the stock market, and this may have inhibited the creation of bank credit. If so, it would have been detrimental to the competitive position of those businesses which were too small to raise money through the stock market, for they would have had to pay a higher rate of interest on borrowings than their larger competitors who had the advantage of access to the bond market.

Since 1971 governments have preferred the pretence that market forces and competition determine interest rates. As a result each bank is expected to announce its own base rate, to which the rates of interest it charges and allows are now related. No formal relationship is revealed between the level of base rates and the level of the Bank of England's Minimum Lending Rate, but a fairly consistent relationship seems to exist. In practice Minimum Lending Rate and most of the banks' base rates have been the same. Market forces also prevent one clearing bank's base rate from deviating from any other bank's base rate for more than the briefest period of time. Real cut-throat competition would destabilise the banking system.

The success of Chancellor Howe in 1979 in fixing interest rates at an artificially high level removed any remaining doubt about the ability of the government to control the trend of short-term interest rates. The government can control them so long as it controls the Central Bank. In Britain, unlike Germany or the United States, the Central Bank was then under total government control, and had been since 1946. Total control was abandoned by the government which came to power in 1997, but only after it had stripped the Bank of England of most of its powers, the powers of supervision of the banking system, and transferred them to the Financial Services Authority (FSA).

Despite the events of 1979, many economists were for a while convinced that the market will ultimately determine interest rates. In the Institute of Economic Affairs Hobart Paper 90, *How to End the Monetarist Controversy*, in 1981 Samuel Brittan wrote,

> *When the Vietnam War and the budget deficits of the late 1960s rendered conventional interest rates incompatible with stable United States monetary growth, the whole post-war monetary system exploded.*

His opinion seemed well justified at the time he wrote, for US interest rates had risen to a record level in the late 1970s. Later events proved however that government policy, not market forces, was responsible for the high rates. By 1992 the US had returned to very low interest rates despite an even bigger budget deficit, which happened to be coupled to an enormous trade deficit. Provided it does not want to use interest rates to bolster the exchange rate of its currency, a government can usually defeat the market and keep short-term interest rates low, it seems.

4

Credit Control by Interest Rates

The modern world is filled with men who hold dogmas so
strongly that they do not even know they are dogmas.

G. K. CHESTERTON

MONETARY THEORISTS believe that there will be a much greater inclination to borrow if the interest rate is low.[1] This is an acceptable proposition, for no-one could sensibly deny that the demand for credit would probably be infinite if the nominal interest rate were nil and no repayments were required.

The theorists also firmly believe that banks and other lending institutions will be more willing to create money if interest rates are high. Lending is a risky business and the risks are more acceptable if the rewards are high. Economists therefore assume that the supply curve for money is one which rises as interest rates rise. This proposition too is acceptable provided one remembers that banks are affected in two different ways: on their checking (current) account balances they pay no or little interest, so a rise in the rates they can charge brings a sharp rise in income, a phenomenon known as the *endowment effect*; on the rest of their deposits they do pay interest, and it is not the absolute level of interest which matters to them, but the margin between what interest rate they charge and what rate they allow. That margin is not a function of the general level of interest rates, but of competitive effects.

The two propositions above can be illustrated by two graph lines as in Graph 1. The graph assumes that there would still be some supply of credit even at a zero rate of interest. This is because there is always some need for money, regardless of the income it earns, and there will always be people prepared to lend their savings regardless of whether there is any return on them. Indeed experience proves that there will still be a demand for a store of wealth, even if interest rates are negative, though the graph does not illustrate that fact.

One could claim that the point of intersection of the curves of the graph determines the market rate of interest. The composite graph pro-

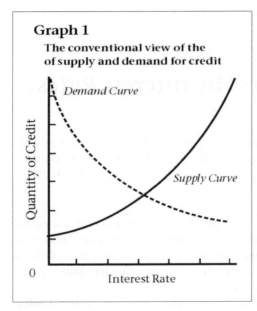

Graph 1

The conventional view of the of supply and demand for credit

vides an elegant, simple, logical, and readily comprehensible example of the operation of the laws of supply and demand. Nevertheless it cannot be correct because interest rates – and especially the short-term interest rate – can be administered: the empirical evidence is that the government can fix them, unless there is some extreme crisis which is beyond the government's control. If the government can fix interest rates, it should follow that, provided the government's economists can discover the mathematical function which determines the relation of the supply of credit to demand for credit, it can also determine the amount of credit to be created. The government would do this by choosing an interest rate at whatever point on the supply curve relates to the quantity of credit it wishes to have created. If that quantity is also under the demand curve of the graph, its determination should, in theory, be effective.

Discovering the mathematical function which determines the position of the supply curve on the graph is not an easy task. Nor is there any reason why the function should be a constant, never varying. Unfortunately the numerical value of the function can never be ascertained with a precision that is better than a vague assumption. The ascertainment can only be completed long after the event, by which time the value will undoubtedly have changed.

An untenable theory

Unless the function is variable over an extremely wide spectrum, a phenomenon which would make any attempt to use it quite hopeless, the empirical evidence of two separate twelve-year periods leads one to the firm conclusion that the theory does not work.

During the twelve years following 1948 the Bank Rate was never higher than 7 per cent. During the twelve years succeeding 1979 the Minimum

Lending Rate, the modern name for Bank Rate, never fell below 7½ per cent. If the theory were correct there would have been lower inflation in the later period than in the earlier, and a slower growth of the money supply. Sadly for the arm-chair theorists, the opposite was true: both inflation and the level of bank deposits grew more slowly in the first period than in the second. Clearly influences must have been at work which over-rode the supposed effect of interest rates, or alternatively, there were factors which caused the supply and demand functions which pertained in the two periods to be very different from one another.

In the twelve years which followed Chancellor Howe's action in 1979, the Retail Prices Index (RPI) showed about 150 per cent inflation. In the twelve year period which commenced in 1948 the RPI registered 46 per cent inflation, and London clearing bank deposits grew by no more than an average of two per cent per annum. Their growth was lowest when interest rates were lowest. Two per cent was well below the growth rate of the Gross National Product. In the period 1979–91 the popular measure of the money supply was corrected to include building society deposits, for they had come to constitute a vast share of the money supply. The new measure, known as M4, was recorded by the Office for National Statistics from 1985 only. Its growth in the three years ending the 31st December 1990 was very large. A growth rate of 18 per cent per annum of this, or earlier, monetary indicators was quite common throughout the whole period of comparison. That rate was several times greater than the growth rate of the economy (GNP), quite the reverse of what happened from 1948 to 1960.

Thus the empirical evidence suggests that the measures which were supposed to stop the intermediated money supply from increasing rapidly were causing it to grow very fast, thus providing the fodder for inflation. Unfortunately some supporters of the policy adopted by Chancellor Howe reject this interpretation of the empirical evidence. They are firmly convinced of the truth of their theory, no matter how much it is discredited by real events. They will not look for the reasons for their errors, so we must do it for them.

The real demand for credit

The theorists had neglected to take into account the interaction between the separate influences which determine the supply and demand curves; the supply function and the demand function are not independent of one another. The public's willingness to take up credit is not an inbuilt, genetically-determined instinct, unaffected by the environment. On the contrary the public's desire for credit can be strongly influ-

Graph 2

Bank marketing can make this happen

Demand Curve

Quantity of Credit

Supply curve

0

Interest rate

enced by an environment of good salesmanship, and effective advertising and marketing. As was clearly seen in the late 1980s, whenever high interest rates make lending very profitable, lenders do not wait for the borrowers to appear. They go out and find them. The pressure they bring upon potential borrowers clearly tilts the demand curve around so that it goes up as interest rates rise, not down. The true graph may look very roughly as in Graph 2, and certainly not as in Graph 1.

It may well be that it is only lack of capacity to service a debt which eventually discourages borrowing, rather than a high rate of interest itself. Admittedly a high rate of interest will lower the borrower's capacity to service loans, but the empirical evidence is that the propensity to borrow seems to resist the influence of high rates of interest for much longer than the theorists expected, and for much longer than is safe.

How the standard theory arose

On one occasion when the Bank of England had recently raised interest rates, I asked a businessman what his reaction was to the higher rate. *'Interest is a cost like any other, and will be reflected in my prices.'* His response has many precedents. In the seventeenth century English merchants complained that the Dutch merchants had an advantage from the fact that they had the benefit of paying lower rates of interest than the English and could therefore set lower prices. In 1621 Sir Thomas Culpeper wrote *Tract against the High Rate of Usurie.* In 1668 his son, another Sir Thomas Culpeper republished the tract with one of his own with the enormously long title, *A Discourse showing the many Advantages that will accrue to this Kingdom by the Abatement of Usury together with the Absolute Necessity of reducing Interest of Money to the lowest Rate it bears in other Countreys.* Clearly the importance of low rates of interest on competitiveness was well understood. Why, when and how did that understanding vanish?

The belief that lower interest rates could lead to lower prices caused many to agitate for legislation to set a maximum rate of four per cent. John Locke went berserk at this proposal and, in a very wordy and overlong paper he published in 1691, he showed that it was impossible to enforce such a law. Nevertheless Usury Laws were later enacted, and the maximum rate was fixed at five per cent. The Bank of England's official discount rate, the *Bank Rate*, remained at five per cent from 1746 to 1826. This was however a purely notional rate, as actual discounts took place at a much lower rate.

In 1832 a Parliamentary Committee was appointed under the chairmanship of Viscount Althorp to look into the question of the effect of interest rates as part of a review of the banking system and the continuation of the Bank of England's charter. One consequence of the review was the repeal of the Usury Laws in 1833, though some limits were retained. The committee was very thorough in its enquiry. The printed report of the committee is held in the archives of the Bank of England as part of the records of *The Committee of Secrecy*. Over 5,300 questions were asked and among those whose gave answers are famous names like 'Mr Baring' and 'Mr Rothschild,' but the person whose answers had the most malign long-term effect was J. Horsley Palmer, Governor of the Bank of England. He replied to the first 913 questions.

It was question 678 which had the profoundest effect on academic economists, and it is still of world importance today. It read as follows:–

678. What is the process by which the Bank would calculate upon rectifying the Exchange, by means of a reduction of its issues?

The answer was:–

The first operation is to increase the value of money; with the increased value of money there is less facility obtained by the commercial Public in the discount of their paper; that naturally tends to limit transactions and to the reduction of prices; the reduction of prices will so far alter our situation with foreign countries, that it will be no longer an object to import, but the advantage will rather be upon the export, the gold and silver will then come back into the country, and rectify the contraction that previously existed.

This answer was taken to mean that if one raises interest rates there are fewer borrowers, therefore less money available to pay for goods and services, and therefore prices fall. The rest of the answer is wrong.

Joseph A. Schumpeter, in his study of *Money, Credit and Cycles* which is chapter seven of his *History of Economic Analysis*, discusses Palmer's evidence:–

> *Slightly reformulating Palmer's answer to question 678, we may put it like this. Accepting an unfavourable turn of foreign exchanges as a sign of an 'unduly' great expansion of credit, he averred that the Bank could prevent or stop an outflow of gold by raising its rate: the increased rate would reduce borrowing; reduced borrowing would mean a smaller volume of transactions and employment, and lower prices; reduced prices would increase exports and decrease imports; and this would turn the balance of payments, hence exchange rates. It is gratifying to note that this proposition does not stand in the name of some professor of economics. But it sounded too academic for professors to miss it. And it became the basis of the 'classic' theory of central-bank policy as taught in nineteenth century textbooks. The much more important short-run effect of an increase in bank rate—that it will attract short balances from abroad—was also discovered as we shall see.*[2]

It is doubtful if any statement of economic analysis has had more effect than the answer to question 678. The monetary policy committees of the Central Banks of all the great industrial nations are expected to take Palmer's thesis as sacrosanct. To question it is to invite incredulity.

Other answers of Palmer seem to back up his thesis:–

159. Have you ever seen that alteration in the market rate of interest, that discounting at five percent, the extent to which the law enables you to go, would not meet?

Not since the peace. (That will be the peace of 1815.)

160. Suppose there was no maximum rate of interest, could you check the demand for discount, gradually advancing the rate of interest?

Yes I think that in such a case, by advancing the rate of interest, that affect (sic) might be produced.

At the time the maximum legal rate of interest was five per cent. Bank rate had remained at that level from 1746 to 1826. Palmer had experimented with a four per cent rate between 1826 and 1832. But Bank Rate does not seem to have been applied. The Bank discounted at lower rates.

The answers to the next two questions provide some empirical evidence about the effect of raising interest rates. They totally conflict with Palmer's later assertion in answer 678, showing that what he says later is mere armchair theorising, and has no empirical basis.

161. In 1825, during the height of the panic, when you raised the interest to 5 percent, what effect did that produce?

None whatever.

162. Do you mean that the same amount of discount took place after that as before?

Yes, I should think at that period a much larger amount of discounts.

163. What was the reason at that time that induced the bank to raise it?

I was not on the Court at that time. I cannot answer the question.

170. Do you think it desirable for the Bank should vary frequently their rate of interest with the alteration in the market rate?

No, I think not. I am of a opinion that with the object of keeping their security fixed and steady in amount, it is not desirable frequently to vary the Bank's public rate of interest; I should deem it to be preferable that the Bank's public rate of interest should be generally above the market, and thereby not interfere with the employment of money actually in existence.

171. Have there been periods when the bank's rate of interest has been considerably above the market rate of interest, of late years, and what has been the effect?

Yes, and the effect has been that the Bank have had very little demand for discounts, special cases excepted, for some years past, in the London markets.

Other answers show that that meant that the country banks got the discounting business which the Bank of England priced out of its reach.

370 Have you any idea that the banks can mount a larger circulation in their discounts than the wants of the country of the time require?

No.

One would love to know how he came to that conclusion. It sounds as though he is saying that the credit supply is determined by the needs of the economy, an opinion later adopted by some monetary theorists.

380. Is it not your view that single articles have their prices affected frequently by circumstances wholly unconnected with the state of circulation; but when all commodities together are affected and affected in the same ratio, then you suppose that to arise from something that has been done with the money, and not to arise from the particular articles?

Yes.

382. Do you hold that the interest of money depends upon the amount of money in circulation?

No; I mean that the effect upon the interest of money is the first effect produced by the contraction or expansion of the circulation, but that as soon as the prices are adjusted by the state of circulation the rate of interest may be high or maybe low, according to the nature of the demand for money.

Does he mean that a new equilibrium position is attained?

383. Then your opinion is, that the interest money, regulated as most other commodities are, by the supply and demand, and that

the money maybe increased in its extent without diminishing the rate of interest?

Certainly, the rate of interest maybe high and the currency may at the same time be depreciated.

That conflicts with other answers, but is probably right. But there is an underlying assumption that the market decides interest rates by balancing supply and demand for credit. But only secondary lending is affected by supply constraints. The supply of primary credit (newly created credit) is potentially infinite, and only prudential considerations restrict it.

384. What do you mean by depreciated?

I mean when its state is exhibited by an unfavourable exchange.

It is clear from the tenor of the enquiry that Palmer was dealing with a very different state of affairs from what we know. The Bank's rate of interest did not affect market rates generally, so the fact that the rate stood at 5 per cent from 1746 to 1826 is not significant. Market discount rates could still be in the range 2.5 to 4 per cent. The Bank of England was the capital's bank, and was in competition with the country banks outside London. Gold and notes were of course interchangeable, the most important difference of all. Palmer's approach is mostly practical, and not imbued with dogma, so some of his statements do not accord with modern theory.

Palmer's only empirical evidence, that in his answers to questions 161 and 162, has been ignored by almost all academics; they have preferred to adopt an intellectually satisfying theory, and ignore the fact that all empirical evidence is against it. They also ignored the arguments of Henry Tooke that if the interest rates in one country are higher than in others, then money/credit is attracted into that country, and prices will rise.3 Conversely, if the interest is lower, then money will be driven abroad. The empirical evidence for this contention became obvious to all in the late 1990s. Japan had low rates of interest, and a stagnant economy as money/credit flowed to America and Great Britain where interest rates were higher. The flow of credit financed flows of goods and both America and Great Britain experienced growing trade deficits. Employment was high in both countries as people were employed to distribute the imports.

Internal costs rose, but the consequent inflation was masked by the lowering of import prices due to high exchange rates, themselves an effect, exactly as Palmer stated in his early answers, of higher interest rates. Import prices also tended to fall because the demand induced in Britain and America lowered unit costs of the exporting countries.

Palmer's Rule

In my cursory investigation of the Minutes of the Secrecy Committee of the Bank of England and the 5,300 questions asked, I did not find any mention of *'Palmer's Rule'*, the rule which Schumpeter says was adopted in 1827, *'namely the rule to keep the Bank's "securities" (discounts, loans, investments) approximately constant so that changes in the circulation would occur only as gold flowed onto or out of the country and circulation would behave as if it were wholly metallic. This rule – not meant to be obeyed strictly – anticipated the principle of Peel's Act to some extent.'*

It is difficult to believe that Palmer could have been so stupid, as the British economy was dramatically advancing and he would by this act condemn it to deflation. If it **was** followed, then we can see why there was so much economic distress later. However, I am inclined to think that the effect was small as the public found another way of creating the liquidity that was needed.

The answer is found in Tooke's paper of 1844 in which he gives the figures for the clearing. More about that later. See Appendix A.

Keynes steps in

Palmer's theory became dogma, but it was of little significance during the rest of the 19th century, as no attempt was made to make use of it. Prices tended to fall because there was so much technical innovation. In 1801 Marc Brunel designed the first machine tools for mass production to be made entirely of metal and thereby reduced the labour costs of making rigging blocks for the Royal Navy by 90 per cent. His example was followed, and price deflation accelerated. From then on the norm was deflation, not inflation, except during wars and the post 1939–45 War era. Wars always cause inflation, and the 1914–18 War repeated the inflationary experience of the Napoleonic Wars. Preparation for war brought inflation back in 1938, but really severe inflation did not take place until the policy of defeating it with very high interest rates was adopted.

John Maynard Keynes was one of those who needed a new job after the 1914–18 War, and he determined that his would be that of economic publicist. What better way of making one's mark than by urging an outrageous proposal. In 1920 Keynes called for an eight per cent Bank Rate to ward off inflation. 10 per cent was the highest rate ever set. Only once had Bank Rate been set that high. It was for seven days only at the commencement of the 1914–18 War, and the purpose was to deal with a banking crisis caused by bills of exchange drawn on enemy countries becoming worthless. Keynes later called for a rate of 10 per cent. Montague Norman, Governor of the Bank of England, supported him, but Austen Chamberlain, the Chancellor of the Exchequer, vetoed it.[4]

Keynes' calls may have been ignored at first, but a little later Bank Rate was raised to 7 per cent, and kept at that level for ten months. The effects on employment were horrific, and Keynes denied that he had ever intended anything so severe. Prices did come down, but only because a dramatic recession was induced just at the time when industry was trying to switch from wartime production to peacetime needs. Easy credit was desperately needed for that purpose. Production fell by 15 per cent.

Keynes' misgivings about a high interest rate were immeasurably enhanced when in January 1923 he opened the Bankers' Magazine, and perused an article headed *The Future Course of High Class Investment Values*. It was written by A. H. Gibson of Harrogate, author of a textbook about Bank Rate. The title gave no indication of its importance for monetary theory. Perhaps Keynes read it only because he was interested in stock market investment.[5] Gibson argued that the price of gilts would depend on the long-term interest rate, and that in turn would be determined by the level of wholesale prices, for his research indicated that the long-term interest rate and the trend of inflation were positively correlated. To substantiate his point he produced statistics for 131 years, 100 years of which were illustrated by a graph.

Gibson would have found the modern theory of the relationship of interest rates and inflation rather curious. He suggested that low interest rates on gilts encouraged the application of savings to real investment in the hope of a better return. Real investment (research and development, plant, machinery, and other productive assets), if effective, should reduce real prices because it should lower production costs. Gibson's reason for the fall in the prices of basic commodities at the time he was writing was the big investment made in food and raw material producing countries in the period 1907–13. He states,

All economic history proves that the cost of foodstuffs, for man and beast, regulates, directly or indirectly, the ultimate costs of commodities in general consumption.

At the time he was writing food was 60 per cent of workers' expenditure. In the later decades of the twentieth century it has perhaps been more correct to say that the cost of energy, and especially oil, is the ultimate regulator of costs (if indeed there is one).

Keynes must have received a shattering surprise from Gibson's paper. It caused him to do some research of his own, and he found that the correlation was true, and, to a lesser extent, of short-term interest rates too. In 1930 he published *The Treatise on Money.* On page 198 of the second volume Keynes makes this fascinating comment on Gibson's theory,

> *The Gibson Paradox – as we may fairly call it – is one of the most completely established empirical facts within the whole field of quantitative economics though theoretical economists have mostly ignored it.*

Expanding Gibson's own figures, Keynes prints a comparison of the yield on Consols with the wholesale price index for the period 1791 to 1928. The two sets of data march in step. It is more than likely that the data could be extended up to the present day with the same high correlation that Keynes revealed except for the unusual wartime period, 1939 to 1946; but even during five of those seven years, throughout which Bank Rate was kept at two per cent, the rate of price increases was remarkably low by the standard of the 1980s. As the level of interest rates between 1940 and 1946 was strongly influenced by Keynes, who was a director of the Bank of England, he must have applied *Gibson's Paradox* as part of his successful anti-inflationary strategy. During the period Keynes was at The Treasury, 1940–45, total official inflation was 9½ per cent, a remarkable achievement.

It is long-term interest rates which the *Gibson Paradox* correlates with prices. The correlation, which was very high, was not quite so strong for short-term rates of interest. One interesting thing about Gibson's data is that it clearly shows that the rise in interest rates follows the rise in prices, not the other way around. This is surprising as one expects rising interest rates to push up prices. The much higher interest rates of more recent times certainly pushed up both costs and prices, but it is a one-off effect.

Price variations which arise from natural variations in costs of production, such as the variation brought about by investment in more efficient machinery, are quite a different thing from what we now know as inflation and deflation. Inflation, which was the main bugbear of the second half of the twentieth century, is not necessarily a rational phenomenon. It may have very little to do with underlying costs. Instead it may have as one of its main causes excess demand arising from the unregulated creation of credit. One can see a dilemma: even if it were true that high interest rates discourage the creation of credit, it would still also be true that they discourage the investment which might reduce real costs of production and expand the economy. Surely the latter objective is more important than the former? However, if the monetarist economists are wrong, as the empirical evidence seems to suggest, and high interest rates cause both inflationary **and** real price rises, and they also lower the rate of investment, one threatens the economy with a triple jeopardy whenever one raises interest rates in pursuance of an erroneous monetary theory.

Keynes and the Paradox

Keynes' reference to Gibsons's Paradox is in the second volume of his Treatise on Money. Volume one, which is the least satisfactory part of the work, reveals little evidence that he was yet taking note of Gibson's Paradox. It could be argued that what is bad in modern monetary theory has its origin in volume one of the *Treatise on Money*, except that Keynes is, very wisely, much more cautious than later theorists have been. At page 132 he writes,

> *It is even conceivable that the cash deposits may remain the same, the velocities of circulation may remain the same, and the volume of output may remain the same: yet the fundamental price levels may change.*[6]

On page 194 he states,

> *There is no simple or invariable relation between the effect of an alteration of Bank Rate on the price level, whether of liquid consumption goods or of output as a whole, and the associated alteration in the quantity of bank money.*

Yet if Figure 2 is the correct graphical representation of the inter-relation of the credit supply and demand curves with the interest rate, the theory of credit control by interest rates is, in its simplest form, untenable. As all the empirical evidence tends very strongly to support our graph, there is a strong case for revising, or refining, the theory of credit control. Also we must look for an alternative method of control which does the job without the need to resort to absurdly high rates of interest. The next step, therefore, is to examine whether there is greater virtue in the method which uses reserve assets as a means of controlling credit creation. This we shall do in the Chapter Five.

Some modern empirical evidence

Three graphs in Appendix B show the relationship over a 22 year period of three month interbank interest rates to the rolling figure for annual inflation at monthly intervals. They appear to show an immediate positive relationship between the two sets of data.

The standard belief is that the solution to the interpretation of the data is to lag the inflation effect by 18 months, and this should make the correlation negative, not positive. For short-term effects the lag makes the graphs sometimes give the result which modern monetary theory predicts. Does that mean that a Gibson graph is totally misleading? Gibson, I accept, would interpret these graphs, as with his own, as showing interest rates following slightly after prices. Unfortunately for the mainstream theorists, the long-term trend of the graphs shows very clearly that low inflation is associated with low interest rates, whatever may happen in the short term. Moreover there are some surprising anomalies in the graphs when the lag is introduced. Sometimes it does indeed show a dramatic fall in inflation in response to high interest rates, especially if the high rates have caused a recession, but at other points on the graph the correlation is completely the opposite. On the other hand, if is it assumed there is no lag, the correlation remains much more consistent, and it is positive.

One must also ask whether the 18 month lag preferred by mainstream monetarists is a justifiable assumption. There is as yet no proven answer to that question.

One cannot in fact deduce with certainty the existence of a lag or the lack of one from a graph; it has to be demonstrated by external evidence. One way of testing the existence of a lag would be to poll all businesses, asking them what is their reaction to an increase in interest rates: do they immediately try to raise prices in order to maintain the level of profit? For 15 years no University Department of Economics accepted my suggestion that such research be done. In 2005 one department accepted the idea, but at the time of writing has not found the funding for the research.

Note that the graph indicates that sometimes inflation rises slightly in advance of an interest rate rise. That was especially true in 1988. This phenomenon needs to be researched. One can however suggest an explanation: finance directors can easily tell when there is a likelihood of a rise in interest rates, and their correct reaction should be to raise prices before it takes place. That is the sensible policy to instruct managers of the businesses to follow. It was my own policy.

The Cost Channel of Monetary Transmission

The above was the title of a paper published in June 2001 by Marvin J. Barth III, of the Federal Reserve Board of governors, and Valerie A. Ramey of the National Bureau of Economic Research at the University of California. On page two the following appears.

> *The response of prices to monetary contraction is a second empirical puzzle that may be explained by the cost channel. Standard VAR methods suggest that the price level rises in the short run in response to monetary contraction. This 'price puzzle' was first noted by Sims (1992), and that has been confirmed by much subsequent work. It is our view that this may result from short-run, 'cost push' inflation brought on by an increase in interest rates.*[7]

Targeting Inflation

If one is going to target inflation, as the Bank of England is instructed to do, what inflation does one target and whose? Does one target consumer prices, or industrial costs, and if the latter does one target only domestic costs, or does one target the costs of countries from which one imports? If the latter how ever does one do it? Surely it is ludicrous to target the inflation of retail prices if a huge proportion of what one consumes comes from foreign countries. The only mechanism for keeping import prices low is to keep the value of the currency high, which can be done by having higher interest rates than other countries, but that in turn attracts money from abroad which both raises prices and the trade deficit. None of these problems seem sufficiently to bother the British Monetary Policy Committee (MPC), but they did bother Dr. Don Brash when he took on the job of Governor of the Reserve Bank of New Zealand, and entered into a commitment to keep inflation in the region of two per cent. Dr. Brash realised that he had no control whatsoever over the prices of imported raw materials such as oil, nor could he control the level of taxes. Being a truly clever man, he wrote his own definition of inflation which differed from the All Groups Consumers Price Index which was the basic target. The changes were incorporated in his contract dated the 16th December 1992. His formula for working out the changes must have been complicated for it was possible to calculate his inflation index only every three months. He would not give me any more details of his formula.

When one compares the level of intelligence with which Dr. Brash approached the problem and that of the members of the British MPC, one can only shudder with shame.

Dr. Brash was interviewed at length on New Zealand television. A kind acquaintance recorded the programme and sent me a copy. Dr. Brash was asked whether the effect of interest rates should be taken into account in the calculation of inflation. He replied *'The government quite correctly said, "No". It should not, because if it does you get into a circular reasoning situation where, because interest rates rose last quarter and therefore the inflation rate appears to be rising, then you are forced to increase interest rates again, and you quickly find yourself in a spiral of rising interest rates.'* Perhaps Dr. Brash was referring only to mortgage interest rates which are included in the All Groups Consumers Price Index, but this statement could mean that he realised that interest rates are a cost wherever they fall, and that they tend to increase all prices. He has read my arguments to that effect.

High interest rates cause inflation

Let us now look, hopefully with a deeper insight, at the opposite contention to the mainstream wisdom, that a high interest rate, far from curing inflation, is truly a principal cause of it. There are a number of reasons why this should be true:–

* High interest rates raise the cost of all business borrowing and thereby increase unit costs, causing cost inflation throughout the business sector of the economy.

* High interest rates cause recession, which leads to reduced turnover and a consequent rise in unit costs.

* Recession induced by high interest charges leads to greater expenditure on unemployment benefits, which can also translate into higher costs through the tax system.

* The most compelling reason is even more apparent. High interest rates immediately raise the cost of servicing mortgages. That stimulates wage claims by workers.

The unorthodox British system of financing long-term housing loans with the short-term deposits of savers enables mortgage borrowers to be charged short-term interest rates, which are commonly lower than long-term rates. This once seemed an inspired arrangement as it meant that in the 1940s, for instance, mortgagors paid only four per cent interest. When the government in pursuance of orthodox monetary theory tried to cure inflation by increasing interest rates, the most marked effect was on the short-term market: interest rates not only rose, but were higher for short-term money than for long. This was a traumatic blow to mortgagors, most of whom are economically active young wage-earners. Hit by high interest rates, which transfer purchasing power from the young to the old because the level of wealth ownership increases exponentially with age, the young fight back with unrelenting demands for compensating higher pay, and they always win. The circulation-seeking popular press supports them sympathetically. The annual round of wage rises becomes an ingrained habit, and wage-cost inflation becomes endemic, especially so in the public sector where workers are sheltered from competitive pressures.

This was the simple genesis of wage inflation in Britain. A unique feature of the British system of financing house purchase amplified normal inflationary pressures.

To illustrate the effect on borrowers, here are the figures for the annual repayments on a loan of £100,000, repayable over a period of twenty years at interest rates of four per cent and 16½ per cent, roughly the lowest and highest house mortgage rates during the second half of the twentieth century. The first figure is £7,358 per year, and the second is £17,316, more than double.

Many young mortgagors are intelligent and perceptive enough to see that inflation favours debtors. They are happy to encourage it actively. They are told that inflation will cause unemployment, but they are unconvinced. It is, as we have already stated, the foolish things done in response to inflation which cause unemployment, not inflation itself which can stimulate economic growth as post-war history has shown. The oft-repeated statement that inflation causes unemployment is irrational. There is no compelling reason why it should. The argument that it makes export industries uncompetitive is true only if the government acts to reverse the natural decline of the exchange rate which inflation generates. Only if the money supply is restricted as part of an anti-inflationary policy will inflation necessarily and directly cause unemployment.

'Facilis descensus Averni: noctes atque dies patet atri ianua Ditis; sed revocare gradum superasque evadere ad auras, hoc opus, hic labor est.' Thus wrote Virgil in book Six of *The Aeneid*, and the translation should decorate the walls of Whitehall and Washington offices to inform those who are more conversant with classical economics than classical poetry that, *'Easy is the descent to Hell; the doors of the dark ruler of the underworld are open day and*

night; but to retrace one's steps and escape to the upper air, that is an achievement, that the labourious task.'

It is the government's own actions, not inflation, which causes unemployment. Nor does inflation necessarily cause high interest rates, as is so often alleged without logical justification. Deflation is a much more horrifying experience. Only hyperinflation is worse, declared Keynes, and some brave souls might be tempted to dispute even that qualification.

Experience in other countries

In other countries mortgagors can still borrow at a fixed rate of interest, not at a variable rate as has long been the norm in Britain. Consequently a rise in interest rates in those countries does not stimulate wage inflation so intensely or so immediately as in Britain. Commercial borrowers too are more likely to pay fixed rates of interest.

In America, instead of causing inflation, an increase in interest rates paid to depositors bankrupted the Savings and Loan Associations, as the Associations' interest payments rose higher than their fixed-interest income. This effect was precipitated by two unlucky events. The first was that the government abolished a statutory limitation ('Regulation Q') on the rates of interest which could be paid to depositors, but did nothing to enable lenders to charge more interest on existing mortgages. The Savings and Loan Associations were crippled by being bound to the rates of interest which they had contracted to charge when the original mortgage agreement was made, while they had to make higher payments of interest to depositors as the Federal Reserve Bank pushed interest rates up to unheard of levels. Circumstances had changed in a way it was impossible for them to anticipate when they made the loans. They could not help making massive losses as interest income fell below interest payments. The second unfortunate event was a decision by an American court that existing mortgages could be assumed by, that is transferred to, the purchaser of a property which was already mortgaged. The mortgage went with the house, regardless of the credit-worthiness of a buyer. Thus the time that a mortgage with a fixed low rate of interest might continue without revision was not ended by a sale of the mortgaged property.

That these two unfortunate decisions were made showed an appalling lack of understanding by those who regulate a great country's capital system. The court decision revealed a total ignorance of banking by the judges who hold absolute power over American business affairs. With such great authority should come a parallel responsibility for judges to ensure that they fully comprehend the economic consequences of their judgements, and they should not be bound by foolish legal precedents if the result is to bankrupt the trustees of the nation's savings. The legal system can have profound effects on the progress of an economy and some changes in the law should first be subjected to criticism by competent economists before they reach either the statute book or the body of Common Law.

In Germany the level of home ownership has always been far lower than the British level. Not only have housing loans there usually been at fixed rates of interest, but also the amount lent to each borrower has been much more prudent. Consequently a rise in interest rates is less of a burden, and therefore has less influence on workers' demands for wage increases. Moreover for decades Germans have not paid interest on their mortgages at anything near British rates.

Low interest rates and low bank profits

In the 1930s the major factor which restrained monetary growth was surely that with low interest rates there was little profit in banking, and consequently the propensity to increase lendings was muted. Just how small the profits of the banks were in the low interest rate era is not known, as true banking profits were then secret. If banking is not profitable, banks can neither attract new capital nor plough back profits in order to increase their capital bases. If they cannot get new capital, they cannot expand their lendings because they must keep a reserve of their own shareholders' capital which is directly proportional to the amount of their rising liabilities.

It might be thought odd that banking profits were so low for until 1971 the clearing banks maintained a cartel of interest rates. In theory they should have been able to use the cartel power to raise profits. For reasons which can only be guessed at they sustained the rate of interest at a level which happened to be just high enough (five per cent) to make borrowers prefer to resort to the bond market. The rate seems to have been too high to tempt borrowers, and too low to encourage lenders to try to overcome borrower resistance by effectively marketing credit.

When competition between lenders was fully established in 1971, it produced a rise in interest rates charged and in interest margins, and a rise in banking profits. But by then the bond market had been destroyed by inflation, so that there was no serious competition.

High interest rates, high bank profits

But even before the cartel ended, in the particular environment of the late 1960s Corporation Tax had already helped cause interest rates to rise and thus made banking much more profitable. Capital-raising exercises by banks then became more frequent. The resultant high level of bank profits even prompted a Labour Party election poster in 1974 which read *'Bank Robs Man'*, though in their book of evidence to *The Wilson Committee on the Future of the Financial Institutions*, which reported in 1980, the clearing banks were rightly able to show that their high profits were partly an illusion of historic cost accounting. Inflation-adjusted accounts showed a very different picture. The adjusted profits may not even have covered the dividends paid.

British clearing banks had been sleeping giants, unaware of their potential. They were at last awakened to their great profit opportunities, and the government policy of encouraging competition was also effective in stirring them to life. In 1972 Barclays Bank, led by the dynamic Derek Wilde, subjected all its staff to intensive training in marketing, and backed it up very successfully with a very powerful management tool called *Management by Objectives* (MBO). MBO produced agreed targets for all staff to achieve, including very specific sales targets. Bank managers quickly found that proper marketing could make nonsense of economic theories that high interest rates discourage borrowing. People were eager to borrow more than they had previously been allowed to, and only needed the opportunity to do so, even if the percentage rate charged was as high as 31. It is now clear that the limitations on the appetite of the public for credit are first, the borrower's ability to service his loan, and second, the lender's prudence. The latter was relaxed. Few now remember, for instance, the time when building societies refused to lend money on houses built before 1919, or would not take into account for loan limits the earnings of a married woman of child-bearing age. Partly under pressure from do-gooders, such restraints have long been abandoned by lenders who, once their protecting inhibitions had been sloughed off, or flayed off by the whips of the popular press, rushed to find new customers who would soak up the ever-expanding supply of credit.

Any inflation of the price of houses beyond the level of general inflation increases the value of building plots. Even at a rate of interest of 14½ per cent or more the willingness of the public to borrow on mortgage, once the credit was available and well-marketed, was sufficient to push the value of houses up so much that in 1989 the value of the plot of a new house rose to perhaps 40 per cent of the total price, and as high as 60 per cent for larger houses. And it has remained that way. In the 1950s it had been normal for 85 per cent of the price to reflect building cost, and only 15 per cent the cost of the site. It seems right to attribute much of the rise in house prices to credit creation rather than to underlying demand. Admittedly demand was strong for another reason as well. With house prices rising on average three per cent faster than the Retail Prices Index from 1957 onwards, houses for occupation had become a very popular investment, largely because they appeared to be an investment that hedges against inflation. Because they were a hedge against inflation their prices rose faster than inflation. Chicken and egg! Which of the two comes first? No-one thought to try to answer the question for thirty-five years. When the house-price bubble burst, and house prices headed sharply downwards to correct the anomaly in values, no-one in government had a sensible remedy to prevent hundreds of thousands of people from suffering bankruptcy and poverty.

Of the leading press commentators one, Anatole Kaletsky of *The Times*, was brave enough to suggest that even increased inflation was preferable to such fast increasing homelessness.

Asset price inflation

When interest rates were at last allowed to fall after 1992, the banks found that corporate loans were more difficult to make, because corporations preferred to lock themselves to low interest rates by borrowing long from a revitalised bond market. It made sense to repay short-term bank loans. The banks had either to return unneeded capital to their shareholders, or to lend more to other sectors; they did both. The loan markets they developed included consumer finance and mortgage lending. Leveraged take-overs and management buy-outs were a market for short-term corporate lending. Both the mortgage lending and the take-overs and buy-outs enhanced asset price inflation. Despite the efforts to find new borrowers, capital adequacy ratios rose. Bank capital was not earning its full potential. After the 1939–45 War the raising of capital in Britain was for a long time controlled by *The Capital Issues Committee* (CIC), acting under the authority of the Borrowing (Controls and Guarantees) Act which became law on 12th July 1946. Did the CIC reject any applications from banks to raise new capital or were none made? Because of the very long period of low interest rates bank shares were not then a profitable investment. One financial journalist, it may have been Harold Wincott, sarcastically dubbed them *'vaguely participating preference shares.'* The raising of new capital for banks by way of rights issues did not recommence until 1961. There was a jump in the aggregate capital adequacy ratio of the banks about that time; it had fallen to a very low level in the 1950s. The rights issues made possible the rebuilding of the banks' portfolios of loans to the private sector. Retentions from growing profits helped the process.

Bank losses as a method of credit control

The expansion of the money supply after 1965 could have been even more rapid if the banks had not experienced some occasional severe losses by misfortune or government action.

There was a secondary banking crisis in 1973–74. From 1971 to 1984 there was confusion over leasing, a clever contrivance which had its origin in an anomaly in the rules of Corporation Tax. Leasing would eventually have caused taxation problems for the banks even if in 1984 the Chancellor of the Exchequer, Nigel Lawson, had not made it less profitable by his changes in the depreciation rules for Corporation Tax. The banks' object in engaging in leasing was to secure the deferral of tax liabilities, but the trick depended on the continuance of inflation if it was to achieve an indefinite deferral of the liabilities. By the time the Chancellor acted to reduce the taxation advantage, falling inflation was already threatening to make the huge postponed tax liabilities mature for payment.

Lawson's action followed only three years after the imposition of a windfall tax on bank profits which also savaged the banks' capital bases. The enormous reduction in capital resources which followed these two actions of the government may have helped the marked reduction in inflation which followed them. A little later the banks also ran up huge losses through recycling the deposits received from Latin Americans and other foreigners (possibly including illegal deposits from Eastern Bloc citizens) back to the free-spending governments of the countries from whose citizens the deposits originated. Then came an interest swap crisis. Finally there were the huge losses which resulted from the over-expansion of credit in 1988, 1989, and 1990, resulting from a vain attempt to compete for market share of the loan market with Japanese banks which had lower capital adequacy ratios, and therefore lower costs.

We will write more about these topics later.

Current cost accounting

In a paragraph of Chapter Three (*'How to create money electronically'*) it was assumed that some interest will in many cases be charged to an overdrawn account, with the result that the bank will be lending the customer the money to pay the interest. Technically that makes it a non-performing loan, and a provision should be made against a potential loss.

But a paper published by the Bank of England in the May 1988 issue of its *Quarterly* put forward an argument which implied that the Bank was not concerned about this technicality. It was as follows.

The real rate of interest (that is after deducting inflation from the nominal rate of interest) was, the Bank averred, lower in Britain than the real rates experienced by Britain's trading rivals. It therefore urged industrialists not to hesitate to go ahead with schemes of investment, and not to be inhibited by high nominal interest rates. It also argued that as interest was deductible against profits for the purpose of assessing Corporation Tax, it was the *net of tax* real rate of interest which should be taken into account. It was suggested that the net of tax real rate of interest at that time was negative!

There were three faults in the paper. One was a matter of fact about the rates of interest experienced abroad. Confidential information from the treasurer of a major multi-national company revealed that the rates of interest his company was paying at that time in the countries mentioned was lower than those stated in the paper. The author of the paper said that special care had been taken to get the rates right. Nevertheless something must have gone wrong.

The second fault was the author's lack of knowledge of the detailed procedure for inflation accounting. The third error was his assumption that all money borrowed for business expansion is spent on assets whose prices rise with inflation.

Money borrowed to provide capital for a business may well finance debtors and work-in-progress. Indeed something like one half of all borrowing by small businesses may finance debtors. In the terminology of inflation accounting, debtors give rise to *a holding loss*. Borrowings, on the other hand, give rise to *a holding gain*. In less technical language this means that one profits from inflation in respect of borrowings, and loses from inflation in respect of lendings. If money is borrowed to finance debtors, a holding gain is cancelled out by a holding loss. Therefore one may not deduct the rate of inflation from the rate of interest on the loan. The real rate of interest is absolutely identical with the nominal rate of interest paid on any money borrowed to finance debtors.

The same may or may not be true of borrowing to finance stock or work-in-progress. Which way it goes will depend on whether the industrialist is able to charge selling prices which reflect the increased cost of future purchases of stock and of future work-in-progress. Very often public opinion prevents him from doing so. As any increases in selling prices will be wholly profit for tax purposes, in practice he not only needs to raise his prices by the amount of inflation, but by the inflation rate *grossed up at his marginal rate of tax*. Only that way can he obtain from his sales all the cash he will need in order to restock to the same level and to continue to finance the same physical level of production.

If borrowings are invested in plant and machinery, there may be a holding gain from inflation, but additional depreciation will need to be charged in order to depreciate at replacement cost, not historic cost.

The author of the Bank of England paper was also mistaken in suggesting that the true rate of interest is the net rate less the allowance for Corporation Tax. He was wrong in two ways. The first was his failure to appreciate that for any industrialist all taxes are effectively a cost of production. That is perhaps best proved by pointing out that without a tax burden a producer could cut his prices. It does not matter a bureaucrat's paper clip to him whether he pays Corporation Tax on his profits, or the receiver of his gross interest payments is liable for tax on them. The money goes to the Revenue either way. The second fault is that Corporation Tax may not be an issue if the loan finances new capital equipment. Capital allowances of at least 25 per cent a year (40 per cent in first year from 1992) would probably eliminate any tax charge in the first couple of years, and by the time there is a tax charge, cash flow may have substantially reduced the loan. For that reason too the nominal rate of interest reflects the full cost of the borrowing.

If an industrialist had increased his borrowing in pursuance of the advice of the writer in *The Bank of England Quarterly*, what would have subsequently happened? The answer is that within a year the company would have been paying nearly twice as much interest, and the expected profit would have turned into a very substantial loss. It is very likely that their inflationary expectations played a far smaller part in the minds of company directors in 1988 than their expectations regarding interest rates. Those whose expectations about interest rates had been optimistic in 1988 went on to see their companies go into receivership.

5

Credit Control by Reserve Assets

Money is like a sixth sense without which
you cannot make use of the other five.
W. SOMERSET MAUGHAN

THE BEST KNOWN ADVOCATE of the policy of the control of the money supply by government is Professor Milton Friedman.[1] He does not favour the use of interest rates as the means to achieve control. The method he prefers is to insist that a fixed part of a bank's assets be invested in a particular form of security whose supply should be firmly under the control of the government. This may be what economists term *High Power Money*, (HPM), that is the balances the banks keep at the Central Bank. Another choice of security for the purpose is Treasury Bills. They are a promise by the Treasury to pay a fixed sum of money three months (usually) from the date of issue. They are an excellent example of non-intermediated transferable debt. Because of their short maturity, it is very easy to alter the supply of the bills. The supply may also be regulated more directly by sales and purchases of the bills by government agencies.

If all banks and lending institutions were forced to keep at least 10 per cent of their assets in the form of Treasury Bills, the intermediated credit supply (money supply) could, in theory at least, never be more than ten times the amount of Treasury Bills currently in issue. This would appear to be a perfect way to control the intermediated credit supply, and one would think that control is so easy that the only real problem – the ultimate and most difficult one – would be to decide the most effective level for the intermediated credit supply. Ideally banks alone should be permitted to hold whatever asset is chosen to be the reserve asset. If it were available to any investor, there might not then be sufficient for the banks. On the other hand, if ownership were limited to banks, the asset would not be freely marketable. Yet that is usually considered to be an essential characteristic of any reserve asset. It could be objected that unless an asset is marketable, it is not a suitable reserve asset at all. The objection, if indeed it matters, is easily overcome, for the asset is purchased by the Central Bank when a bank needs liquidity, in much the same way that the Bank of England bought and sold gold in the days of the full Gold Standard. By such reasoning have we perhaps deduced a modern and improved successor for the alleged discipline of the Gold Standard?

So far no such interesting tactic has been tried in precisely the form suggested, though something near it has happened. One should warn, however, at this point, that history shows that when an attempt is made to limit the supply of the officially recognised form of credit supply, the public invents another one. More about that later.

American banks are required to deposit ten per cent of their checking account balances with the Federal Reserve Bank, and some think that this limits the lending capacity of the banks, because the Central Bank can control the supply of HPM, the bank itself being the sole source of HPM because HPM is Central Bank debt. (Readers will recognise HPM as much the same as *category one money*.) No other bank can create it. But the government is spewing out HPM at a huge rate all the time if it is running a deficit, as it usually is. If it is not running a deficit, but has a surplus, it is of necessity retiring debt, and this too injects masses of HPM into the system.

The reserve asset system

In the past reserve asset ratios have been imposed upon British banks for long periods, yet Brian Kettel in his textbook, *Monetary Economics*,[2] stated, rather surprisingly, that reserve ratio changes were not designed to control monetary growth. In the 1950s and 1960s liquidity ratios of two levels were imposed, one tranche of assets to be in cash (that is Bank of England notes) and deposits at the Bank of England, and another, and bigger, tranche to be in easily realisable investments such as Treasury Bills and short-dated gilts. *The Radcliffe Report* of 1959, which described the functioning of the money markets in the 1950s, also denied that these ratios were intended to control the money supply. Throughout the period when such liquidity ratios were imposed, £M3 grew less violently than under later control systems. But the matter is so complex that there could be many explanations of that phenomenon.

At the time the old reserve asset system was coming to an end, the clearing banks were under an obligation to keep 28 per cent of their *eligible liabilities* (in effect short-term deposits) in liquid assets. That meant that 28 per cent of the assets of the banks were forced loans to the government, and that proportion of clearing bank deposits was consequently unavailable for the financing of industry. Unfortunately a parallel requirement to maintain such a high level of liquid assets was not imposed on other lending institutions, such as building societies. As a result the dam of regulation, which should have held back the flood of credit, became increasingly leaky as building societies and 'near banks' expanded.

In 1971 a much more elaborate system of credit control was instituted to replace the former 28 per cent liquidity rule. The manner in which the new system was applied made it totally unsuccessful in controlling the growth of intermediated credit (money), even though the theory behind it may have been sound. The new form of control was related to some of the banks' deposits, but not all. Those deposits which were affected were also referred to as *eligible liabilities*. A reserve ratio was imposed which was related to the total of eligible liabilities. The reserve had to be invested in a range of specific securities, some of which were capable of being kept in short supply, but none were investments which were exclusively for banks. They were:–

- Balances at the Bank of England (special deposits, coin and notes held as till money were excluded),

- Treasury Bills, tax reserve certificates,

- Money at call with the London money market,

- Local authority and British commercial bills eligible for re-discount at the Bank of England, but subject to a limitation of commercial bills to two per cent of eligible liabilities,

- British government securities with one year or less to maturity.

The clearing banks were required to keep 12½ per cent of their eligible liabilities in these reserve assets, and finance houses (effectively the hire purchase companies) had to keep 10 per cent of their eligible liabilities in reserve assets. It was intended to subject all the other banks or near-banks, often referred to at that time as 'fringe banks', to reserve requirements. But at the time of the introduction of the system there were still many deposit-taking companies which were not required to hold reserve assets. The legislation covering banks and deposit-taking companies was very complicated. Some fringe banks were covered by the Protection of Depositors Act of 1963, and others were exempt. Some qualified under the Companies Acts for exemption from publishing true accounts, while others had to send copies of their accounts to depositors. Experts on the classification of banks bandied around cryptic expressions such as *Section 127 banks, Section 123 banks, Section 25 banks*. What these titles meant exactly is now merely ancient history as they were swept away by later legislation. If memory of these statutory complexities is accurate, the crucial classification was *Section 123 banks*, referring to a section of the Protection of Depositors Act 1963. *Section 123 banks* seemed to be able to get away with financial mayhem.

The Bank of England's intention to control all banks was slow to come into effect. Questioned as to the current position in September 1973, the Bank of England answered that the reserve system would soon be applied to *Section 123 banks*, but in the following May further enquiry revealed that nothing had yet been done.[3] Academic writers on banking history may not be aware of this divergence of practice from announced intention. Certainly one otherwise excellent history of banking states that the 1971 system was applied to all banks, but enquiries at the time indicate that this did not take place for at least three years.

A large bubble of credit was inflated. By 1974 the bubble had burst and the Bank of England had a major banking crisis on its hands. The Bank had probably delayed the implementation of the reserve requirements in order to avoid precipitating a crisis, but it came anyway. Some fringe banks used short-term deposits to finance long-term projects such as the construction of large office blocks. Catastrophe was inevitable at the first downturn in confidence in any of the fringe banks.

The failure of the system

The system of reserve assets which was started in October 1971 never worked properly. It was not allowed to work! The clearing banks found useful loopholes in the system, but perhaps the most important reason for the failure of the credit control system in the 1970s was that despite its superficial sophistication, a section of the banking system which was growing very rapidly was not subjected to all its rules. The fault lay with government officials and the technical experts of the Bank of England. They were using a very narrow definition of what was a bank. Logically a bank is any institution which takes deposits and makes loans, but the government had not followed that logic. On the other hand the clearing banks were too stringently controlled. If their interest-bearing liabilities rose above a predetermined level, they had to make additional deposits – called special deposits – at the Bank of England. This stringency encouraged them to exploit skilfully the loopholes in the system.

It may seem odd that the system of special deposits was used to control the banks' interest-bearing eligible liabilities (IBELS) more strictly than non-interest bearing liabilities. It is possible, though not likely, that the reason can be found in the experience of the United States of doing the opposite in the 1920s. Because they required much smaller reserves, banks in the US greatly expanded their interest-bearing liabilities in the late 1920s. The expansion was helped by a convenient linking with a corresponding increase in loans to stock market speculators. In 1929 the US stock market crashed. That was followed by the crash of many thousands of banks. The experience may have persuaded British banking supervisors that it was particularly important to control the expansion of interest-bearing deposits. Certainly from 1971 special deposits were applied for that purpose. Britain did not thereby succeed in avoiding a stock market catastrophe. It struck in 1974.

The interest-bearing liabilities which were affected by special deposits included only those which were repayable within two years; later maturing liabilities were excluded. Any attempt to exploit this loophole was ineffective, as there was no worthwhile incentive for depositors to tie their money up for more than two years. In fact the opposite incentive existed. Consequently long-term loans could not prudently be made by banks because they lacked long-term deposits with which to finance them. At least that was the theory taught to students of banking.

The growth of the fringe banks

The many deposit-taking institutions which were unrestricted grew very fast. They included the building societies, which were becoming a truly major force in the monetary system. Building societies were beginning to allow depositors to operate, often semi-officially, what were truly interest-bearing current (checking) accounts. The building societies were ignored by the monetary authorities because there was a quaint assumption that their balances represented permanent savings, having a low frequency of circulation. They were totally exempted from the provisions of the Control (Borrowing and Guarantees) Act 1946 by a Statutory Instrument issued in 1958.

The building societies were in the habit of reporting the turnover on their accounts, something the banks had never done, and the figures began to look very impressive. Indeed, the turn-over was equivalent to about 10 per cent of GNP by the end of the 1970s, when the total liabilities of the building societies had risen to a level no less than 80 per cent of the liabilities of the banks as measured by £M3. By 1991 the turnover on building society accounts was equal to 20 per cent of GNP, despite the conversion of Abbey National, a major society, into a true bank, so that its turnover figures were no longer included. Withdrawals from building societies are probably used in the main to pay for major items of consumer expenditure, and that must surely make them very significant for the economy.

Since that time, most of the larger building societies have become full banks, owned by shareholders. Formerly they were *Friendly Societies*, owned mutually by depositors and borrowers. Many former building societies have been acquired by commercial banks.

In the period immediately after the 1971 regulatory reforms a host of other deposit taking institutions escaped the effect of credit control regulations. They did not have to make special deposits and were operating without prudent free capital ratios or liquid asset ratios. They did not accept that there was any need to balance the maturity of assets and liabilities, although what were effectively long-term lendings, financed by short-term deposits, may have been deliberately window-dressed to look like short-term loans. They were only taking to its logical extreme the established but unacknowledged practice of the big banks.

The lack of any requirement to hold officially denominated reserve assets (which tended to give a low return as they were scarce) gave the fringe banks a competitive advantage over the clearing banks in seeking deposits. Inevitably they could afford to pay a higher rate of interest on deposits than the recognised banks which were subjected to reserve asset requirements, because their assets were on average earning them a higher yield. The result was that the fringe banks enjoyed mushroom-like growth.

If you cannot beat them, join them

Eventually the clearing banks decided to fight back. They set up their own subsidiaries which were not officially recognised as banks and were therefore exempt from the reserve asset rules. Some may have been taxed as investment institutions instead of as banks, with the result that their profits on gilts were free of tax. The consequence, rather fortuitously, was a big change in the character of the deposit-taking business of the clearing banks. Up to that time the bulk of their deposits had been obtained direct from the public, and were therefore called retail deposits, as distinct from wholesale deposits obtained through the London Money Market. Of the two, retail deposits were much the cheaper, and it was a profitable privilege of the clearing banks to have ready access to them. In the early 1950s as much as 67 per cent of clearing bank deposits were on current accounts and therefore cost free, no interest being payable. The clearing banks' new subsidiaries began to accept wholesale deposits, even though long-serving and experienced staff of the banks considered the margins obtainable to be ridiculously low. Some senior officials of the clearing banks, including the Chief Accountant of Barclays Bank, Sir Bernard Sharp, were savagely contemptuous. Nevertheless the change was to become a permanent one, with far-reaching consequences for the role of the clearing banks in capital markets.

A strange mood of optimism gripped many of the fringe banks and they happily ignored prudence, borrowed short, and lent very heavily on big construction projects to property developers. A senior employee in London of an American bank which was active in the same market later admitted privately that they were even careless about obtaining formal security for their loans, due to overoptimism about their customers' financial status. Some of the deposits of the fringe banks came from the treasuries of the clearing banks themselves and of their subsidiaries.[4] If the fringe banks had any conscious philosophy behind their policy, it must have rested on the belief that they would always be able to pay the top rate of interest, and would, therefore, never be short of deposits. Perhaps it was for that reason that they did not worry about the need to keep a prudent level of liquidity, or about preserving a balance between the maturity dates of assets and liabilities. It is more likely, however, that no deep thought was ever given to such important issues. The history of financial services to the public is that competitive pressures are totally effective in anaesthetising prudential instincts.

The government breaks the fringe banks

It appears to be a peculiarly British assumption that the purpose of a bank is to convert short-term deposits into long-term loans. A more prudent view is that the government's banking regulations should encourage a closer matching of the maturity dates of assets and liabilities. It is true that if no-one foolishly rocks the boat, the practice of mismatching the maturity dates of assets and liabilities can continue for a long time quite harmlessly, but what happens if the government itself rocks the boat suddenly and violently?

In the early 1970s the government began to pursue yet more firmly the traditional British practice of trying to keep the pound overvalued. In order to succeed in this objective it engineered high interest rates. Then in 1973 the price of oil leapt five-fold, causing a panic. British interest rates were pushed up to unprecedented levels. The fringe banks were plunged into disastrous trouble since many of the property developers to whom they had lent money were unable to afford such high interest payments. Nor were the major banks exempt from disasters. For instance, one of them found itself in the hotel business as a result of the failure of the Garden House Hotel Company in Cambridge. That company had borrowed for rebuilding at an interest rate of 8½ per cent, and the rate rose to 18 per cent.

It was very regrettable that the fringe banks were hit so hard because their lending, though technically injudicious in terms of prudent banking, was nevertheless promoting the construction of buildings and other forms of real capital formation. It thereby expanded British industrial activity, whereas some other expansions of the money supply have tended to finance imports, aiding thereby the expansion of foreign economies instead. Credit expansion has also financed asset price inflation, especially building society lending which increased house prices at a rate faster than the general level of inflation, thereby creating some serious social problems, besides making overnight multi-millionaires of those who sold building land.

The fiction of short-term lending

At that time the clearing banks were still maintaining the fiction that they were following the dogma, preached in all banking textbooks, that banks should provide comparatively short-term loans only. Indeed, up to the 1914–18 War, bill-broking was the clearing banks' preferred activity. They experienced pressure from the 1920s onwards to make medium-term loans to industry but lacked medium-term liabilities with which to finance them. The Macmillan Committee of 1928, of which Lord Keynes was a member, reported accordingly:–

> *There is substance in the view that the British financial organisations concentrated in the City of London might with advantage be more clearly coordinated with British industry, particularly large scale industry, than is now the case; and in some respects the City is more highly organised to provide capital to foreign countries than to British industry.*[5]

In 1932 Lloyds Bank advanced £3,000,000 to Stewarts and Lloyds to start the steel plant at Corby. This is reckoned to be the first example of industrial participation by a British bank.

Otherwise the banks did nothing of any significance at that time except that they formed one of the institutions which later became the 3i's Group. The Macmillan Committee was wrong in saying *particularly large scale industry*, for a more urgent need was finance for small scale industry, which normally lacks access to market sources of capital which big business can tap. That problem was addressed in 1946 by the founding by the clearing banks of the Industrial and Commercial Finance Corporation, which also in due course became part of the 3i's Group, but the supply of long-term finance for industry from banks remained weak.

Pressure upon banks to lend to industry for development was renewed in the early 1970s. Some clever person at National Westminster Bank suggested that the most solid deposits held by banks were the bottom tranches of their current accounts, because customers rarely ran their current account balances down to zero. A proportion of the balance on most current accounts has no frequency of circulation whatever, so the bottom tranches of the balances are in practice, though not in theory, very long-term deposits. The more incautious but persuasively clever people in banking therefore argued that the banks could quite safely lend these deposits long term.

It is an attractive proposal and has a large element of truth in it. It is dangerous nevertheless. That the proposal was put forward reveals just how frustrating and injurious was the banks' lack of long-term liabilities.

The fringe banks simply went ahead regardless of risk. But for the oil crisis they might have escaped danger for much longer. But why were they not restrained? That is the mystery. What went on at The Treasury and the Bank of England? What discussions took place? Was there any relevant discussion at all?[6]

The efficacy of the reserve asset system

Whether or not a reserve asset system can control the intermediated money supply has not yet been fully established in Britain. No conclusion should be drawn from an experiment such as that described above because of the incomplete way in which it was implemented. Some academic comment on the problem has been woolly in certain details. In a lecture in 1980 on the British situation even Professor Milton Friedman showed concern only for M3 as a measure of the money supply. That attitude came to look very silly in the late 1980s when the Central Statistical Office (since renamed the Office for National Statistics) ceased to print M3 in the official statistics. M4 came to be looked on as the correct measure of the intermediated money supply, for it includes the liabilities of building societies.

We have an insight into what the discussions were like at the Bank of England at that time as Professor Charles Goodhart, then a monetary adviser to the Bank, has written about them, and published discussion papers which he presented to the Bank. His account provokes the irreverent thought that many of those involved were trying to play a

---

Official Measures of the Money Supply
Abbreviated definitions

MO = Notes and coin in circulation outside the Bank of England plus
     bankers' operational deposits with the Banking Department of
     the Bank of England.(ONS table VQKT)
M1 = MO plus private sector current account balances. (M1 is not
     published by the ONS but its components are. They are ONS
     tables VQKT and AUYA.)
M2 = M1 plus some short term and smaller retail sight deposits at
     banks and building societies. (ONS table AUYC)
£M3 = MO plus all sterling bank deposits, whether on current or
     interest-bearing accounts, (but not building society accounts) of
     UK residents in the private sector. (No table published.)
M3 = £M3 plus the foreign currency bank deposits by UK private
     sector residents. (No table published.)
M4 = £M3 plus building society deposits less deposits by building
     societies in banks. (ONS table AUYM)
M4c = M4 plus bank and building society deposits in foreign
     currencies. (No table published.)
M5 = M4 plus certificates of tax deposit, sterling Treasury Bills, bank
     bills, deposits with local authorities, and National Savings
     deposits and securities. (No table published.)

---

complex computer game for which they had the wrong instruction
manual. Take the following quotation from page 206 of Goodhart's book
Monetary Theory and Practice as a very simple example:–

> *If banks have to maintain a minimum ratio of cash to deposits and if
> the central bank exercises sufficiently vigorously its undoubted potential
> power as 'the' source of cash, then clearly the size of the high-powered
> money base imposes a ceiling on the level of bank deposits and thus,
> indirectly, on the stock of money, however defined.*

Cash has many meanings, but in this context means cash balances at
the Bank of England, and banknotes and coin. We need to consider the
two categories separately.

We will call the second 'currency' for the purposes of this discussion.
The amount of currency required by an economy is determined by

market forces of supply and demand. Any attempt to diminish the supply provokes the market to find a substitute. Otherwise a situation would arise in which banknotes have a premium value over bank deposits of the same nominal value. In the present era, an attempt to limit the currency supply would increase the use of plastic money. In the 19th century it encouraged the use of bills of exchange as currency. It is therefore somewhat doubtful whether Professor Goodhart is wholly correct in ascribing so much influence to the power to limit the supply of that element of *High-Power Money*. Market forces may over-rule that power.

As regards bank reserves held in the form of deposits at the Central Bank, that might be another matter, and the textbooks of yesteryear were enthusiastic, an example being the textbook of 1957, *Outline of Monetary Economics*, by A. C. L. Day.[7]

But is not the government pumping HPM reserves into the system all the time it is running a deficit, as it most often does? The theorists claim that those reserves can be mopped up by what are grandly called 'open market operations', by which they mean the sale of government debt to the public. If a customer buys a new government stock by drawing on his account at his bank, that bank automatically loses HPM to an amount exactly equal to the purchase price. If that happens, it puts the banks totally at the mercy of the Central Bank, because only the Central Bank can provide the liquidity they need.

It sounds perfect, but there is a catch. Customers have to want to invest in government stocks. If their liquidity preference, that is their desire to hold money in the form of a bank deposit, happens to grow in line with the government deficit, then the policy will fail. Judging by the effects that have been seen, that is exactly what happens. A government deficit expands economic activity, and the increased level of activity causes those affected by the demand to have need of higher liquidity.

Reserve movements

But one has to concede that bank reserves can drop dramatically if there is a sudden influx of tax payments into the government's account at the Central Bank, a movement of funds which automatically diminishes the banks' deposits at the Central Bank. It is in such circumstances that the Central Bank may have to create more money by buying assets from the banks. In theory, if it did not do so, the banks would not be able to maintain their required reserves. Does this mean that the government, as a result of its control of the Central Bank, really does have some control of the money supply, or does the Central Bank always provide whatever funds are needed in order to prevent a collapse of confidence in the banking system? The suspicion is that it is the latter, despite what theorists may say. The skill and knowledge that is needed to control wisely the enormously complex financial systems of the present are unlikely to exist.

The point has been well discussed by Professor L. Randall Wray, and he is confident enough to state, *'The central bank never has controlled, nor could it ever control, the quantity of money; neither can it control the quantity of reserves in a discretionary manner.'* [8]

So open market operations are impotent. One can add a further argument: the successful operation of a reserve system does not exist as it predicates at least the following:–

- A completely balanced budget, so that the government is never supplying surplus HPM to the banks by running a deficit, or maintaining their HPM holdings by running a surplus and using it to redeem debt.

- The creation by the Central Bank, with the cooperation of the government of precisely the amount of reserve HPM required for the required level of the money supply for the predetermined level of GDP.

- No leakage of deposits and balancing lendings from the banking system as a result of the securitisation of existing loans.

Readers should be able to think up a few other prerequisites that are unlikely to be fulfilled.

Interbank market

A bank which is short of HPM will look first to the money market for the necessary funds, as it is normal for one bank to have surplus funds when another bank is short. As shortages are often caused by short-term lags, an overnight borrowing may be all that is needed. On occasions the rate of interest for overnight help can be enormous, rates of 100 per cent being asked at difficult times. The man who ran Barclays Bank's treasury operation in the 1970s put it as follows, *'If we are short of funds, we know they must be somewhere. It is just a matter of finding them and paying the price for them.'* But when the whole banking system is short, possibly as a result of heavy tax payments by customers, the resort has to be to the Central Bank.

One should mention for the record that Britain had a unique element in its money market system, the Discount Houses. The banks were not allowed to deal direct with the Central Bank when needing funds, but applied to a Discount House for assistance. On the other hand, temporary surpluses would be lent to a Discount House. The surplus of one bank could be passed by a Discount House to another bank which would have the corresponding shortage. When the whole market was short the Discount Houses would have to apply the Central Bank. One odd effect of this system was that the Bank of England had no direct influence on individual banks, for it would seem to be impossible to punish a profligate bank by imposing a high interest rate when accommodating its needs. The Discount Houses are no longer necessary to the system as the European Union has insisted, presumably in the cause of harmonisation, that all banks should have direct access to the Bank of England.

Exogenous forces

Academic economists discuss constantly the question of whether the money supply is determined endogenously or whether exogenous forces can affect it, that is forces which affect an economy, but are not themselves affected in return because they are external to the system being studied. Exogenous forces in economics are not readily perceived. In real life there is probably no such thing as a completely exogenous factor. The factors which some economists are proposing as exogenous are, on close examination, not truly so. They are really endogenous, and therefore subject to the natural law that for every action there is a reaction. The money supply is certainly entirely endogenous.

What happened to the money supply control system of the 1970s is a perfect example. The controls imposed were thought to be exogenous, but the reaction of the lending institutions in exploiting loopholes defeated their purpose and expanded the credit supply. This book discusses whether the intermediated credit supply could be controlled by physically limiting the capital base of the banks. Obviously a reaction to that limitation would be an expansion of the non-intermediated credit supply, and consequently that too has to be controlled, and so on, and so on.

It may be argued that we are defining exogenous too strictly. Maybe so, but the point is that any attempt to control human beings must take into account that there are reactions from those controlled. They are at least as clever as those who attempt to do the controlling. Some are cleverer, especially the very highly paid participants in the Financial Services Industry.

So what about the non-intermediated capital market? The reserve asset system makes no attempt whatever to control it. Surely it must play a part in promoting inflation? One cannot assume that disintermediated capital does not have a capability to circulate. Stock market securities are readily convertible into cash when needed, provided every holder does not attempt to make the conversion at the same time! The yearly turnover on the stock market is measured in trillions of pounds. There are forms of cash balances which have a lower frequency of circulation than wealth held in the form of securities which are readily and frequently traded. It is the combined effect of the intermediated and non-intermediated capital markets which determines the effective credit supply, and therefore decides the rate of expansion or contraction of the economy, and ultimately the potential rate of inflation. Amazingly there has never been any control on the creation of trade credit, which can be new credit creation just as surely as that in the banking sector.

Effective control?

A truly effective system of monetary control would have to be expertly operated. The damage which imprudent or inexpert manipulation could wreak is immense. Judging by past performance there is as yet no convincing evidence that any government department or government regulator such as the FSA would manage the control with sufficient finesse. Nor are the necessary techniques yet available for determining what is an ideal level of credit supply. Nor would Professor Friedman's ideal, a steady year by year, month by month, increase in the money supply as the economy grew be appropriate. It is a dangerous, and arguably ridiculous, proposition. It would however appeal to the tidy-minded planners and perfectionists he despised, rather than to the pragmatic believers in the market economy whom he claimed to favour.

A need to increase the intermediated money supply can arise quite suddenly. An illustration was the decision to build the Channel Tunnel using largely borrowed capital. To enable that project to reduce unemployment and be an addition to real capital formation, a substantial and out-of-the-ordinary increase in the intermediated credit supply was required. It is wrong, of course, to finance such a risky project with variable-rate intermediated loan capital, but the days are regrettably long gone when such a project could be financed with debentures paying a fixed rate of interest, as was the Manchester Ship Canal earlier in the same century. The Channel Tunnel has proved no more profitable than the Manchester Ship Canal; arguably the Channel Tunnel is a project of such long-term benefit that an assessment of its financial viability using the standard techniques of investment appraisal is not appropriate.

The Institute of Economic Affairs has published a small book as *Occasional Paper 86* called *Monetarism and Monetary Policy* written by

Professor Friedman's collaborator, Dr. Anna J. Schwarz. She makes the following recommendation:–9

> *The monetary policy recommendation that follows is that to combat inflation, a central bank should limit the growth rate of a monetary aggregate to the long-term growth rate of the economy.*

The reference to '*a monetary aggregate*' seems more than somewhat vague. The British government changed its choice of monetary aggregate during the 1980s whenever it discovered that the monetary weevils had fouled a particular aggregate.

The recommendation is based, like so much unsuccessful economic theory, on wishful thinking. The wish might be to achieve an '*x*' per cent rate of growth of GNP. Applying the function, a '*y*' per cent growth of the money supply is calculated to be correct to achieve '*x*' per cent growth. One could aim for it, provided one knows how. Then the gremlins take over, probably in the form of a batch of aggressive trade union leaders who are trying to justify their existence. One's nicely planned growth in the money supply is absorbed entirely by wage inflation, and no economic growth takes place at all. Any expansion of the money supply affects the future, not the present, and somehow one has to find out what expansion of the real economy is about to take place. The only way one can come near to being sure what growth will take place is to plan it ruthlessly. That takes Friedmanism full circle, right back to the national socialist/communist fully-planned economy, something to which Professor Friedman is wholly opposed.

To reconcile strict and planned monetary control with a completely unplanned, or market, economy, is very difficult, if not, indeed, a logical impossibility.

The two themes of Friedman's policy are from different and independent philosophies. He is an ardent and persuasive advocate of the market economy, but he is also a convinced interventionist in monetary matters. The only way to reconcile the two attitudes is by means of a compromise, albeit an uneasy one. That is what the long struggle between Friedmanism and Keynesianism is all about. It is what the doctrinal conflict between socialism and capitalism is about. At what point does one compromise between freedom and intervention? We shall be commenting further on this point in Chapter Fourteen. There we shall show that compromise between planning and freedom is essential, and indeed inevitable.

Fractional reserve banking

One cannot leave the subject of reserve assets without referring again to the heretic fringe of monetary theorists. They regard fractional reserve banking as the invention of Satan. They argue that if $100 is deposited in a bank, the bank places it with the FED as its fractional reserve, and can then lend $900 of newly created credit. The $900 is deposited in a bank which credits it all to its balance at the FED, and lends $8100 of newly created credit. And so on ad infinitum. The theorists also say the bank is getting interest on money it has created out of thin air. They ignore the fact that banks create money solely for their depositors, not for themselves. The most the banks get from the operation is the margin between interest charged and interest allowed, plus any agreed commitment fee.

Indeed it is wrong to say that banks create money, for money is created by a borrower and a depositor. The bank merely assists. The bank may be likened to a surgeon who carries out *in vitro* fertilisation. The egg and sperm come from his patients; he merely brings them together. The same is true of banks; they bring borrowers and depositors together in a credit creating nexus. The bank gets only the margin between the interest charged and that allowed. But what about the huge multiplier effect? Is it real? Of course not. To be available as HPM the deposits would have to be of money created by the Central Bank, *category one money*. So the deposit would either have to be FED notes or a cheque drawn on the FED. The first would take some notes out of circulation, and they may be needed by someone else, so an equivalent number of notes are likely to be withdrawn. If the deposit is by way of a cheque drawn on some bank other than the FED or the receiving bank, then it can only be cleared by a transfer from one bank's HPM balance to another bank's HPM balance. Of course the effect is neutral.

The Central Bank alone can create HPM, for it is Central Bank debt.

Fractional reserve banking is a technique believed in by many Americans, but faith in it is not universal. The required HPM level of British banks is determined in a totally different way. Professor L. Randall Wray states that the compulsory reserve requirement of American banks is about the amount they would need as working balances if there were no reserve requirement. The British government does not prescribe a set level of bank reserves (HPM); they are determined pragmatically by the Financial Services Authority, taking into account liquidity needs for the next week and month. Details are in the FSA's Handbook on its website.

Independent Central Banks

The above analysis predicates a system where the Central Bank is under the control of the government. At the time of writing there is a fashion among politicians and some economists for independent Central Banks. Such fashions come and go. The Bank of England was founded as a private bank, and the Federal Reserve Bank of the United States is in theory owned by the private sector banks. Both cases have caused great ire among left-wing campaigners. They mistake nominal legal ownership for effective beneficial ownership, a very different thing. Although the Bank of England had long been under effective government control, though privately owned, before the Labour Government of 1945 took power, nevertheless ideology dictated that that Government's first act must be to nationalise the Bank. It made no noticeable difference.

Fifty-two years later a new Labour Government enacted that the Bank of England, though still state-owned, should exercise its powers independently of the government. But of course, the Bank was at the same time deprived of the power that mattered, the power to regulate the banking system. That power, and others, were assumed by the Financial Services Authority. Moreover as soon as the Governor of the Bank retired he was replaced by an academic economist, not an experienced banker. That act alone showed that the Bank had become an academics' debating playground, not a serious force. As a concession to its pride and former glory, the Bank is allowed to produce statistics, though it is a mystery why that role is not left to the Office for National Statistics.

The Federal Reserve Bank of the United States is not openly under government control, but its powerful chairman is appointed by the President, so there is some indirect influence. The Central Bank of the German Federal Republic, the Bundesbank, is run by a committee consisting of the chairmen of the individual state 'Landesbanks'. These state-owned banks control a considerable share of German banking, 18 per cent is a figure often quoted, so banking experience, not academic theory, is the most effective force in the German monetary system. Perhaps that is why German borrowers have never been subjected to the ridiculously high interest rates well-known in the United Kingdom and the United States during the period when academic monetarists were so influential.

6
Credit Control by Special Deposits

Sound finance may be right psychologically:
but economically it is very depressing.
JOHN MAYNARD KEYNES

A THIRD TECHNIQUE for controlling the money supply is the use of *Special Deposits*. It was applied with most enthusiasm in the 1960s and 1970s. In 1990 the Labour Party announced that this was the control technique which it would use if it ever gained power. When Labour got power in 1997, the promise was very sensibly forgotten.

The services of Central Banks, such as the Bank of England, are available only to a very few customers. The principal ones are the government, government departments, important financial institutions such as discount houses, the clearing banks, market-makers in government stocks, and the former Guardian Royal Exchange Assurance which had a historical connection. A clearing bank's deposit at the Bank of England is conventionally regarded as its most liquid financial asset after cash, and it is the deposit on which it may need to draw in order to make a remittance to another clearing bank.

There is little point in any bank drawing a cheque upon itself in order to pay money to another party, for that cheque could only be honoured by the recipient using it to open an account with the bank on which it was drawn, a procedure which does nothing at all to change the initial creditor-debtor relationship. Therefore a payment from a bank should ideally be by a cheque, or other form of remittance, which is drawn on an account with some third party, preferably one with the Bank of England.

The Banking Department of the Bank of England, like any other financial institution, must balance its books. If it holds a bank's deposit, it must either make a loan to match it, or buy an investment (an investment is just another form of lending), or else it must hold some form of currency. The currency can be its own, in which case it becomes a creditor of its own Issue Department, which, in turn, holds investments to balance the liability created by the issue of currency. Fortunately the government is usually a ready borrower from the Bank, whether from the Banking Department or the Issue Department, and it is usually not only willing but eager to mop up surplus funds. Consequently in normal times much of the lending made by the Bank of England is to the central government.

When inflation began to be a cause for special concern in the 1960s, the idea that it was attributable to an excess of money caused economists to apply their minds towards the possibility of reducing the supply of money by artificial means. One fashionable method for doing this was to force the banks to deposit more money with the Bank of England than they might otherwise prefer. These additional deposits were called *Special Deposits*, and they were to be fixed and frozen: the banks could use them neither for their ordinary business nor as reserves. The size of the special deposits was fixed at a stated percentage of the banks' own deposits, though the percentages might differ with regard to each class of deposits, long term deposits tending to be totally exempt. In order to make special deposits into a kind of punishment or discipline they commonly earn less than a market rate of interest, and sometimes earn no interest at all. Unless special deposits are required pro rata from every deposit taking/lending institution they can be discriminatory and grossly unfair.

Negative feedback from banks

It is worth noting the reaction of the banks to special deposits; it is an example of the reactive relationship between economic planners and those subjected to planning. The banks examined all their accounts, and eliminated every possible offset account, so that the special deposit was levied on the smallest possible sum. As a result of their action, there is a small but incalculable discontinuity in the published statistics of the money supply.

A close look at the detailed bookkeeping of special deposits reveals that the only way a bank can make a deposit at the Bank of England is to obtain, directly or indirectly, some form of financial instrument which is drawn on the Bank of England. That financial instrument could be banknotes, but they are an unlikely payment medium because, as currency does not earn interest, the banks keep only sufficient to enable them to cover their customers' day by day demands for it. As already explained, it is pointless for a bank to give to the Bank of England a cheque drawn on itself: that can only force the Bank of England to lend the money back to the originating bank. If the bank has money owing to it by another bank, it can draw on that bank instead. This would cause the second bank to draw on its own balance at the Bank of England at the very time when the Bank is probably requiring it also to make special deposits.

Therefore the only practicable way in which the banks can increase their aggregate deposits at the Bank of England is to pay into the Bank cheques, or other forms of payment, drawn on the Bank (i) by the government, (ii) by some other customer of the Bank of England, or (iii) by the Bank on itself.

When the banks increase their deposits at the Bank of England, the Bank lends or invests the deposited money. It has the usual options, (i) to lend to the government, (ii) to buy gilts, (iii) to buy bills of exchange (iv) to buy repos. Sometimes it will lend money to the government which will itself use it to buy investments. It is, of course, likely, if not inevitable, that the investments bought either by the Bank or by the government will be the same ones as those which have been sold by the banks in the first place. All that has happened is that there has been a change of lender. Nothing more significant has taken place.

The special deposit procedure, vaunted by 1960s economists, is at best a zero-sum game. As a control technique it is useless, and can even cause inflation if it raises interest rates and therefore costs. Whether it raises interest rates will depend on the price at which investments are bought by the government. If the purchase of stock is direct from the banks, the liabilities side of their balance sheets, that is their customers' deposits, remains unaltered. The assets side total also remains the same, but the make-up of the assets is now slightly different. The figure for government stocks has fallen, and the figure for deposits at the Bank of England has risen. Meanwhile the Bank of England's deposits and liabilities have both increased. Therefore, if one chooses to include the Bank of England's balances in the money supply figures, something the government is careful not to do, the money supply will have gone up. Since the purpose of the exercise was to bring the money supply down, the whole mechanism has failed. Economists who subscribe to the efficacy of the special deposits regime must disguise their mistake by refusing to include the totals from the Bank of England's balance sheet in the calculation of the money supply. That is neither sensible nor logical: the assets (loans) of the Bank of England **are** part of the credit supply.

A bank could always acquire some of the special Bank of England money by another route. The government or the Bank of England could purchase stock from an investor other than a bank. The purchase price would be deposited by the seller in his own bank, and that would increase that bank's deposits. The bank could then make its special deposit at the Bank of England because it would have received from its customer a cheque drawn on the Bank of England. In other words it would have acquired some Bank of England money, 'HPM'. The money the bank received from its depositor would have increased the money supply further. That arises solely because the Bank of England has provoked an increase in intermediation in the capital market, and simultaneously reduced non-intermediated investment.

In this scenario the Bank of England would have precipitated two increases in the money supply, one in its own books, and one in the books of the bank at which the vendor of the stock holds his account. Thus a technique has been used which has had exactly the opposite effect of that intended. *The intermediated money supply has been expanded, not contracted.* Moreover the vendor of the government stock may go on a potentially inflationary spending spree.

Unpredictable effects

However, the additional deposit created in the banking system may do more than just increase further the amount of special deposit required. It could also prevent the bank concerned from using its capital base to support the creation of further credit. The bank might even need to reduce some other lending, probably by encouraging a customer to fund his debt by raising finance in the non-intermediated capital market. That might appear to achieve the government's objective, but it is rather hit and miss. The consequent limitation of credit growth, if any, will be difficult to predict as it depends to what extent the borrower can resort to the bond market. If the result is merely to replace intermediated with disintermediated credit, surely nothing of significance for the economy has taken place.

There is yet another defect. Special deposits do not necessarily pay the banks as high a rate of interest as the assets which they have been obliged to sell. Indeed, when *supplementary* special deposits were invented in 1973, they were made interest free. The banks, therefore, must charge higher rates of interest for other loans in order to cover the interest payable on their deposits. These higher rates may be determined partly by market forces. The banks cannot dictate them absolutely. But they will try to raise the margin on their variable rate lendings. If the result is that a higher interest rate has to be charged to producers of goods and services, costs will be raised, and, therefore, there will be price inflation. Remember, *'Interest is a cost like any other and must be reflected in prices.'*

If market circumstances allowed the banks to reduce the rates of interest paid on deposit accounts in order to effect a widening of margins, what would be the effect? It could further encourage wealth owners to disintermediate in order to get higher yields in the bond market. If that were to happen, it would free some of the banks' capital base to support the creation of additional credit.

One can, therefore, envisage a wide variety of possible effects from special deposits, each tending to have a different effect on inflation. All the effects are generally unpredictable, a common result of trying to override market forces. The argument embraced by A. H. Gibson was that any fall in deposit interest rates caused wealth owners to contemplate real investment in order to achieve a higher yield. A fall in interest rates also causes bond prices to rise, which may increase the capital base of the banks, if that base is invested in bonds. If bond prices rise investors feel wealthier and are inclined to spend. The permutation of possibilities is potentially as great as the number of people who own financial assets.

For special deposits to have any success in stifling an overheated economy it is therefore essential that they do not cause the interest rate on deposit accounts to be lowered. On the other hand, if the technique of special deposits is implemented in such a way that it reduces demand, that too can increase producers' unit costs, and thereby give rise to price inflation.

Did special deposits cause inflation?

Special deposits were introduced from 1960 onwards as a means to control inflation. In the years thereafter inflation increased from 1.8 per cent in 1960 to a peak of 24.9 per cent in 1975. The five years 1974 to 1979 saw the highest ever inflation, but before one rushes to conclude that special deposits cause inflation rather than cure it, it would be as well to note that other factors were at work also, such as those described in Chapter Four. Special deposits were used twice in 1960, then again in 1964, 1966, and 1970. Between 1973 and 1980 the punitive scheme of supplementary special deposits, also known as *The Corset*, was used several times.

The period 1965 to 1973 is very interesting. The total deposits of the clearing banks rose in that period from a nominal £9.4 billion to £21.1 billion. However, the inflation-adjusted figure was unchanged, a strikingly neutral result. By coincidence or otherwise the whole increase is equal to the additional loans made to industrial and commercial companies. About £5 billion of the increase in loans was covered by increases in deposits by similar companies, the money coming in the main, no doubt, out of the £39 billion of savings of the corporate sector. The main source of disintermediated credit was in shareholders' funds as a result of ploughing back profits. New issues of disintermediated credit (bonds &c.) through the stock market were unimportant by comparison. Building societies were of course unaffected by special deposits. Their annual level of lending quintupled during the same period, with the inevitable result that house price inflation was 200 per cent, well ahead of retail price inflation.

A significant occurrence which coincided with the use of special deposits was the reappearance of unemployment as a serious problem at the same time that inflation was increasing, a phenomenon which was given the name *stagflation.*

It is more than possible that special deposits had exactly the opposite effect of what they were intended to achieve. It would not have been the first – or the last time – that an anti-inflationary device promoted inflation rather than cured it.

No money is taken out of the system

Special deposits do not, cannot, never have, and never will take money out of the system. The technique of special deposits was abandoned after 1980. It had been in fashion for twenty years – two decades during which inflation went soaring. One might reasonably expect its demise to be permanent. But 13 years later it was resurrected by Mr. John Smith, MP, leader of the Labour Party, who appeared to have adopted it as Labour Party policy. In a long televised interview with the redoubtable and respected Mary Goldring he seemed to imply that he favoured the reintroduction of special deposits as a weapon of monetary policy, *'...so that the money cannot be lent.'* Since all money is assignable debt, the stated purpose is unattainable. All present day money is lent. Money is created only by lending it. It is more than time that all prominent politicians grasped that concept. John Smith died before Labour returned to government. His promise was not implemented by his successor who, perhaps, knew more about the operation of the principles of double-entry bookkeeping.

7
Credit Control by Overfunding

The debits are on the side nearest the window.
BANKER'S AIDE MEMOIRE

A PURCHASE of government stock by the government or the Central Bank from the public can cause a problem for the banks. It brings about an increase in their deposits, and as a consequence the banks may have to increase their reserves. This limits the banks' ability to expand further the amount of credit given to the public. Surprisingly, the monetary theorists are under the impression that it is better to do the opposite if the government wishes to restrict the money supply. Indeed, they advocate that the government should over-fund, by selling government stocks to the public rather than purchasing them; overfunding simply means that the government borrows money it does not need.

The theory behind their policy is this:–

A member of the public buys a newly issued gilt and makes out a cheque in payment to the Bank of England. The bank on which the cheque is drawn can only honour that cheque by acquiring some Bank of England money. It does this by selling a gilt or other investment (directly or indirectly) to the Bank of England.

The resulting bookkeeping when the overfunding takes place is:–

The Bank of England's liabilities increase, because the government's cash balance in the Bank's books rises. Its assets also rise, because it has acquired investments from a bank. The bank which holds the account of the customer who has bought gilts sees its deposits and its assets fall by exactly the same amount by which the Bank of England's deposits and assets have risen.

Is this a reduction in the money supply? Only if balances at the Bank of England are ignored when measuring the money supply. How can it be justifiable to ignore them when the Bank of England's deposits are being used to finance investments which are active components of the credit supply, and indeed are probably identical with the investments removed from the banks? Therefore balances of the Bank of England *ought* to be included in the total of intermediated money supply. It is quite wrong to ignore the Bank of England's own banking activities.

Money used to buy gilts is likely to have been previously kept as an investment and therefore had no frequency of circulation. Nor would it have circulated in its debit form on the other side of the bank's balance sheet, if it was represented by a static holding of gilts in the bank's name. Has anything worthwhile been achieved by the manoeuvre of selling gilts to the public? No.

It may, however, have increased the bank's capital adequacy ratio, unless all the investments sold by the bank are those government obligations against which it may not have to hold a capital reserve. We shall have more to say about capital adequacy ratios in Chapter Eight, and all we need say here is that the capital ratio has to be at least eight per cent of risk-weighted assets. The bank's capital base earns interest by being lent, but it does much more than that; as has already been mentioned in Chapter One, it sets the effective limit on the amount of deposits which the bank can accept, and the amount of money it can lend.

How banks make profits

Because the rate of interest a bank charges on loans is more than it pays to its depositors, a profit is earned on its own capital over and above the interest earned by that capital itself. Suppose the following parameters apply: the difference between income on unsecured loans and borrowing costs, after deducting overheads and bad debts, is a quarter of one per cent; the capital ratio is eight per cent; the interest rate is 10 per cent; the risk-weighting is 100 per cent. The calculation of the resultant profit on a loan of £1000 should be as set out in the box overleaf. Our calculation assumes that for the purpose of profit planning it is correct to have first set off all non-interest earning assets, (cash and infra-structure) against non-interest bearing deposits.

With a trivial margin of a quarter of one per cent the basic return on the shareholders' capital is increased by over a quarter, from £8 to £10.30. If, as is now permitted by international convention, only £40 of the £80 capital is shareholders' capital, the other £40 being subordinated loan capital, the return on capital rises to over 25 per cent (because £10.30 is 25.6 per cent of £40).

In 1991 Lloyds Bank achieved a net interest margin on its domestic banking of 5.33 per cent. In 1987 it had been even higher at 5.84 per cent. In 2004 the margin was 2.89 per cent, a reflection of how lower interest

---

Profit on a bank's capital

Bank's capital	£80	x 10.00 per cent	=	£8.00
Deposits	£920	x 0.25 per cent	=	£2.30
Total income after expenses			=	£10.30

Return on capital = $\dfrac{£10.30 \times 100}{£80}$ = 12.88 per cent

---

rates lower the cost of finance, and therefore potential inflation. The post-tax return on total shareholders' assets in 2004 was still a very acceptable 23½ per cent. The tier one capital adequacy ratio was 8.9 per cent, much higher than in 1990, and more than twice the prescribed minimum. A typical balance sheet of a bank in 1990 showed shareholders' funds at five per cent of unweighted liabilities, the rest of the capital base being derived from subordinated loans. The latter capital structure is potentially much more profitable for shareholders.

The directors of some clearing banks have set a target of 20 per cent as the return they aim for on any investment of shareholders' funds. Naturally those banks whose capital adequacy ratio is lower than eight per cent can make do with lower interest margins, because the multiplier is higher. This may explain the aggressively priced loans which Japanese banks were able to offer in Europe before they had to increase their capital adequacy ratios to comply with the Basel Capital Accord.

A bank's capital base must fully earn its keep

The purpose of this explanation is to show why the directors of a bank should not waste the earning power of their shareholders' capital. They must keep the capital adequacy ratio as low as possible, if profit per share is to be maximised. Therefore when overfunding of government debt has the effect of increasing a bank's capital adequacy ratio, as it will if the bank has to sell assets such as bills of exchange which have a high risk-weighting, its directors will be most anxious to reduce the ratio by increasing lending. So when a government funds or over-funds its debt, the effect can be to stimulate the banks very strongly to create more credit. In that case the money supply is fully maintained, and the overall credit supply is increased. The policies pursued since 1979 in the name of controlling inflation, which for a while included overfunding, were effectively sabotaging that objective.

There is evidence that the bankers of Britain have rarely been prepared to waste the earning power of their capital bases by leaving them idle for any lengthy period. On the contrary the history of capital bases is one of increasing risk being taken, though caution has recently become much more fashionable as a result of some nasty experiences, hence the high ratio for Lloyds TSB in 2004. It has been reckoned that in the early 19th century the average capital ratio was 35 per cent. In reality it was higher, for until 1858 shareholders in banks risked unlimited liability, and therefore the reported capital base was only that part of their capital which was employed in the business. The total amount at risk then included all the personal fortunes of the bankers.

The capital base gradually fell to 20 per cent in 1880, to 13 per cent in 1914 and six per cent in the 1920s. The lowest ratio was around two per cent in the 1950s. That does not mean that bankers were then taking exceptional risks since only about 20 per cent of their assets consisted of advances to private sector borrowers. Most of their loans were to the government and therefore deemed risk free. Measured as a percentage of advances to non-government borrowers, the capital base in the 1950s was more than adequate. Around 1959 banks began to increase the proportion of their assets invested in advances and, as a result, found it necessary to raise additional capital.

The published balance sheets and profit and loss accounts of banks for the period before full disclosure began in the early 1970s may not give a true picture. If the banks wished to mislead, it would surely be with intent to exaggerate the strength of their capital bases. Popular myth at the time was probably foolish to credit them with the opposite attitude. In the light of the evidence that no bank has ever done other than try to make the shareholders' funds earn their keep, and that except for rare interludes the capital base has been fully employed, it must be apparent that an economic stratagem which depends for its success on the willingness of directors of banks to forego profit on their shareholders' capital must at most times be ineffective.

Admittedly in the late 1990s the capital adequacy ratios of the banks rose sharply, as we have just seen from the figures of Lloyds TSB. This was partly occasioned by the fact that a large reduction in long-term interest rates caused borrowers to look to the bond market for finance, instead of to the banks. Left with huge reserves they could not safely make use of, some banks took the step of returning unwanted capital to their shareholders. This was done by buying in shares. Barclays Bank in particular carried through several buy-backs. That was interesting, as in

1988 that bank had made the largest rights issue of all time, and had lost all of it by foolish lending.

The results of overfunding

Overfunding was pursued in the period 1980 to 1984. In his book, *Money, Information and Uncertainty*,[1] Professor Charles Goodhart states that '*Within its own framework of reference, the overfunding exercise (of 1980–84) was remarkably successful.*' This claim seems to be belied by his next sentence: '*Although bank lending to the private sector surged ahead over the years 1980–84 at an annual rate of no less than 19.6 per cent...*' Thirty years earlier that rate must have been nearer three per cent. But the full sentence explains his reasoning. He tells us that despite a huge overrun in public spending, the sales of government stock had managed to hold the average annual rate of growth of bank lending to 12½ per cent.

I decided to examine what I regarded as key statistics for the five-year period. I found that gross domestic fixed capital formation (that is real investment) by industrial and commercial companies had been uncannily consistent for the first four years, but with a leap of nearly a fifth in 1984. Borrowing by the companies from banks had been consistent for the first three years, but in 1983 it collapsed by three quarters, then jumped nearly five times from that level in 1984. Total borrowing had been very consistent for all but 1983, when it was a third down. Obviously non-bank borrowing had made up in 1983 for a lot of the fall in borrowing from banks. The savings of the personal sector had also been uncannily stable in the five years despite dipping a little in 1983. Investment by the personal sector in fixed assets and stocks had increased 60 per cent.

There is no purpose to be achieved by trying to interpret these figures as they stand for they need to be adjusted for the huge inflation which took place during the five years. With an index figure of 100 representing the level of prices in 1985, 1979 was 61.3, and 1984 was 94.8. An inflation adjustment would show that there had been a nearly catastrophic fall in company real investment, and a huge fall in personal saving, though personal sector investment had somehow remained stable. It is investment by industrial and commercial companies which is vital for controlling inflation, as it lowers costs, and therefore prices. It had been inhibited. By what? Interest rates, of course. The interbank rate at the start of 1980 was 17.68 per cent and never got below 9.25 per cent during the whole five years. By 1984 the rate had come down sufficiently to raise the level of real investment somewhat.

The theoretical analysis outlined earlier in this chapter leads to the prediction that if lending to the government is blocked, lending to the personal sector is enhanced, the phenomenon which Professor Goodhart reports. It increases the overall credit supply nominal terms, and it may also replace money having a low frequency of circulation with money of a higher frequency of circulation. That the ploy had the opposite effect of that intended may have been a godsend to the British people. It helped slightly to end the recession of the early 1980s. That was important except to those for whom an inflation-free pound is a sacrament. The fact that real investment by industrial and commercial companies was severely reduced was doubtless not the result of overfunding, but of extremely high interest rates at the start of the five years.

The overfunding exercise stripped the banks of Treasury Bills. Having eliminated that reserve asset, the Bank of England responded by accepting commercial bills of exchange in return for increasing commercial banks' reserve assets. To quote Goodhart again, *'The overfunding exercise led the authorities to accumulate a bill mountain.'*

The sad story does not end there. By the end of 1990 the gilt holdings of Barclays Bank were down to a half of one per cent of its assets. As the overfunding exercise had stripped the clearing banks of gilts, the Bank of England had to continue to buy commercial bills from the banks, no gilts being available. Thus it was buying investments for which the banks selling them had to have a full eight per cent capital adequacy ratio. Therefore the government was freeing the banks' capital base for further credit creation. Perhaps the banks instructed their staff to foster the use of bills of exchange as a lending medium so that they always had plenty of bills available to sell to the Bank of England. Professor Goodhart states that the overfunding policy put so much money into the bill market that it had the effect of reducing discount rates on bills of exchange. That means that, among other things, it cheapened the financing of imports, which are often paid for with bills of exchange! Far from restricting the availability of credit, the Bank of England was fuelling it. But the beneficiaries were importers of foreign goods, not British companies wishing to pursue fixed capital formation.

Would underfunding be better?

If overfunding can have the opposite effect of what is intended, could that also be true of underfunding? Underfunding has been suggested as a way of expanding the money supply. That would seem logical, for if the government does not fund its debt by selling gilts, it must borrow from the banks. That must increase the supply of intermediated credit and also increase cash holdings with the power to circulate. If the government monopolises the intermediated credit supply, which is limited in size by the required capital adequacy ratio, then surely private sector borrowers are squeezed out?

Not necessarily, for government borrowing direct from banks can be zero risk-weighted for the purpose of the Basel Capital Accord, and no capital base is therefore required. Admittedly the United Kingdom is not taking advantage of the authorisation of a nil risk-weighting for all government debt. Gilts appear to have been given 10 or 20 per cent risk-weightings.

Underfunding however implies some direct borrowing from banks to cover a budget deficit, and that lending by the banks requires no capital base. If the required capital ratio of the banks is calculated on loans other than those to the government, underfunding would not reduce the supply of credit to the private sector. Nor would it increase it. The hope of those who have advocated some underfunding seems to be that the increased deposits which would be created would circulate freely, and have a multiplier effect on the money supply. Unfortunately, for a credit multiplier effect to take place there has to be an increase in the capital base of the banks as it is bound to mean increases in loans which attract a full risk-weighting. So we are back to square one!

But is there really all that much difference for money control purposes between a cash deposit and a holding of gilts when the latter can be traded for cash in minutes? Any competent investor knows that gilts are as good as cash. That is why gilt turnover on the stock-market is counted in trillions.

8

The Basel Capital Accord

Debt is the worst poverty.
THOMAS FULLER, M.D.

I F THE FRACTIONAL RESERVE THEORY described in Chapter Five is a technical error, is there any effective restriction on bank lending?

Yes there is. As we have already seen the amount a bank can lend is a function of its capital base, and the capital base can be neutered by raising capital adequacy ratios, or the growth of the capital base can be regulated. The latter would be very controversial. This is the first truth about the money supply.

We have already looked at the matter of capital adequacy ratios (CARs) but it may be useful to state the principle again. For the purpose of monetary theory the capital base of a bank consists of its shareholders' funds, plus its subordinated loan capital,[1] minus any capital which is invested in intangible assets such as goodwill, minus trade investments such as shares in subsidiary or associated companies not involved in banking and which may not be readily realisable, and minus any other asset which is difficult to sell. Ideally the capital base should consist of comparatively liquid assets.

In the published accounts of a bank the total of shareholders' funds is nowadays clearly identified, but it may also be broken down into several components. One of those components will always be the nominal value of the ordinary share capital in issue. Other items contributing to the total of shareholders' funds will be the nominal value of preference share capital, undistributed profit, share premium account, and possibly other reserves. Some reserves are not part of shareholders' funds: for instance a reserve for deferred taxation is not normally shown as belonging to the shareholders, even though it does not belong to anyone else. It can be huge.

Loan capital can also take a multiplicity of forms, but the common attribute is that in a liquidation of the bank, owners of the loan capital will not be repaid until the depositors have been paid in full, though they will be repaid before the shareholders get anything. Technically deposits are also loans to the bank, so in order to distinguish loan capital from deposits it is described as subordinated loan capital.

The 1988 Basel Accord on Capital Adequacy

Under the provisions of the original 1988 *Basel Accord on Capital Adequacy* (since revised), the capital base of a bank determined lending capacity in the following way. First, the risk value of the bank's assets was calculated in accordance with a scale of weightings decided by the Central Bank under the discretions given to it by the Accord. Most assets counted in full, but mortgages by occupiers of residential property might be reduced by 50 per cent. The obligations of governments which are members of the OECD could be ignored completely. After all the permitted reductions, one arrived at *the risk-weighted value of assets*. The 1988 Accord is still valid, but a newer version permits a different, more sophisticated, approach to determination of risk for those banks which have computer systems capable of making use of it.

The Accord stated that the capital base of the bank may not be less than eight per cent of the risk-weighted value of the assets. The percentage the capital bears to the risk-weighted value of the assets is known as the capital adequacy ratio, or just *capital ratio*. The Accord broke the capital base down into two tiers: tier one is roughly shareholders' funds, and tier two is subordinated loans plus other liabilities. There are however some grey areas because some more exotic varieties of capital do not fit neatly into either category. Some forms of capital, such as convertible loan stocks, even have the capacity to change category. Initially tier two, on conversion into shares they become tier one. Unrealised profits on investments are not looked on with unqualified favour, and they may not necessarily be counted in full in the capital base. That has caused a problem for Japanese banks. In Japan it has been very common for the bank's capital base to be invested in the shares of quoted companies rather than in loans to customers.

Although an international agreement on capital adequacy was not achieved until 1988, the Bank of England as semi-official regulator had been applying capital adequacy rules for a long time, though how long it is difficult to ascertain. All the regulatory work of the Bank used to take place in secret, and amazingly was rarely mentioned among practising bankers. All we knew about capital adequacy was culled from occasional announcements by the Bank of England, and references in the financial journals and financial press. We gathered that an eight per cent capital adequacy ratio was required, and that illiquid assets could not be counted. Some work, and very good work must have been going on somewhere, but it was not a hot topic, even in high level banking circles.

Earlier attempts to ensure capital adequacy

Capital adequacy had not always been ignored. Indeed it became an issue shortly after the formation of the Bank of England in 1694. Readers will recall that the Bank was founded in order to fund on a more permanent basis some £1,200,000 of government debt. Investors were invited to subscribe that amount for shares in the new bank, and the Bank would take over the existing debts, which were presumably evidenced originally by government tallies. The Bank in return would receive an annuity of 8 per cent on the money, plus a service charge of £4,000. The Bank was granted a monopoly of banking within 65 miles of London. The £1,200,000 became the capital base of the bank. The Bank accepted deposits, and with them was able to commence the business of discounting bills of exchange.

Within a couple of years or so the amounts of the discounts were worth twice the value of the Bank's own capital, and this caused some worry and comment. In the modern age a capital adequacy ratio of fifty per cent would be regarded as grossly excessive. It looks as though for the first time in banking history a bank had its capital base invested in government debt, a not very liquid debt and historically a rather risky thing to do. Surprisingly it worked, and the Bank was able to lend depositors' money to private borrowers, and provide some finance to the government. The historic riskiness of lending to a government caused the Bank to be very cautious in its banking operations, and for much of its history it was a drag on the economy, and was probably not very profitable. Besides banking it also dealt in bullion, at a ridiculously low margin, about 0.16 per cent. It is difficult to see how the bank could ever have made any worthwhile profit out of its investment in gold bullion unless the turnover was very, very fast. It would be interesting to research the Bank's business success.

To follow up the question of the practice of capital adequacy rules I asked the librarian of the Chartered Institute of Bankers (also known as the Institute of Financial Services) to help me, thinking that the library might hold copies of Bank of England directives. It did not. The librarian suggested that the best he could suggest was that I read *Money and Banking in the UK: A History* by Michael Collins,[2] and he also produced *Supervising International Banks: Origins and Implications of the Basle Accord* by Ethan B. Kapstein.[3]

Collins' excellent book included a survey of the capital adequacy of banks from the early nineteenth century onwards. It showed that in the days of small private banks before joint stock banking was allowed the adequacy ratio was as high as thirty per cent. That meant that nearly a third of the money which bankers lent was their own. It would be difficult to give a precise figure of the capital reserves of banking partnerships, as the partners were, of course, liable to depositors up to the full extent of their own assets, whether they were in the banking balance sheet or not. When joint stock banking with limited liability became the norm after 1844, it was quite common for banks to have a level of uncalled capital which could only be demanded from shareholders in the event of a liquidation. Even in the 1950s Lloyds Bank had shares with an uncalled liability; that is the shares were partly paid.

Collins says that the adequacy ratio fell to around ten per cent at the beginning of the twentieth century, and during the 1939–45 War it fell to two per cent. But during the war 80 per cent of bank assets were in the form of government debts, so the low ratio was deemed not to matter. Governments were no longer the pariah borrowers they were in mediaeval times, as their ability to tax had strengthened greatly. At the end of the war, the banks slowly started to unravel their dependence on lending to the government. The change meant that capital reserves had to be strengthened, and Barclays Bank had its first issue of new shares for perhaps more than a generation in 1961.

The world was not over-eager to adopt the British system of capital ratios. The story is that ten of the twelve members of the Bank for International Settlements were reluctant. The Bank of England put pressure on the Federal Reserve Bank to join it in pushing the others to agree. A slightly reluctant FED gave way, and the Accord came into being.

The Accord is born

The year chosen for the implementation of the Basel Capital Accord was 1993, following the end of each bank's financial results for the accounting year ending in 1992. Under the system already enforced by the Bank of England shareholders' funds in United Kingdom banks hovered at around five per cent of risk-weighted assets, slightly more than the internationally agreed minimum of four per cent.

The upper limit on a bank's risk-weighted lending capacity is twelve and a half times its capital base, and twenty-five times shareholders' funds, whichever was the less. With the sole exception of some government borrowing, the intermediated credit supply is therefore strictly limited by the capital base of the banks.

The nil risk-weighting allowed by the Accord for the obligations of OECD governments looks like a huge loophole, which might allow the infinite expansion of the credit supply by profligate governments, and could even lead to hyperinflation. I understand that some national regulators have not permitted the full exemption authorised by the Accord, and it appears that 10 and 20 per cent weightings are required for some government liabilities, the exact percentage depending on the length of maturity.

When the United States Government gave thought to the subject in the mid 1980s, it decided that the weighting for government securities should be 30 per cent. The United States government appears to have been a late convert to the concept of weightings, for its original proposals ignored them. A fixed capital adequacy ratio of shareholders' funds to assets of 5½ per cent was applied, regardless of the quality of the assets. Under such a regime the limitation of the money supply by the capital base is total. The fixed ratio did not take into account off-balance sheet items; subsequent regulations did so. In January 1986 the United States Federal Reserve Board announced its proposals to apply risk-weighting – thereby adopting the line already taken by the Bank of England – and to keep the 5½ per cent fixed ratio.

The proposal to allow the obligations of OECD governments to be given, at national discretion, a nil risk-weighting has worried many commentators. One point which may however have escaped notice is that if there is no capital base needed in respect of bank lendings to governments, the return on assets for the bank is infinite provided it has some profit margin on the loans. A bank could use this profit to subsidise its other loans, or to pay for the money transfer system. It is possible that this took place in Britain during the period 1939–60, when a huge proportion of bank lending was to the government.

Slow recognition

General recognition outside the banking world of the importance of CARs was a long time coming. Until the 1980s it was notable by its absence from the literature on monetary theory. The most famous book on monetary theory, *The Treatise on Money* by J. M. Keynes,[4] contains no suggestion that bank capital adequacy ratios set the upper limit of the money supply. Familiar textbooks on economics were also silent. A large number of the publications by the Institute of Economic Affairs has been searched in vain to find references to it. The Chartered Institute of Bankers used to recommend to students of monetary theory Brian Kettel's book, *Monetary Economics*. Kettel mentions the discussion paper issued in 1975 by the Governor of the Bank of England on capital adequacy ratios, but he is silent about their significance in limiting the money supply.[5]

Professor Charles Goodhart, once an adviser on monetary policy to the Bank of England, wrote two important books on monetary theory and practice. The earlier, *Money, Information and Uncertainty*,[6] was first published in 1975. A second edition appeared in 1989. It has no reference in its index to the capital base of the banks. Nevertheless Goodhart must be given the credit for raising the subject, for in his other book, called *Monetary Theory and Practice*,[7] the importance of capital adequacy ratios is discussed at pages 115, 167–169, and 179. One suspects that Professor Goodhart, in his role as adviser, may have originated the Governor's paper of 1975 on capital adequacy ratios. His discussion of them appears to be more concerned with banking prudence rather the control of the money supply, but it is implicit in his remarks that he is aware of the point, even though he may not have highlighted it to the extent one would wish.

In January 1992 the truth finally received proper recognition when Professor David Llewellyn of Loughborough University stated categorically in an article in *Banking World* (then the journal of the Chartered Institute of Bankers) that the capital base of the banks is the ultimate determinant of their lending capacity.[8] As money is created only by the process of granting loans, it follows that the banks' capital base is also the final limiting factor on the money supply. The only loophole is the one already mentioned, the generous treatment of loans to OECD governments.

The effect of the Accord on Japan

If Japanese conspiracy theorists were to claim that the first Basel Accord on capital adequacy was part of a plan by Japan's economic rivals to destroy the Japanese economy, they could make a very convincing case.

We set out above some of the history of the level of capital adequacy ratios in Britain. In Japan things were managed rather differently, and far more dangerously.

The Japanese have a very admirable characteristic. They are not ashamed to look at what other nations do, to copy it if it appears good, and to improve upon it. As an example, Richard A. Werner, in his book *Princes of the Yen*,[9] describes how in 1938 the Japanese abandoned their free market, US-style, economy in order to copy the national socialist economy of Germany. They adopted aggressive state planning, but seemed to have avoided the worst pitfalls of the national socialist system.

In the 1960s Japan became a powerful economic force, and the need to improve its financial systems became apparent to the government and to the banks. The banks set up offices in London and went systematically about studying every aspect of British financial practice. They got full co-operation from the British banks, and in 1972 and 1973 I found that a lot of my working time had to be devoted to arranging study courses for Japanese bankers, especially officials from the Japanese Trust Banks. In return they were most responsive to my requests to learn more about Japanese practices. Unfortunately my interest was not shared by the officials of the Bank of England. In 1976, at a banking conference in Cambridge, I asked a very senior Bank of England official if he and his colleagues ever went abroad to study foreign banking and capital systems, to see what they could copy and improve upon. He looked as though he was going to explode. *'Of course not! We might occasionally go abroad to tell the foreigners what to do.'*

What he had consequently missed was that the Japanese had perfected systems for mobilising the savings of the general public for the medium-term financing of Japanese industrial growth. It was popular capitalism on a gigantic scale. When I asked an official of a Trust Bank what percentage of the Japanese public invested in Loan and Money Trusts, the investment media of the Trust Banks, his idiomatic reply was *'Every percentage.'* The mobilisation of the savings of the Japanese people was necessary because the war and inflation had destroyed the wealth of the prewar rich. The Trust Banks had originally specialised in servicing the oligarchy of rich families, but by 1952 had concluded they had to find a new function. I was given a translation of the statutes under which they operated and I noticed with interest that the legislation had been influenced by British Trust Law.

The Japanese must have also studied the German banking scene, and here they made what was to turn out to be a serious mistake. They noted that the German commercial banks invested in the equity of the companies to which they lent money. One assumes that one of the reasons the German banks can invest in long-term assets is because they have long-term liabilities in their balance sheets in the form of their pension liabilities. Unlike British practice, pension funds in Germany can be internally invested. If Barclays Bank were allowed to do the same thing it would add £13 billion of very long-term liabilities to its balance sheet.

The Japanese banks decided to copy the German practice, even though they did not have similar long-term liabilities.

The other thing the Japanese did was to cut the capital base to the minimum. What Professor David Llewellyn wrote for the January 1992 issue *Banking World* include the following:–[10]

> *Capital is an important dimension in banking for several reasons. Firstly, because it is the ultimate determinant of banks' lending capacity; assets are funded by deposits and capital but they cannot be expanded beyond the limit of the multiple of the minimum required capital-assets ratio. Thus the availability and cost of capital determines the maximum level of assets.*
>
> *Secondly, because capital has to be serviced, it represents a significant cost to banks and hence the amount of capital a bank needs to hold (and its price) has an impact on the pricing of banking business.*
>
> *Thirdly, the structure of capital (especially the balance between debt and equity) may have an impact on various aspects of the banking business because the cost of different components varies and because, as not all forms of capital perform all the functions required of capital, they are not perfectly substitutable.*
>
> *Fourthly, capital is a principal aspect of regulation which defines minimum capital adequacy standards, the form in which capital can be issued, the characteristics of allowable capital instruments, and the balance between different forms of capital...*
>
> *Fifthly, the cost of capital together with the amount of capital banks maintain, has a decisive impact on their competitive position especially compared with the capital market. If a bank faces a shortage of capital, or if the cost is high, it loses business to competitors, including the capital market and other suppliers of credit. There is, therefore, no aspect of the business of banking that is not either directly or indirectly influenced by the cost and availability of capital.*

Professor Llewellyn's article also compared the 1988 capital adequacy ratios of the National Westminster Bank (NatWest) and of Dai-Ichi Kangyo (DIK), the former being at that time the largest bank in the world by equity capital, and the latter the largest measured by deposits. The Japanese bank was able to earn a higher rate of return on equity with a return on assets half that of the British bank. The reason was that DIK had an equity capital ratio 60 per cent lower than NatWest. Respectively they were 2.4 and 6.1 per cent. As the Basel Accord set an equity capital ratio of at least 4 per cent, it was obvious that the implementation of the accord would mean that DIK would either, 1) have to raise more equity capital, or

2) cut back on its lending. Professor Llewellyn discussed several strategies in detail.

Lending to Robert Maxwell

The Japanese practice of keeping low equity reserves made them formidable competitors internationally. A rough calculation indicated that they could offer a loan at an interest rate half a per cent below a British bank, and yet still maintain the same return on equity capital (shareholders' funds). In the 1980s British bankers saw their good quality corporate lending disappear, won by the Japanese, who could offer a lower interest rate. A senior director of Barclays remarked in my presence that he did not know why the Japanese could offer such low rates of interest. At that time no-one present had the knowledge to enlighten him. In May 1988, ignorant no doubt of the reason for the anomaly, Sir John Quinton, Chairman of Barclays Bank, decided to fight back. He raised £920 million of new capital and went on a lending spree. In the next 19 months he raised the Barclays balance sheet total by £41 billion, and raised lending on mortgage by 50 per cent. Unfortunately the industrial lending available to Barclays at that time was what one might call 'The Robert Maxwell layer of lending.' According to his successor as Chief Executive, Quinton lost the whole £920 million and more. Some Barclays staff allege that they were inspired by a slogan, *'Number One, by Ninety-One,'* but that is hotly denied by the management.

In 1988 DIK's return on capital was 29.8 per cent. Nat West's was 23.3 per cent. If DIK raised additional capital to equal the requirements of the Basel Accord, its return on equity would fall to 17.33. To equal the CAR of Nat West, its return would fall to 11.72 per cent. One imagines that that would not have pleased the market or have been digestible by Japanese pride. One must assume that they therefore cut back on lending, beginning with the loans to foreign borrowers, and continuing by reducing lending to property owners. The whole experience needs researching in detail, but no research has yet come to my attention.

The banks had four years to comply. The Basel Accord levels of CAR had to be implemented by Fiscal 1993. During that period, 1) Japanese bank profitability fell, 2) the Nikkei Share Index fell from above 37,000 to under 17,000, reducing the value of bank reserves, 3) reduced availability of borrowing caused company growth to falter, triggering falls in share prices, 4) reduced lending to property speculators sent land prices down 60 per cent. (Figures for the level of prices are available on the web-site of The Japanese Real Estate Institute.) This fall reduced the collateral for existing loans, and revealed bad debts. Attempts were made by the authorities during the following years to support the Nikkei, but in 2000 the slide from 20,000 became relentless until a level of around 8,000 was reached.

The banks became far too unprofitable to raise new capital from investors, and everything else they did to meet Basel CARs just aggravated the problem. There were other reasons for the collapse, and these have been brilliantly revealed by Professor Richard A. Werner in his amazing book, *Princes of the Yen*, but the experience also supports very strongly the valuable point made by him in his later book, *A New Paradigm in Macroeconomics*.[11] He perceived that the Basel Accord acts pro-cyclically '*worsening both the state of the economy and, ironically the state of the banking system.*' The idea that banks should have adequate reserves is a good one, but they must be free to use them when a crisis occurs. Under the present arrangements that does not happen. They have to maintain the reserve regardless of what is happening, and if that means that loans have to be cut back, a worsening of the recession is inevitable, and has no theoretical bottom limit.

Another point of concern is property taxation. The taxes on company assets of land and equipment are in Japan at such a level as to amount to confiscation of the equity in a country where very low returns on assets are the norm. In additional a general property tax of 0.15 per cent on all property was introduced, perhaps the result of agitation for increased property taxation. The capitalised value of property taxation comes straight off the price, so any increase reduces property values, and the value of the property as collateral falls. Although 0.15 per cent does not appear to be much by British standards, in a country where yields on investments were minuscule, it was a serious imposition. The general property tax is at the time of writing in abeyance, but has not been abolished.

Derivatives

In 1998, after long negotiations, the Basel Accord was extended to cover derivatives trading. I was no longer in the financial services industry, but for a while I heard a little about the negotiations that went on from an official of Standard Chartered Bank with whom I was in touch. I gathered from him that banks were finding that they could not make enough profit out of the commissions charged for futures trading, and therefore wanted to take positions in order to increase their profits. As derivatives trading, like all gambling, is a zero-sum game, this was remarkable. It goes against the experience of the ages in the second oldest profession, that of bookmaker. Bookmakers do not gamble themselves, if they can help it. The principle of making a book is to set such odds that will, firstly, create a margin of probability in favour of the bookmaker, and secondly tempt as much money to be bet one way on a happening as is risked the other way. The losses and profits of the gamblers should be equal, but for the small cut which the careful setting of the odds should ensure will go to the bookmaker. If his book is not balanced, the bookmaker will try to lay off the difference with another bookmaker whose book may be unbalanced in the opposite direction.

If this practice is rigorously followed, the risk to the bookmaker is minuscule. Derivatives traders are lucky in that they have another source of income, not available to bookmakers. They charge commissions. They should not need to gamble on their own account.

If banks involved in derivatives trading do take positions, that is gamble on their own account, reserves are needed. The Bank for International Settlements (BIS) imposed capital adequacy ratios in respect of the risks, and this move may have caught Far Eastern banks with inadequate reserves. The date for implementation of the reserve requirement was the 1st January 1998. The 'Far East Crisis' started three months before, and it seems very likely that it was caused by the need to reduce the amount of trading, and that the unwinding of deals in panic circumstances triggered a crisis. Research is needed to ascertain what happened. Economists did not wait for research to be done, but assumed another cause for the crisis.

There is now a Basel Accord Mark II to be implemented. It is very technical and complex compared with the first Accord. It does not necessarily increase the size of CARs, but it makes the way of calculating risk more sophisticated and could, perhaps, be used to ease the problems of banks. Indeed there is a suspicion that the new Accord is a complex fudge to allow big international banks to reduce their CARs, but it would require a master statistician to decide what the effect will be. Perhaps it is more than a cynical guess to suggest that the new Accord is academic flim-flam to hide a lowering of standards.

Conspiracy theorists would probably be wrong to believe that the Basel Accord was an Anglo-Saxon plot, deliberately intended to wreck the Japanese Banks, but it certainly achieved that, with a little help from other factors. The Japanese banks all became insolvent and had to be recapitalised by the State. That cost the tax-payers nothing directly. The banks were given access to additional funds, created out of thin air, at a very low cost, and were able to re-lend the funds at very profitable rates, and thus restored their shareholders' funds. The reduction of the discount rate to zero must have been a great help to that process.

A weapon of control

Could capital adequacy ratios be used to control the credit supply? If the above analysis of the Japanese banking crisis is correct, and further research is needed to establish that, then the empirical evidence would appear to suggest they could. But the case is not completely clear. The public might quickly find other ways of creating credit. If it did work, it might be a very powerful weapon indeed. Would one want to place such a powerful weapon in the hands of government bureaucrats? Do they have a proved record of competence in understanding such matters and in making policy? No, they do not. Dr. Don Brash, governor of the Reserve Bank of New Zealand appointed a committee to consider the use of this weapon. While accepting the validity of the argument in favour of it, the committee decided to continue as before.[12]

The Exchange Rate Mechanism

If there had been real competence available in Britain, the 1992 affair of the Exchange Rate Mechanism (ERM) would never have come to the result it did. To remind readers of what happened, the British government had decided to try to keep Sterling within a narrow trading band in relation to a basket of other European currencies. Speculators saw this as an opportunity to gamble on a certainty, and they were able to muster more funds to attack Sterling than the British government could muster to defend it. Britain was forced to exit ignominiously from the ERM and resume a free float of the pound. The irony is that the pound stands in 2005 at a level higher than that at which it was supposed to stand within the ERM. The loss to the British people from the action of the speculators has been variously estimated at between three and five billion pounds, the lower being the official guess.

Much of the money gambled by the speculators was borrowed from banks. Why did not the Governor of the Bank of England take action against the banks involved? One can imagine with relish one of those famous meetings between the Governor and the Chairmen of the banks at which the Chairmen got their knuckles metaphorically rapped. But it really required something bigger than that. The meeting should have been with the heads of all 460 banks listed as 'UK Banks', and the governor should have asked those who had lent money to the speculators to own up. Those who confessed should have been punished by having their banking licenses withdrawn. To sabotage an attempt to maintain the stability of a currency just because it presents a guaranteed way of making a profit without risk should be regarded as a act of economic treason.

What sets the exchange value?

While we are on the subject of exchange rates we can look at one of the technical factors which determines them.

Britain decided not to be in the first batch of members of the European Union to join the Euro-system. A possible rational reason for not doing so, as distinct from the emotional factors which probably decided the question, was that at that time Sterling stood too high against the other currencies. But the result of not entering the Euro-system was to drive Sterling higher still. The Euro-system countries each held some reserves in the currencies of the others. Once within the system, they could no longer do that; their reserves had to be placed in non-euro-system currencies. They were hardly likely at that time to wish to place substantial reserves in those many currencies whose names begin with an 'R', though in the longer-term there could be good profit in doing so. No, they chose Sterling and the US Dollar. As a result both appreciated sharply. It was a one-off effect, but the new level was maintained by sentiment. A look at the web-site of the European Central Bank (ECB) reveals that the Bank is proud of the fact that all its reserves are invested externally. But the Bank's reserves are not the only Euro-system reserves, for there are still reserves, nine times greater, maintained by the eleven Euro-system Central Banks, bringing the total Euro-system reserves to over 400 billion euros. All but a trivial part of these reserves are externally invested.

One can speculate with some confidence as to what would happen if Britain announced it will join the Euro-system. All the Euro-system reserves which are currently in Sterling would have to be re-located. Sterling would flop instantly. We know this would happen as there has already been one false start. Rumour that the British government was planning to push to join the Euro-system sent Sterling immediately plummeting, recovering again when the rumour was firmly denied.

9

The Currency Principle

There are two problems in my life. The political ones are
insoluble, and the economic ones are incomprehensible.
SIR ALEC DOUGLAS HOME

ALTHOUGH MONETARISM may be thought by many to be a modern economic theory, its essential belief has been part of economic history since money was invented.

Wealth owners, that is the possessors of financial assets, are very anxious that the purchasing power of their financial assets shall be maintained, and preferably increased. It is this concern which inspires monetarism. Debtors, on the other hand, would prefer to see the real value of their liabilities reduced, and certainly not increased. The final transfer of control of the British government from the monarch to a wealthy elite in the eighteenth century put deflation at the head of the menu. The further transfer in the twentieth century of control from a wealthy elite to representatives of trade unions and the poor, enabled the inflators, after a long battle which initially they seemed to lose badly, to get the upper hand of the deflators.

In Britain the debasing of the currency by the ruler himself was developed to an advanced art by King Henry VIII. The coinage became so debased that what were supposed to be silver coins in fact had only a thin coating of silver. This wore off with the result that the King became known as *Old Copper Nose*, as the first place for the silver to wear off was on the King's effigy.

Queen Elizabeth I was urged to restore the silver content of the coins to its former level. Her adviser was Sir Thomas Gresham, a banker himself, who carried on business at 'The Sign of the Grasshopper' in London's Lombard Street. The street got its name from the Italian bankers who set up business there, coming mostly from cities such as Sienna and Florence in Lombardy. Gresham advised the restoration of the real worth of the currency, and in 1572 his wish was fulfilled. This must have been a disaster for debtors, as the real value of their debts was markedly increased. The resultant deflation caused a recession, and it is estimated that GDP dropped substantially during the remainder of Queen Elizabeth's reign. Her income from taxes was so far below expenditure that she kept things going by selling state assets. At her death in 1603, Queen Elizabeth's debts totalled £400,000.

Sir Thomas Gresham survives in economic history as the author of 'Gresham's Law' which states, *'A bad currency drives out the good.'* If it were true, it might be no bad thing, as the encouragement of the opposite process has been very harmful.

Another revaluation

The Napoleonic Wars cost Britain an enormous sum of money, some say around £1.5 billion. Government debt rose sharply. As is usual, the war caused inflation which in turn forced the Bank of England in 1797 to abandon the practice of guaranteeing that banknotes could be exchanged for gold at a fixed price. Despite, or more likely because of, the great expenditure on war and subsidies for allies, the economy boomed, and Britain became the leading industrial power. The great benefits which flowed from the cutting of the link with gold were not appreciated enough by the economists of the time.

Once peace had been achieved in 1815, the question arose as to whether the 'gold standard' should be resumed, and if so at what rate. David Ricardo is quoted as saying that he would not contemplate trying to restore a currency which had depreciated 30 per cent (it was probably more.) Nevertheless in 1821 the decision was taken to restore the gold value of the currency to the level which had obtained prior to 1797. The enormous debts incurred to fight the wars therefore became far greater in value in real terms than they were when they were incurred. Those who had been made wealthy by the wars received a gigantic bonus. Those who held government bonds received a double bonus as yields fell. The big winners included the Rothschilds.[1]

Once again the effects were terrible, and particularly so on agriculture. The war had brought a boom to agriculture, and farmland reached a price level in 1814 it was not to see again until about 1949 in nominal terms, and 1968 in real terms. The destruction of agriculture led to great suffering, and the episode of *The Tolpuddle Martyrs* in 1834. Prices were forced down by the deflationary measures, and the price of wheat fell so much in nominal terms that it triggered the implementation of a tariff on imports. The legislation, known to history as *The Corn Laws,* had been in existence for some time, and in 1811 Professor The Reverend Thomas Malthus had prepared a paper which discussed the pros and cons of protection for agriculture. He tried not to judge the issue; his object, he claimed was merely to provide the legislators with the arguments either way.[2]

At the time he was writing, wheat prices were above the level which triggered the protection of an import tax, but Malthus speculated as to what would happen if the currency appreciated and prices fell far enough to trigger an import tax. The fall in wheat prices, and the imposition of an import duty came at a time when the population was rising rapidly, and the economy was rapidly industrialising. Workers moved from the land to work in the factories, often in terrible conditions. Agitators protested that the workers were being prevented by the Corn Laws from getting cheap food. The *Anti-Corn Law League* was formed, and its supporters went the length and breadth of the country to argue their case. I came across the records of some of these meetings in the public library in Lockerbie in Dumfries and Galloway, a very rural area, and it was fascinating to read what the protesters said. Honesty of argument was not apparent, and no-one was perceptive enough to put the blame for the problem on the return to the Gold Standard, or on an over-valued currency. The fact that deflation had increased the purchasing power of a given nominal amount of money was not understood.

The Leaguers were not concerned at the suffering their proposals would cause to farm-workers, and they bravely went into the countryside itself to campaign, hence the meeting in Dumfries-shire. They used the argument that the real beneficiaries of the Corn Laws were the landlords, and the farm-workers believed them. Like all good campaigning deceptions it had, of course, an element of truth in it, as rents had been slow to fall, but the future was to prove that the workers would suffer as well, and suffer terribly.[3]

Nor were the campaigners the slightest bit concerned about the effects their proposals could have in the countries which were expected to send Britain cheap food. As events were to reveal, the repeal of the Corn Laws was to be a disaster of hideous magnitude for the native peoples of North America and South America, and to many other peoples too.

A government dominated by landowners tried to resist the agitation, but the arrival of potato blight in the British Isles caused an appalling famine, and in 1846 the leader of the agricultural interest, Sir Robert Peel, was, unexpectedly, the Prime Minister who effected the repeal of the Corn Laws. Significantly perhaps, the Chicago wheat futures market opened in 1848.

Though the tariffs on agricultural produce had protected farming, they must also have delayed necessary improvements in efficiency. So the abolition of protection probably had harsher effects than would have been the case if the deflation of the 1820s had never triggered the imposition of tariffs. Faced with a steady erosion of profit margins over several decades, the industry might have had time to attain the efficiency it was to achieve a century later in different conditions.

The repeal to the Corn Laws became part of a campaign for Free Trade. The centre of the Campaign was the heavily industrialised city of Manchester, and Benjamin Disraeli gave the name '*The Manchester System*' to what was proposed.[4] The intention was that Britain should be the industrial workhouse of the world, and the rest of the world would produce primary products, that is raw materials and food. It was argued that free trade was to everyone's advantage. Even before the Corn Laws were repealed, Disraeli had used great literary skill to expose just what the industrial revolution was doing to the British people. He supplemented his personal experiences by dramatising brilliantly the contents of the reports of Parliamentary Commissions, especially that of 1832, which few would otherwise have seen. The result is an amazing romance called *Sybil: or The Two Nations*.[5] The two nations were of course the rich and the poor. Such was the effect of the book that even today rarely a week goes by without some newspaper leader-writer advocating passionately the need for 'One Nation Politics.' But such was the popularity of free trade at the time, that even Disraeli began to compromise. He was accused of being led by his party, instead of leading it.

Although most modern economics students are automatically indoctrinated with the benefits to the whole world of a free trade system, there are those who see it as far from wholly good. The most informed and articulate of the critics is Professor Michael Hudson, who in a book entitled *Trade Development and Foreign Debt* has argued that Britain's adoption of free trade was a clever act of economic imperialism, for the rewards of free trade to countries which are secondary producers always turn out to be greater than to those which are primary producers. Also economies of scale are greatest in secondary industry. An efficient secondary producer can easily destroy any emerging competition in less advanced countries, because it can sell into those countries at prices which reflect its low marginal costs, not its higher unit costs.

British capital was deployed to develop primary industry around the world. In the Argentine the natives of the Pampas were already being ruthlessly exterminated at the time when Charles Darwin visited the country in HMS Beagle.[6] The Pampas was later to become a source of beef for Britain, and huge quantities of British capital were invested there. It now supplies Germany and other European countries. In North America the Great Plains were cleared of bison and Native Americans, the number of the latter falling from an estimated 4,000,000 in 1520, when Europeans first arrived, to 290,000 in 1890. The depopulated prairies produced cereals, and in the 1880s British capital was applied to beef production. Many ranches were developed with British capital.[7]

The British policy of dependency on foreign food supplies was assisted by the development of the use of the British currency as a reserve currency, with the inevitable result that it became over-valued, and imports were made cheaper still. The effect was reflected in the level of farm rents in England. In 1930, the low point of British agriculture, farm rents in nominal terms were a quarter of the level in 1770.

The policy was strategically dangerous, but the British assumed that the Royal Navy would always assure supplies of foreign food to Britain. Germany had no such protection. The German rulers knew that German borders could be closed to imports in a moment, and, following the unification of Germany in 1875, a policy of self-sufficiency in food was instigated, regardless of the cost. These converse decisions are still reflected in the present comparative efficiencies of the British and German agricultural industries, the former having been forced to become efficient, and the later being trapped in inefficiency by subsidies and favourable tax treatment.

Deflation

During the 1914–18 War Britain spent much of its accumulated wealth. It incurred a colossal addition to the national debt. It had, however, further developed its industrial potential. The urgent post-war task was to find a peacetime use for the massive factories which had been built to supply armaments and other war provisions. Low interest rates would have made good sense.

In 1920 inflation was 20 per cent. John Maynard Keynes urged a Bank Rate of 10 per cent to cure the wartime inflation.[8] His advice was not accepted but in 1921 Bank Rate was pushed to seven per cent, higher than it had been during the war, and stayed at that level for 10 months. The national workforce fell by 2,000,000. In 1921 the previous year's inflation of 20 per cent was fully reversed by an equal deflation. Its effect was to increase to at least 28 per cent the real rate of interest charged to commercial borrowers.

Fortunately from 1922 until 1925 the British economy was able to renew its advance at a steady pace. It was accompanied by falls in Bank Rate to the three to four per cent range. The advance was made despite being accompanied by an initial fall in the intermediated money supply, but from 1922 to 1925 bank deposits were stable in nominal terms. In real terms, that is after adjusting for the deflation which was taking place, the money supply increased quite considerably. The frequency of circulation of bank balances also increased. Whether that was significant is impossible to say, as there is no data to reveal what proportion of the cheque clearings related to purely financial transactions. It could easily be true that after deducting financial transactions (that is transactions which did not relate to sales and purchases of goods and services but to movements of financial assets) the circulation of money was slowing; that would be normal in a period of deflation when debts tend to remain outstanding for longer.

Reserve assets

Under the system of monetary control practised at that time, reserve asset ratios were very important. Whether the supervising authorities also paid attention to free capital bases or capital adequacy ratios is less clear. Academic economists paid no attention at all to capital adequacy ratios. But it is difficult to believe that cautious bankers took no notice of them. Indeed the evidence is that they kept sensible ratios.

The advance falls short

Despite the increase in production of goods and services from 1920, according to figures quoted by Keynes the volume of production in 1925 was still about 10 per cent lower than in 1913. The rate of unemployment fell from over 11 per cent in 1921 to seven per cent in 1923, but then began to rise again. The rise in unemployment seems to have reflected a fall in the real money supply. It may also have reflected greater productivity resulting from an increase in capital investment which had gone forward quite strongly after 1922. The data for this period is contained in the Bank of England's *Panel Paper No. 23*, written by the Bank's panel of academic consultants in 1984. Unfortunately the item of data the Panel never mentions is the level of banks' capital bases. Even when the Panel Paper was published, half a century after the events it describes, the importance of the capital adequacy ratio was still not appreciated by leading academic economists. They remained, it would seem, impervious to all attempts to interest them in its significance. Lacking hard evidence one can only deduce tentatively that the credit supply in the period 1922–25 was adequate to finance capital formation, but perhaps not consumer finance as well. Both are needed if an economy is to grow.

During that period no truly adequate statistical data was collected. Therefore all conclusions are tentative. It may however be legitimate to suspect that economic growth could have been much faster if there had been a better growth in the credit supply, and if the circulation of the existing money supply had not been slowed down, as it very likely was, by deflation.

A media campaign for gold

Economic policies are widely debated in the information media and thereby become the victims of fashion. In the 1920s the restoration of the Gold Standard became, just as in 1820, a fashionable policy. The nation was urged by the media to look forward to the rebuilding of Britain's economic glory, of which the outward and obvious symbol was to have a stable, respected, and highly valued currency. Germany's experience in 1923 of hyper-inflation helped to encourage this attitude. There was a great agitation to prove Britain's European, and indeed global, superiority by going back to the Gold Standard, which the government had been forced to abandon during the 1914–18 War.

A huge mythology has always surrounded gold. Many people believe that its value is somehow sacred and immutable. That is not a rational attitude as gold is a commodity like any other. If it ever has a stable value it is only because governments choose to give it that quality – in so far as they are able to do so. When gold serves as currency it should be given an exchange value in terms of all other goods and services which is far above its market value as a commodity, otherwise its value becomes subject to all the vagaries of the demand for gold for industrial and other purposes, and also subject to the effect of variations in the supply of newly mined gold. The supply of new-mined gold was in the 1920s far more than was needed for industrial uses, and there were also vast stocks in existence. Such an excess of supply over demand would quickly reduce its price dramatically, were that ever to be determined solely by industrial is evidence of such an effect on the level of prices during the 19th century, a period in which the value of the currency was firmly linked to the price of gold. Gold does not automatically give stability.

This principle was not understood by Sir Isaac Newton when he was asked to determine the value of gold for the purposes of the English Mint. He established a price which was as nearly the exact market price of gold as was feasible. He arrived at the figure of £3. 17. 10½, about £3.89 in modern decimal currency. Adam Smith tells us in his chapter headed *Money* in *The Wealth of Nations* that for many years the Bank of England often had to pay £4 an ounce for the gold which it used to mint gold coins. Canny Scots saw a profit to be made.[9] Their banks bought gold coins from the Bank of England, paying with bills of exchange. As there was a continual demand for coins, what must have been happening was that the Scottish purchasers were melting them down and selling the gold back to the Bank of England. The flow of coin was huge, up to a million pounds a year. The Bank of England presumably made some profit from discounting the bills of exchange, but doubtless not enough to cover its loss on its purchases of bullion. Adam Smith does not seem fully to understand what was going on. What prevented total disaster may have been the fact that to make a profit the turnover needed to be very fast, to negate the effect of interest charges, but the demand for gold to be coined was so great that there was often a delay of months in getting the gold coined. Eventually a fall in the price of gold put things right.

Despite his misinterpretation of this phenomenon, Smith was well aware of the fact that coined gold was usually worth more, weight for weight, than bullion, and that this enabled a mint to charge for its services in coining bullion, a fee called 'seigniorage'. He states that the French Government charged eight per cent seigniorage.[10]

From a very early time, governments found they could obtain a regular income by having frequent recoining. Coins were convenient, and people were prepared to pay for that convenience. Saxon kings announced recoinings about every three years. Holders had pay a fee for having their coins replaced by new ones. They had no choice but to comply, for they could not legally use old coins to repay a debt. The practice may have started long before Saxon times. Cuneiform scholars at the British Museum have noticed that in the Seleucid era in Mesopotamia, contracts would routinely require that debts should be paid only in coins of the current ruler at the time the debt was due.[11] Although there are other possible explanations of this term of the contracts, a likely one is that new rulers recoined in order to collect seigniorage, and the coins of their predecessors were not legal tender.

Reality and stability

The public's sentimental yet wholly irrational attitude to gold was to be expected. Such is the mystique of gold it needed little encouragement, though it is surprising that financiers and economists were also infected with gold fever. Gold has the power of a secular religion in distorting reality, and those who have blind faith in gold are very like religious fundamentalists. They could even be described as the victims of an obsessional neurosis which occupies an area of the brain that is not amenable to reason. A gold-based currency was believed to be a reality which gave *stability*. The pressure for a return to the Gold Standard became greater and greater as people yearned for a lost stability. Psychologically they had not had long enough to adjust to the new experience of living with a currency whose buying power had become unstable. The extent of that instability was illustrated by Maynard Keynes, who showed the wholesale price index rising from a base of 100 in 1913 to 308 in our starting year, 1920, and then falling back down to 159 by 1925.

An elaborate theory based on the concept of the Gold Standard can be found in any elementary textbook. There is no need to repeat it here. All that needs saying is that it is believed that when a country is on the Gold Standard, a monetary discipline is imposed on the country, and it prevents the creation of money ad libitum. The theory was no doubt conceived in an academic's cosy armchair and bears no relation with reality whatsoever. The restrictive power of the Gold Standard is easily circumvented by the public, which overcomes the shortage of currency by creating its own. That currency is usually in the form of bills of exchange. In the reign of Queen Elizabeth I the government suspected that merchants preferred to use bills of exchange because they were selling their gold and silver abroad, something which the government considered almost to be treason. Very likely the merchants were doing exactly that, and very wisely too.

Henry Tooke's evidence

The evidence for the wide use of bills, gathered by a Mr. Leatham, was published by Henry Tooke in 1844. His paper was called *An Inquiry Into the Currency Principle*. In the earlier chapters he describes the theory of the Gold Standard but in Chapter Six he produces the evidence which devastates the theory. The whole chapter is quoted in Appendix A, with some textual modernisation and emphasis. Readers should note the figures he gives for the amount of bills of exchange in circulation and the Bank of England's stock of gold. Bills of Exchange were the normal currency of the 1830s, not banknotes nor gold nor silver, and they were created by individuals and businesses. The state issued its own versions, tallies and Treasury Bills, which rely on the same principle, but for a very long time were far less trustworthy. The years for which Tooke gives the figures were no different in kind from the previous 4,000 years or more. Bills, or their ancient equivalents, were the regular currency of the civilised world.

In the period Tooke is describing cheques had not been developed as a means of exchange. What is clear from his chapter is that bills of exchange were superceded as the preferred currency by banknotes, not because the public wished for the change, but because the government taxed the small bill to extinction. Even so the bill was a long time dying.

The data Leatham had collected shows a vast expansion in the effective money supply in a five-year period during which the Bank of England's holding of gold remained unchanged. The theory of the Gold Standard being the base of the credit system is thereby shown to have no empirical support.

The 1925 system

The system proposed in 1925 for the return to the Gold Standard was less extreme than the prewar version, for a high minimum value was prescribed for any sale or purchase of gold by the Bank of England. This served totally to exclude the ordinary person from dealing in gold. Nevertheless, with regard to every matter which had any international aspect a very tight discipline was imposed on the British economy by setting a fixed international price for the pound in terms of gold.

In any system of fixed exchange rates, whether it be the Gold Standard, the Bretton Woods variable peg system agreed in 1944, or the European Monetary System's *Exchange Rate Mechanism* (ERM), which was in use for a while, the effect is always the same: every other economic objective is subordinated to the need to maintain the exchange rates of the currencies in the system at a fixed level. Full employment becomes a lower priority.

The Economic Consequences of Mr. Churchill

A fixed exchange rate does no great immediate harm if it is set at a sensible level. Unfortunately the choice of rate in 1925 for Britain's return to the Gold Standard was more idealistic than practical. The rate was chosen for one reason only: it was the same as the prewar rate, just as had been done 100 years earlier. Nothing could have been less scientific. It reflected the romantic ideals of the more articulate section of the British people, nowadays often referred to as the chattering classes. The one man who dared to expose this foolish nonsense was John Maynard Keynes (Lord Keynes). He stated his arguments in three telling newspaper articles which were later published in a small 32 page book by his friends Leonard and Virginia Woolf at their Hogarth Press. The book was called *The Economic Consequences of Mr. Churchill*, after the Chancellor of the Exchequer who had, rather reluctantly, taken the decision to return to the Gold Standard at the prewar exchange rate.

To facilitate the return to the Gold Standard the exchange rate of the pound was bolstered by an increase in interest rates. The purpose was to make it an attractive currency to hold, and to encourage deflation by discouraging the creation of credit. Bank Rate was fixed at five per cent on 5th March 1925.

Keynes' arguments were expressed with great vigour in his little book which was published that same year:–

> *The object of credit restriction...is to withdraw from employers the financial means to employ labour at the existing level of prices and wages. The policy can only attain its end by intensifying unemployment without limit, until workers are ready to accept the necessary reduction of money-wages under the pressure of hard facts.*

> *It is a policy, nevertheless, from which any humane or judicious person must shrink.*

> *Credit restriction is an incredibly powerful instrument, and even a little of it goes a long way.*

> *No section of labour will readily accept lower wages merely in response to sentimental speeches by Mr. Baldwin. We are depending for the reduction of wages on the pressure of unemployment and of strikes and lock-outs; and in order to make sure of this result we are deliberately intensifying unemployment.*

> *We want to encourage businessmen to enter on new enterprises not, as we are doing, to discourage them. Deflation does not reduce wages 'automatically.' It reduces them by causing unemployment. The proper object of dear money is to check an incipient boom. Woe to those whose faith leads them to use it to aggravate a depression.*

> *It is a question of relative price here and abroad. The prices of our exports in the international market are too high...Why are they too high? The orthodox answer is to blame it on the working man for working too little and getting too much. In some industries and in some grades of labour, particularly the unskilled, this is true; and other industries, for example the railways, are overstaffed...it is not true in those export industries where unemployment is greatest.*

By maintaining discount rates in London at a sufficient margin above discount rates in New York, it can induce the New York money market to lend a sufficient sum to the London money market to balance both our trade deficit and the foreign investments which British investors are still buying despite the embargo. Besides when once we have offered high rates of interest to attract funds from the New York short loan market, we have to continue them, even though we have no need to increase our borrowings, in order to retain what we have already borrowed.

Keynes also demonstrated that Britain's major export, coal, could not compete in foreign markets while sterling was deliberately and severely overpriced.

In order to maintain the new fixed exchange rate at its excessive level, wages had to fall, and they did fall, despite bitter opposition from the trade unions. The unions lost their battles to stop wage reductions, including the General Strike of 1926, but they remembered their defeat with bitterness, and it brought a determination to exact revenge. The opportunity to do so came twenty years later. Trade union militancy in the post-1945 years flowed directly from the painful defeats in the 1920s. There is a great mythology surrounding the General Strike, but I discovered what appears to be the real truth in the Keynes Papers in the Public Record Office. Among them was a note by Ernest Bevin, who in 1926 was the Secretary of the most powerful union, the Transport and General Workers. The gist of his note is this. *'I called the General Strike solely to get the pound down. I did not want to call a General Strike, but I had to.'* His tactic unfortunately failed.

In 1928–30 Bevin served with Keynes on the Macmillan Committee which made a far ranging enquiry into the state of the British economy, and into monetary policy. Bevin questioned very roughly Montague Norman, the Governor of the Bank of England, and Sir Richard Hopkins, the head of The Treasury.[12] At one point he says (paraphrased) *'Your policy meant that wages had to be reduced. No way could I deliver a reduction in wages.'*

A history lesson for all time

Those who ignore the lessons written in the pages of history are condemned to learn them from painful experience. There is a chilling similarity between the debates and decisions of 1821, of 1925–26, of 1944–49, and those of 1990–92, the period when Britain tried to stay in the European Exchange Rate Mechanism. The chill is rendered even icier by the fact that Britain in 1992 was not the world economic power it was in 1925. It was no consolation that it had less to lose because it had already lost much of its manufacturing industry. Keynes' words in his little book still make impressive and instructive reading. They are much clearer in their message than in his later, less lucid books. *The Economic Consequences of Mr. Churchill* should be compulsory reading for every student of economics.

Deflation continued until 1935. But Keynes had inadvertently laid the foundation of a powerful delusion: that high interest rates could cause deflation (or reduce inflation). His own reasoning at the time was not in serious error: he makes clear that lower wages would result from higher unemployment, caused, in its turn, by high interest rates and a consequently overvalued currency. The delusion from which others later suffered was that high interest rates could cure inflation just by the reduction in the demand for credit. Very high unemployment was not seen as an inescapable stage in the inflation-curing process. But in Britain it is an inescapable stage. The attitude of the trade unions, and indeed of the general public, ensures that that is so. While a trade union still retains sufficient power to get a wage increase by using the threat of strike action, and is still motivated to do so, control of inflation by restriction of the credit supply will bring about high unemployment. The history of the 1980s proves that is so.

Academic economists and the Treasury's theoreticians, both remote from the real action, deluded themselves about the progression statement which describes the process of curing inflation. The true statement is, as Keynes knew,

(A) Raised interest rates lead to
(B) Unemployment leading to
(C) Reduced inflation – provided the wind is fair.

By the 1980s that progression statement had been altered into the very different statement that (A) leads to (C), (B) now being redundant. Since (A) is easy, and (C) is considered pleasant, the body politic preferred to draw a convenient veil over (B), which is very unpleasant. Many millions of people in Britain, and in other countries which have pursued similar policies, have discovered very painfully that (B) means unemployment, and is inescapably part of the progression. They are being asked to pay the price of the simplistic and forgetful understanding of Keynes' theories by the powerful economic establishment of the United Kingdom, by the International Monetary Fund, and by many governments throughout the world, especially that of Germany. Keynes would be horrified at the foolish accretions which have become attached to his careful analysis, and at the unnecessary human suffering which is being inflicted as a result.

Keynes was not wholly correct

But even Keynes was not entirely right in his expectation that unemployment would cure inflation. The 1980s demonstrated that if workers and their leaders were intransigent, unemployment and inflation would **both** grow simultaneously, the phenomenon known as *stagflation*. His mechanism does not always work, and when it does work it may take a decade or more to have any effect.

There was, admittedly, a difference between the 1920s and the post 1945 era. It was deflation that took place in the 1920s, not a reduction in inflation which became the quite different objective after 1945. Deflation is a far more horrifying thing than inflation, and its horrors are magnified by its effect on the exchange rate. A deflating currency is popular with foreigners, and especially with those whose own currencies are inflating rapidly. There were many such currencies in the 1920s, not least the German Mark. The deflated pound became sought after internationally, intensifying the problems of British exporting industries even further. No worse fate can befall a national currency than to become a reserve currency which foreigners wish to hold; it inevitably leads to a huge trade deficit, as the United States has discovered.

No capital issues

In his book Keynes implies that, concurrently with the high interest rates, there were also embargoes on capital issues at the time of Britain's return to the Gold Standard. Thus not only was the growth of the intermediated credit supply attacked by high interest rates, but there was also an attack on the expansion of the non-intermediated credit market. Of the two the attack on the latter was the more important. Besides having a direct effect on the creation of credit, it also stopped any attempt by the banks to increase their capital bases, a primary requirement if the banks were to create credit. Without new issues of capital to supplement their capital bases there was no hope of the banks increasing the nominal intermediated credit supply.

Figures quoted by Keynes in *The Treatise on Money* indicate that the deposits of the London clearing banks fell slightly, from £2,023,000,000 in 1921 to £1,843,000,000 in 1925, and then rose to £1,940,000,000 in 1929. In real terms (adjusted for inflation) deposits rose sharply in value. The real meaning of the deflation-adjusted increase is difficult to interpret, but at least it saved the necessity for a capital injection into the banks, for deflation, as we have already noted, makes bank capital stretch further in real terms. Keynes also noted that during the same period bank deposits in the United States grew in *nominal* value and that the volume of industrial production increased, whereas in the United Kingdom production was slightly less in 1927 than in 1907, a depressing indication of Britain's industrial decline.

Deflation is self-perpetuating

Positive nominal interest rates, that is rates above zero, can be raised or reduced. Real interest rates, the nominal rate less the rate of inflation or plus the rate of deflation, cannot be reduced once the nominal rate is down to zero. Britain has never tried a mechanism to apply a negative nominal interest rate, when the depositor pays interest instead of receiving it. The Swiss Federal Government, by contrast, has on occasion ordered the application of negative nominal interest rates to foreigners' deposits.

If deflation is running at five per cent, then even if the nominal rate of interest is zero, the real (deflation-adjusted) rate of interest is also five per cent. The lowest nominal rate of interest ever charged in Britain by the Bank of England is two per cent. This may well be the lowest practicable level for Bank Rate, though the Japanese have taken their discount to zero. Once that level is reached there is no longer an interest weapon available with which to stop the recessionary effect of high real interest rates. How does one break out of a downward recessionary spiral once nominal rates of interest are too low to allow the Central Bank to reduce the real rate of interest any further?

Heretics at large

Ways out of the downward recessionary spiral were suggested by two very controversial but influential amateur economists called Silvio Gesell and Major Clifford H. Douglas. Gesell, who was born in Belgium in 1862, started writing in the 1890s. *Die Natürliche Wirtshaftsordnung durch Freiland und Freigeld* is his major work. *The International Association for a Natural Economic Order*, which was founded to spread his teaching, is still active, and his memory is kept well alive in Switzerland where his theories are respected. Douglas, a Canadian, was the founder in the 1920s of a somewhat similar movement called *Social Credit*, and he too still has many very devoted followers. He disturbed many professional economists, as can be seen from references to him in Sir Roy Harrod's life of Lord Keynes, and in Keynes' own writings.

Gesell and Douglas both made proposals which might have been effective in reducing unemployment and curing deflation, even though the reasoning behind them is faulty. Gesell, like many moralists before him, realised that the build-up of wealth implies the build-up of debt, as the two are opposite faces of the same phenomenon. A wealthy nation is an indebted nation as well. He therefore wanted to reduce the propensity to save, and the consequent necessity for borrowing. In order to encourage people to spend their money rather than save, and increase the frequency of circulation of money, he suggested that the state should make money lose its purchasing power by a fixed percentage each year. His theory as it stood was quite unworkable as it was only the value of banknotes which he proposed to depreciate, and that left bank balances untouched. A system could certainly have been devised to achieve his purpose in respect of the whole money supply. The oddity in Gesell's views is that he was strongly against inflation, and yet moderate inflation has precisely the effect he was trying to achieve.

The buying power 'Gap'

Clifford Douglas's proposals were based on the theory that the costs of production are not matched by an equivalent buying power, and there is therefore a gap which has to be bridged. No modern accountant would accept his reasoning, though there are circumstances in which it can happen. For instance if a worker leaves his wages on a bank account, he is effectively financing his own production, for by not spending he is depriving the world of the finance to buy his production.

Douglas's proposal was that the gap be closed by the state giving everyone some money, a sure way to get out of a deflationary spiral and into an inflationary one!

Would their proposals have been more effective than Keynes proposals? Or do they in pure essence amount to the same thing? Keynes could not accept the theories of either Gesell or Douglas. Nevertheless he wrote about them with sympathy even though he also linked them with Karl Marx as belonging to an 'underworld' of economic theorists. He also refers to them as 'brave heretics'. Present day admirers of both Gesell and Douglas claim that Keynes was finally converted to their views. Such claims merely demonstrate their great anxiety to earn the approval, even posthumously, of the century's best known economist.

Effects of the Gold Standard

In the years immediately following the abandonment of the Gold Standard in 1931 there were some important realignments of relative currency values. Initially the pound fell enough to bring on one of the strongest industrial booms in the history of the British economy. But later the British pound rose against the American dollar, partly as a result of a deliberate devaluation of the dollar by Roosevelt, who may have seen a truth to which the British government was still blind. British deflation was all too effective in making sterling an alternative popular currency for foreigners to hold. Ultra low interest rates in the 1930s may have lessened the tendency of deflation to push up sterling's exchange value, but by 1937 its appreciation was enough to bring a modest economic recovery to a halt.

The danger of averaging

Such statistics as there are of wages for the 1920s and 1930s are difficult to reconcile with the anecdotal evidence of industrial workers of the time. The difference between data and recollection may be caused by the reliance of the economists on averages. Although averaging is perhaps the simplest of all the arithmetical techniques used in statistics, it is probably the most dangerous, and it constantly leads people away from the truth, not towards it. In this case averaging concealed the fact that producers of goods were much the worst affected. Public employees, by contrast, fared exceptionally well in the 36 per cent deflation which took place between 1920 and 1934. By 1935 the treasured jobs in the community were in central and local government. Teachers and bus drivers were envied people. Bank clerks too were lucky: they lost one pay increment in 1931; otherwise their salaries remained as they were.

The economists' averages disguise the fact that manufacturing industry in the 1930s paid very little to its workers: that low pay level must have been determined by the exigencies and realities of foreign competition in an era when sterling was overvalued. The worst effect was between 1929 and 1932 when exports fell by a third and unemployment rose to 23 per cent of insured workers.

In 1925 Keynes had foreseen this inequality of suffering. In his pamphlet, *The Economic Consequences of Mr. Churchill*, he stated in several places that the burden of the necessary cut in nominal wages would be borne by the export industries, and the strong would benefit at the expense of the weak. He said on page nine,

> *...there is no machinery for effecting a simultaneous reduction. Deliberately to raise the value of sterling money in England means, therefore, engaging in a struggle with each separate group [of workers] in*

turn, with no prospect that the final result will be fair, and no guarantee
that the stronger group will not gain at the expense of the weaker.

The result was not at all fair. Wages in the unsheltered industries took
all the punishment. Not surprisingly, the quality of management in the
underpaid export industries declined.[13]

The low value of the dollar and the intricate system of exchange control in
Germany, which was designed to keep export prices low, helped to depress
British export industries. By the time war began in 1939, German consumer
industries were in a fine state. Even high tariffs failed to keep German
products out of the British market. Adolf Hitler's finance minister, Hjalmar
Schacht, seems to have laid the foundation for the German post-1945
success in production of consumer goods. The British worship of a strong
pound proved to be a profound economic tragedy. Perhaps the most deeply
depressed industry between the two wars was British farming, which could
not compete with cheap foreign produce.

Churchill confesses

In the budget debate in Parliament in 1932 Winston Churchill who had
by then been out of office for three years, made his sincere and
emotion-charged apology for his action in 1925.

> *When I was moved by many arguments and forces in 1925 to return to*
> *the Gold Standard I was assured by the highest experts, and our experts*
> *are men of great ability and indisputable integrity and sincerity, that we*
> *were anchoring ourselves to reality and stability; and I accepted their*
> *advice. I take for myself and my colleagues of other days whatever degree*
> *of blame and burden there may be for having accepted their advice.*
>
> *But what has happened? We have had no reality, no stability...*

The quotation shows Churchill honourably defending the capability
and sincerity of his advisers. This he no doubt did because Keynes on page
10 of *The Economic Consequences of Mr. Churchill* had attacked the advisers.
In answer to his own question, '*Why did he do such a silly thing?*', Keynes
had explained,

> *Partly, perhaps, because he has no instinctive judgment to prevent him*
> *from making mistakes; partly because, lacking this instinctive*
> *judgment, he was deafened by the clamorous voices of conventional*
> *finance; and, most of all, because he was gravely misled by his experts.*

Churchill also observed that it had become much more expensive in real terms to pay off a loan because of the deflation. The greatest debt was that incurred for fighting the war of 1914–18. Of the £6 billion cost of that war one third took the form of an issue of gilt-edged stock called 5 per cent War Loan, with a nominal value of very nearly £2 billion. The post-war deflation, triggered by the return to the Gold Standard and intensified by the 1929 crash, made the real cost of servicing the loan about 50 per cent greater. In 1931 the problem was partly resolved by replacing the original 5 per cent War Loan with a new 3½ per cent War Stock, thus restoring the interest cost of the stock to its original level in real terms. Luckily for the government the capital was not yet repayable. One of the bits of trickery involved in the conversion of 5 per cent War Loan to 3½ per cent War Stock was that the original obligation of the government to redeem the Loan by 1946 at the latest was replaced by a government option to repay it, but only in 1952 *or after*. It has never been repaid, and because of inflation its real value has become comparatively trivial. By December 2004 the original £2 billion would have grown in real terms to more than £84 billion. For a heavily indebted government to cause deflation, as it did in the 1920s, is an act of unbelievable incompetence. The inflation of the post-1945 years has left Britain in 2005 with a comparatively low public debt.

Inflation is an arbitrary tax on every wealth owner. By inflating the currency, Governments get their wars on the cheap. When the Premier and Chancellor of the Exchequer in the 1980s and 1990s repeatedly placed *curing inflation* at the top of their priorities, they were reversing the historical self-interest of governments down the ages. Governments can either pay off their debts from the proceeds of taxation, or they can wash them away altogether by inflating the currency.

Inflation has forced savers to pay for everything for which money is borrowed. Some it has beggared; some – the borrowers – it has made wealthy for no effort. The millions who are made poorer by inflation, and they include every owner of United Kingdom 'Gilts', of United States 'Treasuries', of a building society deposit, of a bank deposit, or of a non-indexed National Savings Certificate, lead their lives seemingly unconscious of their loss, even though they complain of rising prices! A government which practises taxation by inflation can be accused of having the low morality of a loan shark. Significantly, National Savings were invented in the 1920s after the swindler, Horatio Bottomley MP, had shown how easy it was to get hold of the citizen's savings by playing up to his patriotism.

But what is the alternative to taxation by inflation? Higher tax rates? The problem is that such a huge proportion of total national expenditure is in the hands of the state that to finance it without inflation necessitates high tax rates which are strongly resisted. Inflation is the easy way out, and the voter supports it. So who is the true shark? Is it the government or the voter? The very government which proclaimed its opposition to inflation won the 1992 election by its stance against higher taxation! In the 1997 election campaign its rival did the same, though having got power it raised taxation enormously by stealth.

Inflation does not destroy an economy as does deflation, though the vain methods used to try to cure inflation may do so. Many economists have claimed that inflation causes unemployment. Have they truly got the progression statement right? It is surely not *'Inflation leads to unemployment'*, but, *'Inflation leads to foolish counter-inflationary measures which cause unemployment'*.

Ultra low interest rates

The 1925 policy of high interest rates and a fixed exchange rate having proved disastrous, a policy of ultra-low interest rates was adopted in its stead. From June 1932 to 1951, with only a brief break at the outbreak of war in 1939, Bank Rate remained at two per cent. Traditional monetary theory predicts that such a low interest rate will precipitate a vast increase in the intermediated money supply, an over-heated economy, and very high inflation. It did none of these things. Indeed, deflation continued for another four years. Unemployment halved but remained high at 1,400,000 (though total employment rose by 2,600,000 in five years). There was a significant boom in manufacturing. By 1937 Gross Domestic Product was 33 per cent above the 1907 level, having been a little below it in 1925. The growth rate of manufacturing averaged about two per cent annually. The long period of deflation ended only when rearmament was started. Then inflation reappeared. That was five years after the reduction of Bank Rate to two per cent. In the meantime the real value of bank deposits had increased. It was not low interest rates which were responsible for ending deflation. The heretical question is therefore prompted: *'Do low interest rates then cause **deflation**, not inflation?'* Regrettably the answer is not yet clear, but if they encourage real investment, it could be well be so.

The main effect of the switch to low interest rates was to alter the proportions which cash, non-interest bearing and interest-bearing deposits bore to one another. When interest rates are low, there is little incentive to switch one's money to interest-bearing deposits. So cash holdings and current accounts rose sharply. The total of cash and bank deposits (not officially known as M3 until much later) surged initially, fell back again, surged briefly when deflation ended, and then resumed a slow rate of growth. A fifth of the increase in the money supply was banknotes. That is interesting as M0 (currency) requires no capital base, and therefore lack of new capital does not restrain its growth at all in the way it does for bank money.

Were there restraining factors at work, hindering the rapidity of the growth of the nominal money supply? Was such a factor the lack of growth in the capital base of the banks? Initially there was ground to be recovered because in 1931 bank deposits were 10 per cent below their 1920 level. The growth in bank deposits petered out when they reached 10 per cent above the 1920 level. The required capital base was presumably already in place at the clearing banks for the restoration of lending to its 1920 level, unless the banks had made secret losses during the period 1920–1931, and concealed them, as was then permitted. Nor would it have required much of a decline in the capital adequacy ratio to enable the growth in lending which took place after 1931. But would the capital base have supported any further growth? There is a very slight possibility that from 1932 it would have done so. The clue to what might have happened beneath the veil of banking secrecy may lie in a prophecy made in A. H. Gibson's article in *The Bankers Magazine* of January 1923. That article not only included the data for the famous *Gibson's Paradox*, but also a prophecy that if the price of 2½ per cent Consols rose to 77 per cent, the banks would make enough profit out of capital gains to cover their dividends for ten years. With the fall in general interest rates after the reduction in Bank Rate to two per cent, Consols duly rose in price to 77 per cent. Did the banks make a paper profit so that their capital bases were thereby sharply, but secretly, increased? Was this the support for the initial surge in the money supply?

Since the 1939–45 War banks have held only shorter-dated gilts, which cannot appreciate as dramatically when interest rates fall as the 'longs' or the undated gilts. But earlier in the century short-dated gilts were uncommon. On the basis of 19th century experience it would not have seemed risky to hold undated gilts. Gibson states some of the details of the banks' investments in 1923. If he was right, and the make-up of the banks' portfolios was still similar in 1932, the banks' profits on gilts could have been enormous. This is an intriguing mystery, the answer to which could prove to be significant to monetary theory. The banks should delve into their archives and reveal the true state of their balance sheets and profit and loss accounts for that era. Information about the true capital base at that time would be most welcome. Much might be explained.

We must observe that the very low interest rate of 1931 onwards did not lead to any great expansion of the nominal intermediated credit supply; between 1932 and 1937 its growth was nowhere near the level of the increase achieved in later decades when nominal interest rates were higher. Indeed in the later 1930s the earlier growth in the credit supply petered out even though Bank Rate was lower than the inflation rate; in 1937 even the long-term real interest rate fell below zero. The root of the problem was almost certainly that the benefit of the 1931 devaluation had been completely eroded by the appreciation of the exchange rate of the pound, measured against a basket of currencies, to the pre-1931 level.

The expansion of both the intermediated and the non-intermediated credit supplies during the period lends support to the contention that studying the intermediated credit supply in isolation is an unsatisfactory way to fathom the depths of monetary theory. A somewhat older example which illustrates the combined effect is provided by Maynard Keynes in *The Treatise on Money*. It concerns the period 1894 to 1896. In 1894, as official gold holdings had recently doubled, Bank Rate was lowered to two per cent. Although bank deposits increased by 20 per cent Keynes noted that trade during the two years was stagnant, employment figures bad, and prices were falling. The reason for this paradox must have been that new issues of stocks and shares were low, and the rise in the intermediated credit supply was not sufficient to compensate for a slowing down of the rate of increase of non-intermediated credit.

War and its aftermath

War is the most catastrophic event an economy can undergo; it can normally be expected to bring both a financial crisis and high interest rates. Yet throughout the 1939–45 War nominal interest rates were as low as they have ever been. Churchill now made good use of the ingenuity of Keynes, the economist who in 1925 had so savagely criticised him. Keynes had an office in the British Treasury from 1940. Over the five years from the time he went to the Treasury in 1940 until 1945, official inflation totalled 9½ per cent. A rather more realistic unofficial calculation puts the rate of inflation at a little over five per cent per annum, still a remarkable achievement in war-time conditions. By the end of the war Keynes and his ideas had achieved supremacy in the world of economics. He did not live very long to enjoy his success. He died in the Spring of 1946.

What people *assumed* would have been Keynes' policies, had he lived, continued to develop. The old mistakes which Keynes had criticised so vehemently in the 1920s were brought back into fashion, even by his self-styled '*successors*', the Post-Keynesians. The pound was seriously overvalued. British determination to keep it high caused an increase in interest rates from two per cent in 1945 to 4½ per cent in 1955. Inflation averaged 3.9 per cent during the same decade. Some temporary inflation was inevitable in a period of recovery and rebuilding after such a devastatingly destructive war, and following the lifting of so many wartime price controls. Subsidies were also gradually reduced though not abolished. The inflation worried people, even though by comparison with later decades it was trivial. A nation which had become used in the interwar period to prices going down found it difficult to adjust to the novel experience of prices going up, and wanted inflation stopped. Inflation is indeed an aberration, though it would be difficult for anyone born after 1940 to accept a statement which sounds so heretical. In an era of high investment, constant technical innovation, and consequently of increasing productivity, falling prices ought to be the norm, as indeed they were until 1937.

Inflation was to continue, becoming endemic in the British economy, though it declined to an average rate of three per cent in the decade ending in 1965. The reason it continued was very simple: it was the practice of regular annual pay claims by trade unions which always won very nearly what they asked for in unequal battles with weakened employers, and automatic rises for executive staff who can be relied on to look after themselves. After the war the general public was very sympathetic to claims by workers for *cost of living increases*, not understanding that such increases could not compensate for the rise in the cost of living when the economy was already at full stretch. Politicians gave in to popular opinion. Trade unions which had lost their battles of the 1920s to avoid wage cuts, won their battles in the 1930s to preserve jobs, and brought so much underemployment into the economy that there was apparently a shortage of labour. From 1945 onwards the cards were stacked in favour of Britain's trade unions by history, by circumstances and by the actions of its first-ever majority Labour Government. The leaders of the trade unions, and many members of the government, were those who had endured the harsh sufferings of the great deflation and were embittered by it. In their determination to avoid a return of the depression they went too far in the other direction. The Labour movement was a victim of its own legends in which the demons were always the employers, but never the foolish politicians of all parties, never the mistaken economic advisers, and certainly never their own leaders.

The great socialist experiment

The immediate post-war government was ultra-socialist, even by world standards. Its unacknowledged inspiration was the National Socialism of Germany, whose social and industrial success it hoped to emulate, but in an environment of free trade unions. Its brave attempts at socialist planning held the economy in check when they did not actually drag it backwards. The government persisted despite all set-backs with that blind fervour which is the characteristic of idealistic do-gooders of all eras. The aim was to bring all key or basic industries, the so-called *commanding heights of the economy*, into public ownership, in that respect going beyond the more practical socialism of Adolf Hitler. *Public ownership* meant, in truth, the de facto ownership by civil service barons, assisted by cohorts of bureaucrats who paid Danegeld to buy off trade unions whose behaviour differed little from that of protection racketeers.[14] Many of the industries made losses, a nearly inevitable consequence, it was later discovered, of such ruthless socialisation, but whose truth was then a lesson still painfully to be learnt. The capital needs of state industries had to be met either by taxes or as part of the public sector borrowing requirement. High taxes became a further stimulus for inflationary wage claims.

It was a most frustrating time for those who saw that Britain had an opportunity to become one of the two leading industrial powers of the world. Small private businesses, which are commonly the growth points of industry, were especially handicapped. With a top rate of income tax of 95 per cent a businessman who started a successful new venture might receive only five per cent of his profit, but he suffered 100 per cent of any loss if it was unsuccessful. Success created another hazard, the possibility of an estate duty charge of up to 80 per cent on the death of the owner. Very few businesses can sustain the loss of 80 per cent of their capital once in every generation. The only answer to the threat of estate duty was to become a public quoted company, and suffer the loss of that freedom to manoeuvre which is the greatest virtue of the private business. Fancy techniques of avoiding destructive taxes were developed, but they too often had the injurious side effect of reducing the businessman's ability to manoeuvre quickly, partly because it was usually necessary to put business assets in trust.

The early post-war governments all ignored the essential life truth which is that human beings are willing to provide whatever goods or services the community wants provided it is made worth their while to do so. The businessman's frustrations were not only financial. Many essential resources were allocated by the planning bureaucrats, and the small businessman lacked the clout to compete with the big organisations in the scramble for scarce resources. Without the planning controls it is likely that many of the shortages would have disappeared: such shortages are a feature of the planned economy which truly causes them.

The wartime controls on prices had the opposite effect of what was intended when peace came: they kept prices up. The new Conservative government which came to power in 1951 saw this and took action. Price controls were abolished on many raw materials, including lead and zinc. The controlled prices of these two materials had been about £117 and £120 a ton respectively. The planners and the socialists screamed that prices would soar, and that it was folly to end the controls. By 1956 the metals were selling at around £60 to £65 a ton.

For 'Keynesian' read 'Socialist'

Because the post-war Labour government adopted those economic policies which were commonly thought to be derived from Maynard Keynes' theories, their right-wing opponents gradually came to identify incompetent interventionist socialism with Maynard Keynes. Keynes' statement on page 145 of *The Treatise on Money* rather encouraged this misleading belief. It reads,

> *Perhaps the ultimate solution lies in the rate of capital development becoming more largely an affair of state, determined by collective wisdom and long views.*

Some governments, also inspired by German National Socialism, have followed that solution effectively. One such is Japan, not normally classified as left-wing. In Britain even Conservative governments for many years pursued policies inspired by Keynes' dictum, though their enthusiasm was sometimes attenuated.

Keynes might well have resented the identification of his economic philosophy with any political system. His political allegiance was to the Liberal Party. He was called a radical, but his brother-in-law, Professor A. V. Hill, a Conservative Member of Parliament, maintained that Keynes grew less radical as he grew older.[15] Though a radical he was clearly a pragmatist and also a supremely successful speculator. He made a great fortune from financial speculation which secured his total academic independence. Professor A. V. Hill may be right in his statement that at the end of his life Keynes was less of a radical. Can one speculate that he had lost faith in the ultimate solution he had proposed in 1930, and would not have supported the policy of the post-war socialist government? He had cynical moments and a journalistic turn of phrase, journalism being one of his professions, and if he had lived, one can imagine him commenting in the privacy of the Senior Combination Room at King's College, Cambridge, that the fault in post-war British planning was that the collective stupidity, not the collective wisdom, of the British electorate was dictating the planning of capital development. In the history of post-war monetary policy one can see the short view predominating in Britain rather than the long views advocated by Keynes, and which have been followed with some success in other countries. Keynes would have been more willing to face reality than were post-war governments.

Keynes died in April 1946 and was therefore unable to tell his followers that many of the circumstances of the post-war era were sufficiently different from those in the 1920s and 1930s to require policies which were also different from some of those with which his name had become firmly associated. Despite his oft-quoted phrase *'in the long run we are all dead'*, it is most unlikely he would have approved the short-termist manoeuvres which were to be a feature of post-war monetary policy.

One wonders too if he would have approved of the attempt, so seriously pursued, of turning his illustrative algebraical equations into computerised emulations of the economy, with real numbers inserted in the place of his mathematical symbols. That many economists were anxious to make use of mathematics is entirely understandable. Powerful mathematical tools were available, and many of them would know the famous dictum of the great scientist, Lord Kelvin, which goes as follows:–

> *When you can measure what you are speaking about and express it in numbers, you know something about it, but when you cannot measure it, when you cannot express it in numbers, your knowledge is of a meagre and unsatisfactory kind.*

Few economists are prepared to be content with meagre and unsatisfactory knowledge, and admit that truly that is all that is available. Moreover, hidden in the obscuring recesses of faculties of economics are serious scholars with great mathematical skills for which they desperately wish to find a practical use. They do not drink to the traditional toast of mathematicians, *'Here's to higher mathematics; may they never be of any use to anyone!'* Such is their desperation that they are prepared to use their skilled techniques in the complex manipulation of spurious data, in spurious formulae, with spurious results.

The science of economics

It was Keynes more than anyone else who had made economics respectable as a science. That was the firm opinion of Professor A. V. Hill, whose own status as a scientist – Director of the National Physical Laboratory, Nobel Prizewinner, and a President of the Royal Society – was unassailable.[16] Many socialists of those days prided themselves on being scientific, and believed all their pet policies to be based on science. Economists of that generation adopted scientific procedures, especially statistical techniques, which were appropriate to the physical sciences, but which were not valid for a human science. They rejected the stricter methods considered correct by other human scientists, and ignored the scathing protests by the physical scientists against their flagrant misuse of statistical techniques.

Not surprisingly the British economy did not function as well as pseudo-scientists and academic socialists expected. The British are believed by many foreigners to be perfectionists who are always seeking the ideal. The ideal was not being attained, and therefore the post-Keynesian establishment in economics came under increasingly sceptical scrutiny, particularly by those on the political right. They inspired a penetrating inquisitor and effective publicist in the form of the best-known columnist of the *Financial Times,* Harold Wincott. A most effective writer, he expressed views which appealed to many businessmen, who found him easy to understand. Wincott argued his case very well and targeted his attacks with precision, even if his line of argument was sometimes rather simplistic. It helped him greatly that Keynesianism had indeed been corrupted, making it an easy target. Keynes himself shortly before his death talked of an economics *'turned sour and silly'*, and may well have been referring to some of his professed followers.

Wincott targeted his attack on monetary policy, continuing week after week until his death in 1969, but it was not until ten years after his death that people with beliefs similar to his own won power in government. In the meantime there was a drift, encouraged no doubt by the International Monetary Fund, towards a more monetarist approach to problems, and in particular towards the use of the weapon of interest rates. Wincott may have exercised some posthumous influence on this trend. His fame was perpetuated by the creation of the Wincott Foundation with the purpose of sponsoring an annual lecture in his memory under the auspices of the Institute of Economic Affairs. Appropriately, the Harold Wincott Memorial lecture for 1970 was given by Nobel Prizewinner, Professor Milton Friedman, a zealot for monetarism, which he put forward as a correction of corrupted Keynesianism (which might be called *post-Keynesianism*, or *keynesianism* with a small 'k'). By contrast the following year's lecture was given by an eminent associate of Maynard Keynes, Professor James Meade, who later won the Nobel Prize.

The influences of J. Enoch Powell

But surely the most effective publicist for monetarist views, and certainly the cleverest, was John Enoch Powell, MP. In the 1950s he had been a Treasury minister in the Macmillan government. He and the Chancellor of the Exchequer, Peter Thorneycroft, along with another Treasury minister, Nigel Birch, all resigned from the government in January 1958 over the issue of the proper control of government spending and its effect on the money supply, a monetarist viewpoint. Viewed more than a generation later the whole affair of their resignation looks bloated out of all sensible proportion. The true problem, as it always is in Britain, was an unwillingness to be realistic over the exchange value of sterling. To avoid devaluation some deflation was needed and monetary restraint, partly in the form of credit controls, was being used. By later standards inflation was so trivial it would be regarded as a Chancellor's bright dream. The money supply position was anything but liberal. In 1951 the total deposits of the London clearing banks had been 49 per cent of GNP. By 1958 the proportion was 35 per cent. The banks' advances to non-government borrowers, which are what really matter in the financing of GNP, and which had been 14.8 per cent of GNP in 1951, were 9.6 per cent in 1957, and 11 per cent in 1958. In 1959 the figure rose to 13.6 per cent of GNP. The 1957 figure was a big decline on the position in 1950, and in such a situation one can conceive that Friedman would have wished to see an expansion of the money supply. It is paradoxical, therefore, that one of his most vociferous allies should have taken the opposite attitude.

The figures are trivial by later standards. In 2005 the money supply was almost four times GNP. So why was not inflation, many, many times the 1951 level? Inflation in 2005 is running at about three per cent, not much different from 1950 and 1952, and a quarter of the 1951 level.

10
Irving Fisher's Equation

I do not believe in mathematics.
ALBERT EINSTEIN

MONETARY THEORY boasts a fundamental equation. It is MV=PT, and its derivation is credited to an American, Professor Irving Fisher. It states that the money supply (M) multiplied by the velocity of circulation (V) is equal to the number of transactions involving money payments (T) times the average price of each transaction (P).

The purpose of the expression 'PT' is to give the total value of all transactions during a period. The period usually chosen is a year. Ideally one would like to know the figure for each day.

The word velocity means speed. It is not the appropriate term for the equation. What is truly meant is the *frequency* with which money changes hands during the chosen period. If the frequency is high, one could rightly say that the money must be moving faster, but as the equation stands MV is an unsatisfactory expression. Only when *velocity* is replaced by *frequency* is the expression capable of calculation.

We will be pedantic and rewrite the equation as M*f*=PT, '*f*' indicating frequency, exactly as in the science of electronics.

How does one discover the average frequency with which money changes hands? It must be axiomatic that it is the total of all transactions in a certain time period divided by the total of money in use during the same period. That seems to be the only way of discovering the value of '*f*'; there is no independent means of calculating its value. Unfortunately the amount of money in use is not constant for a day, let alone a year, and so a calculation of '*f*' that is based on a time scale of a year gives a result which cannot be more than vaguely accurate if the active money supply is increasing or decreasing sharply. For purposes of comparing periods the figures thus derived can be misleading.

Note that we have introduced a new expression, for *the total of money in use* is not necessarily the same as *the money supply*, however one chooses to

142

define it. There is plenty of money on bank accounts which is not used from one year's end to the next for any transaction: it remains static and is financing a permanent investment, not a transaction. No-one has yet found a way of estimating with any precision the proportion of the total money supply which is being used for transactions at any particular point in time. Moreover there are, by contrast, transactions which do not involve money on bank accounts because they are accounted for by bookkeeping entries.

PT or GNP?

Economists long ago introduced what they seemed to think was another form of the equation for, as they had no practical way of ascertaining the number and value of all transactions, they made a mental jump and assumed that PT must be the same as the total of all goods and services produced in the community during a year. For PT they therefore substituted gross national product (GNP). Table 11½ of the 1992 Financial Statistics published by the Central Statistical Office (now the Office for National Statistics) gave frequency (velocity) of circulation ratios for M0 and M4, calculated in just such a way. The ratios showed a big variation, so that over a seven-year period the highest ratio for M4 is 50 per cent above the lowest.

These published ratios are interesting but they have nothing to do with Mf = PT. Money transactions do not relate solely to goods and services; PT includes *all* transactions for which money payments take place. A vast number of movements of money relate to transactions in financial assets which are in no way part of Gross Domestic Product, or Gross National Product. Stock Exchange equity transactions alone reached a total value of over £4.7 trillion in 2004, or more than twice the total of the liabilities (deposits) of the major British banking groups in July 2005 (£2,243,825,000,000), whereas the Gross Domestic Product for 2004 was only £1,164,439,000,000. Obviously a part of the money supply is tactically more important in the economy as the basis of the liquidity of the securities market than it is in financing the supply of goods and services, and another substantial part is just plain savings.

Should one then restrict PT only to transactions which involve the sale of goods and services? If one does, how much of M does one ignore because it is not actively financing our new PT? It does not matter how one answers the first question because no-one knows for certain how much of M is used only for financial transactions. Until electronic transfers made the 'town clearing' irrelevant, a slight indication of the level of purely financial transactions used to be provided by the total of cheque clearings in the town clearing. Much of the town clearing was concerned with activity in financial markets, for it related only to the cheque clearings between branches of banks located in the square mile of the City of London, the branches whose business tended to monopolise the transfer of money around the financial markets. However there is no reason to suppose that the figure would be consistent from year to year, or even from day to day. Money used today for a purely financial transaction could tomorrow be used to finance the purchase of a new Rolls-Royce motor car.

PT is greater than GNP

A second objection to the replacement of PT by GNP is that the sale of goods and services does not take place only at the point of final consumption. An item can be the subject of many sales during its progress to the consumer, and each transaction includes the value of every previous transaction, plus the value added since the last transaction. Every industry would have to be fully integrated vertically for PT to equal GNP. PT *has* to be vastly greater than GNP, and it *must* be PT, not GNP, which dictates what monetary resources a community should need.

Moreover the need for money will be affected by changes in the industrial structure. If a vertically integrated business is dismembered into its smaller components, those transactions which were once inter-company transfers involving internal book entries become external sales and purchases which require the use of the money supply or trade credit. The frequency of circulation will probably increase following such a change, but the quantity of money may need to be higher too. A merger which brought about more vertical integration might have the opposite effect.

GNP a function of M?

It is undeniable that at any one moment in time a certain supply of money, and of credit, is required to sustain a particular level of economic activity. The precise requirement will differ greatly both from country to country and from one time to another. The exact level of money requirement for a given level of production will be dependent on the interrelation of a host of factors. Some will be environmental or customary, some will be legal, some will depend on the structure of the capital market. All the relevant factors are liable to change at one time or another. Predicting the changes or their effects is difficult, if not impossible, though economists have not been discouraged thereby from trying to make forecasts.

Monetary theorists, such as Professor Milton Friedman and Dr. Anna J. Schwarz, having observed that a certain level of economic activity requires a certain level of money supply, went on to claim that if one controlled the money supply one would also control the level of economic activity. But economic man reacts against government controls, and the consequence is that they produce dynamic reactions which are neither intended nor anticipated. Cynical observers are inclined to conclude that the public's reaction will wreck *any* control system. This phenomenon led Professor Charles Goodhart to propose a new law of economics,

> *...that any observed statistical regularity will tend to collapse once pressure is placed upon it for control purposes.*

Goodhart's Law, as it is called, may seem to some economists to be just a joke, but it is undoubtedly true. The public is not a set of programmed robots, mindless and unreacting, to be manipulated by over-confident economists. For every action by a government which is attempting to control the economy there is bound to be a reaction by members of the public, a reaction beyond the expectation of the planner. The reaction does not even have the simple virtue of being *equal and opposite,* as in the Third Law of Motion. Unfortunately Professor Goodhart's cynical but wholly accurate observation has not, it would appear, demoralised enthusiastic monetarists, nor has it dissuaded many interventionist politicians from fruitless actions.

The constant velocity cult

Before monetarists could suggest seriously that monetary controls would be effective they had to prove that they could accurately calculate the money supply requirement for a given level of economic activity. Studies were made of the relationship of GNP and other key variables to the money supply in both America and Britain over a long period of time. The chosen measure of the money supply in Britain was £M3, which was at one time very roughly the sterling deposits of the clearing banks. Important researchers (notably Professor Milton Friedman and Professor Sir Alan Walters) showed that there was a remarkably stable relationship between GNP and the money supply except in unusual circumstances such as war. Can the frequency of circulation of M3 money really be a constant? If so, why?

As a wrong application of the control of the money supply can devastate an economy, there must be no doubt about the answers to the two questions in the last paragraph before any monetarist is allowed to try to exercise control. Unfortunately, the gravest of doubts must remain. Further more, if there were no doubts about past relationships of the money supply to economic activity, would not Goodhart's Law apply in the event of the *statistical regularity* being made use of *for control purposes*?

Irregularities

Those who have carried out the studies admit that they have had to ignore periods of great irregularity such as war, and that raises the question of why war should cause an irregularity in a constant. They have also had to assume that the relationship is a lagged one. Rather tricky statistical techniques have had to be used. Are they reliable techniques, or are they being used to make the wanted result appear? The great *'Why'* question, the root question which any physical scientist will ask, does not seem to have been answered at all. That question is, *'Why should the money supply and the Gross National Product and other "key variables" have a precise and constant functional relationship?'* What mechanism of cause and effect makes the stable functional relationship exist? Why does it cease to be stable in a war?

The detection of lagged relationships is a statistical minefield. The researcher must exercise the highest standard of care and integrity.

Causes of instability

One can readily think of many reasons why there can be no stable functional relationship. Some we have already mentioned, but we must now list a few more of the phenomena which we would expect to accompany, of necessity, a stable relationship between the money supply and the gross national product. They are:–

- The structure of the capital market must be constant. There must be no variation at all in the ratio of the total quantity of intermediated capital to the total of non-intermediated capital. The ratio of capital to GNP must also remain forever constant, or, alternatively, a change in the latter must be compensated for by a change in the former.

- There must be no change in the level of the requirement for consumer finance. It must be a constant ratio of GNP.

- There must be no change in the overall effect of vertical integration in industry, or in the overall effect of mergers. Therefore any move to vertical integration by one business must be balanced by a disintegration of equal effect in another industry.

- The proportions of people paid weekly, two weekly, monthly, or for any other period must remain constant. Any switch from weekly payment to monthly payment would tend to require a greater money supply as the frequency of circulation is likely to be reduced by more than three-quarters.

- The amount of housing finance required must maintain a constant ratio to GNP.

- The introduction of new methods of payment, such as credit and debit cards, must have no effect on the overall demand for currency ('M0'), or on the overall level of outstanding debt. (The Association for Payment Clearing Services state that plastic cards were used in 2004 for transactions totalling £463,800,000,000.)

- The increase in the level of saving through pension schemes which has taken place over decades must be exactly balanced by compensating falls in other forms of saving in order to have no effect on the money supply.

- There must be no big swing towards endowment mortgages from subscription mortgages as the former require a larger money supply. (In practice the use of endowment mortgages went from one per cent or so to 80 per cent in the course of 40 years, most of the swing taking place in a decade, and then down again.)

- There must be no variation in the proportion of the banks' assets invested in government debt. (Over a period of fifty years the proportion went from 67 per cent to 0.5 per cent in 1993 and up to 5.6 per cent in 2005 for major British Banks. For all financial corporations the proportion in 2004 was a little over 10 per cent. I consider the 2005 figures for major banks, as collated by the British Bankers Association to be the significant figures.)[1]

One could surely add substantially to this list of things which would have to remain constant as ratios to GNP or, alternatively, whose changes must be negated by an equal and opposite change in some other influence on the quantity of money required. But is it necessary to go further? Is it not axiomatic that none of those things which are required to remain constant ever do so? Because they are not immutable, it is impossible to arrive at an econometric formula which will determine what change in the money supply is needed for a given alteration in GNP. The Friedman-Schwarz edifice of theory collapses under the impact of reality.

For monetary strategy to work with any precision, a constant relationship between the Gross National Product and the money supply is essential. If there is no constant relationship, how can one determine the desirable level of the money supply? Only by inspired and experienced guesswork.

Some eminent monetarists have long conceded that there is no constant relationship. Professor Sir Alan Walters, writing in 1969 in the Institute of Economic Affairs publication, *Money in Boom and Slump*, puts the position as follows:–

> *We cannot predict at all accurately the effects of an increase in the quantity of money on prices and incomes.*
>
> *On the other hand, it has been argued by Professor Milton Friedman of the University of Chicago, and by a rapidly growing school of monetary economists in the United States that the velocity of circulation, although not a constant, does behave in a systematic and predictable way. Broadly speaking they argue that, as the quantity of money is increased, the velocity of circulation also increases. Thus, money incomes increase even more than the increase in the quantity of money. Similarly, when the quantity of money is decreased, so the velocity follows it down. (This implies inter alia that the monetary leverage is large, i.e. a small change in money has a large effect.)*

Professor Sir Alan Walters was sensitive to the criticism that the velocity of circulation is not a constant. In a footnote on page 28 of the book he writes:–

> *It is remarkable that the 'constant velocity' strawman is the one most frequently attacked by the anti-money school. Sometimes they attribute these views to monetary economists: demonstrating that the monetarists are wrong is then like taking candy from a baby. An example is Mr. Jay's allegation that Professor Friedman is trying to prove that the velocity is constant ('The Times' 29th May 1968.) Professor Friedman has always insisted that only a rigid orthodox quantity theorist would pretend that the velocity is constant; rather one seeks systematic variation and enduring regularities.*

So there is no constant, but there is a regularity. Even if there were, would it survive the intervention of government economists?

When 'M*f* ' does not equal 'PT'

At the beginning of this chapter we defined 'T' as being the total of transactions which involve money payments. That distinction is made in order to exclude non-money, or book entries, of which there are myriads being made every day by way of entries in books of account, and these make no use of the intermediated money supply. If the distinction is not made then M*f* does not equal PT. Popular textbooks on monetary economics do not make this distinction.

How to hide money

It is also possible for accounting practices to hide a great part of the true money supply. Multi-national companies, and other big holding companies, commonly have departments which they call their 'Treasuries', and these act as bankers to their self-accounting subsidiary companies. The use of a treasury diminishes the apparent money supply as the bank accounts of the group are netted down to one bank balance in the name of the parent company.

Some subsidiaries may be borrowers, while some carry large credit balances. The parent company lowers its financing costs a little by using the credit balances to fund the debtor companies. That could also be done by inter-company loans, but it is much more effective for the holding company to act as banker for the subsidiaries so that all daily variations in debit and credit balances are automatically netted out immediately. Possibly the largest treasury operation is that of the British Petroleum Company (BP). If that operation is as large as rumour avers, one would expect the Financial Services Authority to insist that BP's treasury be recognised as a bank, that the individual balances of subsidiary companies be reported, and thus included in the official statistics.

There was once a proposal that the Law Society should act as banker for all solicitors in order to get a cheaper banking service. The aggregate of the balances under the control of solicitors must be enormous. If the debit and credit balances were netted out so that only the net figure was reflected on an account at a recognised bank, the implications for the money supply figures would be very significant. But a more serious practical problem would then be that a slice of the banking system's free capital reserves would become redundant, making it available to support the creation of more credit. If the Law Society had gone ahead with its proposal (it is presumed that it did not), it should have been treated as a regular bank and required to hold reserves equal to eight per cent of the gross credit balances as reflected in the books of each individual solicitor's practice.

A philosophers' stone for economists?

Given the many probable defects in the money supply figures must we conclude that econometricians have been pursuing a philosophers' stone that cannot exist? Their confident assertion of a predictable regularity in the frequency of circulation of money must be rejected for want of proof so long as the money supply cannot be defined and measured. The definition used by Professor Friedman in those of his papers which were published by the Institute of Economic Affairs under the title *Monetarist Economics* was the one known as Sterling M3 (£M3). But publication of £M3 has ceased. Presumably the official statisticians decided that it was no longer valid as a useful measure of the money supply. As British research into the regularity of the frequency of circulation used a measure of the money supply no longer considered valid, the tempting conclusion is that the result of the research into the relation of M3 to GNP is not valid either.

A constant functional relationship solely between M and GNP is impossible because PT, which determines M, has no constant relationship with GNP. Any function relating M to GNP must therefore include in its parameters the variations in the relationship of PT to GNP. Estimating the variations looks likely to be beyond the predictive power of any econometrician.

A true monetary theory must accord with empirical facts. In the latest argument we have sought to prove that some facts discovered by painstaking research are invalid because they are inconsistent with basic theoretical considerations. By relying on theory, not facts, have we betrayed our principles? Would it not have been better to have proved that the facts discovered by the research were wrong? Much as we feel that our theoretical arguments are overwhelming, we accept that they do constitute only a hypothesis, not a proof. However as no factual research is possible without a proper definition of one of the key variables in the function which we are discussing, what more can we do?

The significance of M0

In the late 1980s, after every other indicator of the money supply had proved misleading, the government acted on advice that it should regard M0 as the most significant monetary indicator. M0 is banknotes and coin. One can see that as it is mainly used for retail purchases, it could be a better indicator of overall economic activity than M3, a greater proportion of which is perhaps used for transactions before the point of final sale to the consumer.

However the figure for currency in circulation arouses both one's curiosity, and some suspicion. Why is the figure so large? Sterling banknotes in circulation in 2005 amounted to about £39 billion. That was £650 for every man, woman and child in Britain, or more than £2,600 per household of four. As the pockets of the populace do not obviously bulge, the large figure can only be explained on the basis that a large proportion of the currency in issue is tucked away out of sight, being held primarily as a store of value, and not as a medium of exchange.

Why should this be so? The popular assumption is that it reflects the frequent use of currency in the black economy and by criminals, the two sectors of the population which prefer the anonymity of currency. So for M0 to be a useful economic indicator one needs to assume that the level of activity in the black economy, and in the criminal world, is a constant proportion of all economic activity. Rising crime statistics rule out that assumption. According to the little memo of interesting statistics which the old Central Statistical Office distributed to celebrate its fiftieth anniversary in 1991, crime had increased ten times in fifty years. No doubt it has further increased in the following 14 years. Is that trend reflected in the Treasury's computer model of the economy?

In fact we do know exactly where a little under one third of M0 is; it belongs to financial corporations, and is kept in their tills and strongrooms.

Beliefs

There can be little if any doubt that the level of the money supply, in that it reflects the level of the intermediated credit supply, is of great concern to governments. Professor David Laidler, who is one of the leading philosophers of monetarism, is quite correct when he writes in the introduction to his collection of essays called *Monetary Perspectives*,2

> *Above all, the essays which follow are motivated by the belief that the behaviour of the quantity of money is very important (though not all-important) for the behaviour, not just of real income and employment, but also and in particular of the general price level.*

His very next sentence, however, moves from the realm of belief based on truth to that of belief based on something less solid. He says:-

> *This belief in turn is related to another belief, which, I insist, is the sine qua non of monetarism: namely, that there exists a stable aggregate demand function for money.*

Given the enormous number of variables which one would expect to be included in such a function, this is a remarkable belief, but in Chapter 2 Professor Laidler indicates that he expects the function to include a *'relatively small number of arguments'*. The rest of the chapter, a complex one, leaves one in doubt as to whether he has proved that could be true.

Let us translate the word *money* into *intermediated credit*, as we have advocated, and ask whether the demand function for intermediated credit can be stable, which perhaps means 'regular', when intermediated credit is liable to be converted into non-intermediated credit at any time, and in any quantity, if interest rate conditions favour it, or even capriciously? Does the demand function for money take into account the reasons why someone might prefer to borrow from a bank rather than the bond market, and why an investor should accommodate the borrower's wish? We have suggested that when long-term interest rates are low, the borrower will prefer a long-dated bond, but if they are high a borrower will prefer to borrow short-term from a bank. Professor Laidler's function does not seem to include interest rates as a parameter in his function. In fact he does not appear to discuss at all the reasons why, 'an agent' plans to hold a certain sum of money. That an 'agent' may be influenced by the tactics of borrowers does not appear in his analysis.

Nor is the possibility considered that the ultimate determinant of the intermediated credit supply is the capital base of the banks, so that it is the *supply* of money which is more likely to be stable, so long as the banks' capital base is stable, and the aggregate demand function for money will have to yield to the reality of what is available. The banks are not going to raise new capital every time the demand for money rises unless it is profitable to do. Or is a stable demand function for money equivalent to an *unaltering* demand for money? As the demand for credit and its supply are interactive, there can be no simple answer.

The effect of the level of income

Professor Laidler's stable aggregate demand function for money is commendably subtle in one respect for his function takes into account factors other than the GNP and the money supply. One additional factor is the individual's level of income. There must surely be some relationship between aggregate individual incomes and GNP, though the relationship could be variable because of the irregular supply of, or demand for, credit. The granting of credit increases demand above the level determined solely by income. An increase in the level of personal sector debt relative to personal sector income increases spending, and thereby GNP. At first sight this appears to increase the ratio of GNP to income. But as it also raises aggregate income, because money lent becomes income in the hands of the person supplying the goods and services on which it is spent, there is a tendency for the ratio of GNP to income to be restored. This must encourage Professor Laidler.

Although much research and ingenuity has been devoted to finding an equation which emulates the demand function for money, it must remain very doubtful whether any model can produce accurate calculations. It is right to be very agnostic as to whether the function can be stable, for, as we have already suggested, there are many factors affecting the demand for money which must change erratically and with considerable but irregular frequency. All these factors would have to be emulated in the model. There is, in addition, far too much doubt about the reliability of the estimation of the constants in the function for it to be used for the management of the economy as if it were a truly scientific tool. Finally, it is not *the aggregate demand function for **money*** which is of first importance but *the aggregate demand function for **credit***. The demand function for money *must* be subservient to the demand function for credit, for it is the latter which initiates the creation of money. By looking for a demand function for money one is on the wrong side of the looking glass, as well as on the wrong side of the balance sheet.

Models

In determined pursuit of the philosophers' stone econometricians have constructed mathematical models, which are designed to emulate the functioning of the economy. Such models may look like dubious intellectual exercises but they fascinate many economists. If there were no faults or assumptions in them, they would work in the same way, and with the same accuracy, as an electronic circuit. Put in only one assumption and the emulation ceases to be reliable. All models must contain many parameters which are assumptions, and many constants which are unreliable and not constant at all.

One would certainly not want to travel to the moon if the spacecraft's computer were filled with equations and data of the quality with which applied economists have to be content. Yet the lives and well-being of countless millions are affected by the decisions influenced by such calculations, not just a couple of spacewalkers who know they are risking their lives. Put into such dramatic perspective the complacency of econometricians is horrifying.

Professor Alan Peacock in the Seventh Wincott Memorial Lecture (Institute of Economic Affairs *Occasional Paper 50*, Page 15) put the criticism as follows:–

> ...*the illusion that mathematical skill is a protection against the penetration of ethical bias and a complete substitute for imaginative insight into the workings of the economic system is widespread.*[3]

In such circumstances the inspired guess of an experienced observer of the economy is likely to be more accurate than the computerised emulation. The human brain, when working in its *super-logic* mode (unconscious reasoning, a process sometimes called *intuition*), and when well programmed by long and close experience, can sometimes compute the likely result of a huge mass of varied and variable inputs far better than any computer which has been programmed with conscious logic. Unfortunately, the processes of unconscious logic are not, to use computer terminology, transparent. Therefore one cannot observe them while they are proceeding, one cannot test the programming of the individual's mind for correctness, nor can one decide whether his intuitive reasoning is reliable. On the other hand, the level of unreliability of the most sophisticated economic model is fairly obvious; there are too many assumptions in them.

The real problem for monetarists

At the risk of repetition we again emphasise the importance of the underlying problem in monetary theory, the definition of the money supply. Money is declared to have three purposes. It is a store of value; it is a medium of exchange; and it is a measure of value. But money is not the only store of value, for any debt is a store of value. Other stores of value can in certain money markets be used as a medium of exchange. As a measure of value, money is variable and inconsistent, but it is the best measure, indeed the only universal measure, which can be devised.

Money (or debt) is very easily created and its creation brings prosperity. To reduce the quantity of money (or debt) does the opposite. Much money has been created by the granting of loans which one cannot realistically expect to be repaid. Such debt overhangs the world economy like a sword of Damocles. When the public is overborrowed is it not better slowly to erode away its excess debt by gentle inflation? Is that not preferable to the prospect of banks going into liquidation? Is it not possible that inflation, though wholly condemned by moralists as well as by politicians and economists, has on many occasions saved mankind from more terrible sufferings? In the days when currencies were based on precious metals, and therefore less easy to depreciate, debt led to revolution. The condemnation of usury by several religions must surely stem from this phenomenon.

A flawed concept

Before we leave Fisher's famous equation we should contemplate the possibility that it is based on a conceptual flaw. Fisher was a famous mathematician but his approach to money is just as simplistic as that of the man in the street whose attitude is, *'I have money in my pocket, and some more in the bank, and I shall spend it.'* Fisher has totalled all the money in all the pockets and in all the bank accounts, and considered what that total means for spending potential. He has ignored the fact that there are accounts in debit at the bank totalling slightly more than the deposits, and the *negative money*, to coin an expression, on those accounts can circulate. In fact there is a strong possibility that one-quarter of all money payments are made from accounts with debit balances upon them to other accounts which are in debit.

A bank manager watching the transactions going through his customers' accounts sees four classes of payments:–

1. From an account in credit to an account in credit.
2. From an account in credit to an account in debit.
3. From an account in debit to an account in debit.
4. From an account in debit to an account in credit.

Classes one and three have no effect on the total money supply. Class four increases the money supply by the amount of the payment. Class two reduces the money supply, but how much it does so will depend on whether the payment pushes the receiving account out of the red. For the money supply to remain constant, all the payments in classes two and four must have no net effect. A bookmaker who accepted a bet at odds of infinity to one on that ever happening could sleep very soundly.

Fisher's equation assumes that all payments are class one, yet they may be only a quarter of all transactions. Half of Britain's smaller businesses are in debt to their bankers, and payments taking place among them will mostly be from or to overdrawn accounts only. Such payments must represent a considerable proportion of inter-business transactions.

How does one reflect the power of *negative money* in an equation? Should one add the assets and liabilities of the banks together to arrive at the true money supply? No, that must be ridiculous. How does one take into account the constant change in M because of class two and class four transactions? The equation has a variable in it which needs to be invariable if it is to be of any practical use. Finally, how does one estimate the amount of new credit which may be created at any moment and provide new purchasing power?

Fisher's equation has very little use; it is a classroom curiosity whose variations may have some obscure meaning which patient work may ascertain, but only long after it has ceased to matter. By then the current meaning of the frequency of circulation will be different. The determination of the correct level of the money supply can never be a matter of mechanical computation suitable for a computer emulation; it will remain an affair of inspired guesswork resulting from constant careful observation of what is happening in real time in the financial world. The question to be asked is, *'What tricks are the financiers up to today?'*, rather than *'What is the level of the money supply?'* It was the lack of real time observation which caused the supervising authority of the banking system to fail to check the eruption of the great volcano of new credit in 1988, a volcano which has continued erupting.

Disaggregation of the money supply

We hinted earlier at the possibility of removing from the calculation of the intermediated credit supply (money supply) the element which finances only transactions in existing assets, not current consumption. This is an attractive idea, and it has received the attention of one of the brightest minds among a new generation of economists, Professor Richard A. Werner of the University of Southampton. Professor Werner created a sensation when he published, originally in Japanese, his book *Princes of the Yen*, a study of the highest importance and quality. In his subsequent book, *New Paradigm in Macroeconomics*, he attempted with some success to disaggregate from the figures for the intermediated credit supply that element of new credit creation which relates to the purchase of existing assets. His target therefore is that quantity of money which is created solely to create asset price bubbles and consequent banking crises. He has devised a model, based on Japanese data, to test his analysis and assumptions.

Sadly it is necessary to disagree with the purpose of this work, even though it required very great technical skill, for it seems to imply that asset price inflation is an entirely separate effect from general inflation.

Members of the Creditary Economics Group have examined the phenomenon of asset price bubbles in great depth and over a long period, and far from believing that the creation of credit for the purchase of existing assets has no effect on general inflation, they have, on the contrary, concluded that it is the main source of the fodder for general inflation.

To understand their reasoning, one must follow through the bookkeeping. A sells a house to B, who borrows most of the proceeds from a bank on a twenty-year mortgage. The statistics for the banks lending indicate that this is entirely new credit creation. What does A do with the proceeds?

A has three options: the first is to leave the money on a bank account as a long-term investment. That would mean that effectively he is financing the borrowing. Only in this case does the transaction have no further effect on final demand inflation, other than the possibility that it has inflated the price of one house. The second option is that A may buy another existing house from C, in which case we have to ask the same question about C's intentions for the use of the proceeds. The third possibility is that A, or C, or some subsequent vendor, may use some or all of the proceeds on consumer items, the product of current economic activity. When one thinks carefully about A's initial sale, one can see that unless some part of the proceeds are used for option one, the proceeds **must** eventually be used for final demand inflation, if not by A then by someone at the end of a chain of transactions in assets, however long.

A case study

One can illustrate this with a case study. It relates to an actual house sale and purchase in 2004.

This house sale was wholly financed by new credit creation. This is known because the sale was to a developer who needed finance, not only for the purchase, but for some of the development costs as well. His finance came from HBOS, which increased its loan book during the year, and we can regard the loan to the purchaser as its marginal loan. Not only did the purchaser pay £538,000, but he also had to pay £22,000 in Stamp Duty. His legal costs would have borne VAT at 17½ per cent, and the lawyer's expenses would have included income tax payments. The proceeds went, not on an existing house, but on a new one, so the only element of asset price inflation was the land on which it was built, perhaps £75,000, out of which probably £30,000 went in Capital Gains Tax assessed on the vendor of the land. Part of the costs was a payment of £10,020 in stamp duty, and the builder's expenses would have included income tax and Corporation Tax. Various other expenses arising from the move resulted in VAT of £6,105. The total expenses, including new furnishings and garden landscaping, came to something over £35,000. VAT on a couple of new vehicles bought partly with the proceeds was about £6,800. All these tax payments were spent by the government on current expenditure, which means that what appeared to be expenditure covered by taxes on the national income was in fact financed by new credit creation, that is by borrowing. Thus the published figures for the Public Sector Borrowing Requirement are understated, an accounting delusion.

It must be obvious from this study alone that asset price inflation which is financed by new credit creation must cause an enormous increase in consumer expenditure. The realisation of equity, mostly by elderly people, to finance current expenditure is at the time of writing running at a very high level. But they do not have to move house to spend their profit; they can borrow against the increased value. An issue (2005) of the Bank of England Quarterly discusses it, and tells us the amount raised in the most recent quarter was in the region of £6,000,000,000. In America the figures are far higher. The New York Times of 27th September 2005 reported that in a speech delivered by satellite to a meeting of the American Bankers Association in Palm Desert, California, the Chairman of the Federal Reserve Bank, Alan Greenspan, stated that borrowing against home values had added $600 bn. to consumer spending, equivalent to 7 per cent of disposable income.

As the expansion of the credit supply in recent decades has largely been for asset price inflation, one can say that it is absolutely certain that asset bubbles can cause general demand inflation as well as asset price inflation.

'But inflation is now low', will be the objection, *'so why has not the present huge rise in house prices led to general inflation?'* Of course it has, but domestic inflation has been concealed by the fall in the price of imported manufactured goods. The cost of the most expensive services, such as restaurant meals, have risen recently by exactly the same percentage that the cost of imported goods, such as DVD players, has fallen. The low inflation rate seen in Western Europe and the United States since about 1993 has been entirely an illusion, which concealed very high domestic cost inflation, and equally high import cost deflation. For the cost in the United Kingdom of the most important purchases, such as houses, the rise was twice the rate of the consumer price index.

11

The Unintended Consequences of Taxes

*All money nowadays seems to be produced with
a natural homing instinct to The Treasury.*
THE DUKE OF EDINBURGH

INFLATION is not only a function of trade union wage demands and credit creation, but of taxation too, as the following case study will demonstrate. Although the study starts long ago, it is still relevant at the time of writing in both the United Kingdom and the United States of America.

On this occasion we deal with an additional creditary structure to those we have concentrated on hitherto. Credit is not only supplied to companies in the form of loans, but of course also in the form of equity. Readers may not be used to looking at equity as part of the credit supply, but that is what it is. Companies recognise that they owe something to the providers of equity capital, and therefore shareholders funds are always shown in the company's balance sheet as a debt of the company to them. It is however a liability which is not repayable except with agreement of a majority of the shareholders.

This form of creditary structure evolved very early in economic history, though in the form usually of partnerships rather than limited liability companies such as we know today. Ancient Assyria had a system of state authorisation of what we would characterise as companies or partnerships. Records have survived of Assyrian companies which traded with the Hittites around 1,800 BC. Although they were active on the very edge of the Assyrian sphere of rule, they had to be authorised in distant Assur. Correspondence has survived in which a debt for equity swap is offered by one of the managers of a trading firm, subject to Assur authorising him to form a new firm of which he will be principal.

The *'Debt for Equity Swap'* has a long history.

Equity investors are entitled to share in the profits of the company, but those profits are often taxed in ways which differ from other income. One of the systems of taxing profits is called Corporation Tax because it is levied on incorporated entities.

In April 1965 the new Chancellor of the Exchequer, James Callaghan, introduced Corporation Tax to Britain. He applied it in its classical form, that is a tax on company profits over and above any income tax charged on dividends paid by the company. Previously companies had been subject to the same income tax system as individuals, plus an additional tax called profits tax. Since a company had already paid income tax on all its income, dividends paid out of that same income were regarded as taxed already. Profits tax was charged at a fairly low rate, 15 per cent at its highest on retained profits, and at a rather high rate, up to 45 per cent, on distributed profits, giving an incentive, it was hoped, to plough back profits. Germany did the opposite, taxing retained profits at the higher rate. Many competent theorists preferred the latter system. Their rationale was that investors were better judges of the correct investment opportunities in the general economy than company directors.

The classical Corporation Tax hit distributed profits even harder than the previous system.

Chancellor Callaghan justified his decision by arguing that Corporation Tax was a more modern tax, that it would enable companies to be taxed at a lower rate than individuals, and that it would motivate companies to retain a higher proportion of profits for investment in expansion of their businesses.

But a few days later France abandoned the classical form of Corporation Tax, thereby casting much doubt on its modernity. As regards the second argument, Corporation Tax has never been levied at a lower rate than the standard rate of income tax. In contradiction of the third argument, the proportion of profits retained by companies fell from 44.82 per cent in 1965 to 31.97 per cent in 1969. In real terms the fall in retentions was even greater. Because inflation doubled between 1965 and 1969, much of the profit retained in 1969 and after was truly additional depreciation, charged to comply with the principles of inflation accounting by which depreciation should be calculated on the replacement cost, not the historic cost, of plant and equipment. Although it was logical to believe that Corporation Tax would encourage retention of profits, there were overriding factors at the time which rendered the logic of Callaghan's Treasury officials and academic advisers totally ineffective. These factors were practical ones, not likely to be anticipated by pure theorists. The main one was the need for directors to maintain dividend rates as a way of discouraging take-over bids.

Inflation grows

There was a delay of about 18 months before the new tax became fully effective. Not long after that inflation started to increase.

Year	Inflation rate (per cent)
1966	3.0
1967	2.9
1968	4.73
1969	5.64
1970	6.8
1971	8.6
1972	7.55

The inflation rate measures what one could call kinetic inflation, on the analogy of kinetic energy. It relates to manifest price changes. But just as there is also potential energy, by analogy there is potential inflation too, that is inflation which has already been caused, but whose appearance in the statistics is prevented either by consumer subsidies, or by an artificially bolstered exchange rate which keeps import prices low. It is quite usual to say that a devaluation causes inflation. Professor Sir Alan Walters, in his contribution to the volume of essays published in 1975 by the Institute of Economic Affairs and called *Crisis 75*, made a most perceptive comment about inflation in connection with his own proposal for a devaluation of sterling at that time:–

> *Such a devaluation would not **cause** inflation. On the contrary, devaluation is simply a **consequence** of the inflationary expansion of public spending and the money stock which has persisted since 1971. Nevertheless the devaluation will be associated with a considerable acceleration in the rate of inflation as the prices of imported foods and raw materials rise. And it is likely that cause and effect will be confused yet again and the devaluation will be blamed for the further inflation.*

What Sir Alan believed to be true in 1975 had also been true in 1967, for bolstering of the exchange rate was then taking place. Therefore some of the kinetic inflation of 1968 and 1969 properly relates to the period before the 14 per cent devaluation of the pound in November 1967.

Although there are always very many complex agents at work in the causation of any inflation, in the specific environment of the British capital market it is justifiable to believe that there was a causal relationship between the upward trend of inflation after 1965 and the introduction of Corporation Tax. The effects are still causing problems in both the United Kingdom and the United States in 2005.

The encouragement of debt capital

The classical form of Corporation Tax which Chancellor Callaghan introduced cheapened debt capital relative to equity capital, because it ensured that a net of tax dividend on equity required about 1.8 times more earnings to service it than the equivalent net interest payment on a loan. Corporation Tax therefore encourages the raising of loan capital in preference to equity. The consequence was that whereas in the period 1959 to 1964 58.7 per cent of new company finance had been equity, in the five year period 1965 to 1970 only 27.1 per cent was raised by equity issues.

The collapse of Rolls-Royce Ltd. in 1971 was attributed partly to its directors' over-reliance on loan capital; significantly five of Rolls-Royce's seven quoted fixed-interest loans had been issued on the stock market after the introduction of Corporation Tax. But for the classical Corporation Tax system, Rolls-Royce directors must have preferred to raise new equity capital rather than borrow money.

When an economic slump takes place, many heavily borrowed companies which would have survived if all their capital was in the form of equity are forced into liquidation. Therefore cautious economists favoured equity capital, but Chancellor Callaghan seemed unaware of such important implications, or unconcerned by them. Perhaps it would be fairer to suggest that the failure of understanding lay with his principle economic adviser, Professor Nicholas Kaldor (Lord Kaldor). Later events demonstrated just how dangerous it is to rely on borrowed capital.

Unwanted fixed-interest issues

The change to a taxation system which encouraged borrowing was imposed at a time when professional investment managers were increasingly reluctant to invest in fixed-interest stocks. They were well aware of the depreciatory effects on such issues of the mild inflation which had become endemic after 1945. They no longer regarded issues of fixed-interest or fixed-nominal stocks as safe investments. Moreover, rising interest rates had caused the price of gilts and other fixed-interest securities to fall, and investors feared that the falls could be extended by further rises in rates of interest, a foreboding which was fulfilled. Ordinary shares had come back into favour from 1953 onwards, and the so-called cult of the equity had by 1965 reversed the traditional yield relationship between fixed-interest issues and equities, the latter becoming the lower yielding. No wise investor wanted large holdings of fixed-interest stocks, while the less wise investors were attracted only by the consequent high yields on such stocks. Before Corporation Tax the best British companies had been able to capitalise themselves with equity at very low cost, 3 per cent being an acceptable dividend yield on rights issues of ordinary shares. After Corporation Tax had caused inflation to increase, all the shrewdest investment advisers discouraged investment in gilts, preference shares, debentures, building societies accounts, and mortgages. It was a confident prophecy to make that some day a Trust Corporation would be sued for damages for having invested trust money in gilts. The case of *Nestle v. National Westminster Bank 1984* eventually fulfilled the prophecy. The defendant won the case only because a high proportion of equities had been retained in the trust even in the deflationary period of the nineteen-twenties and early nineteen-thirties. But an expert witness for the plaintiff went so far as to maintain very strongly that there should never have been any fixed-interest investment at all throughout the whole life of the trust which had started in 1922. He went too far; he was not as expert as he claimed to be, for he lacked the necessary historical economic knowledge.

Until 1961 the trustees of trusts which gave them no stated investment powers were restricted almost entirely to fixed-interest securities. The Trustee Investment Act of 1961 ameliorated that restriction which had become more a benefit to borrowing governments than a protection for trust beneficiaries. From 1961 onwards there was a reduced demand by trustees for both fixed-interest investments, such as debentures and preference shares, and fixed-capital investments, such as bank deposits and building society accounts.

The plight of the non-professional investors

Although the professional investor did not then want to invest in debt capital, the general public was still happy to do so, as the growth of the building society movement amply confirmed. Though even an undergraduate economist would advise investment in equity assets in an inflationary period, the evidence of the government statistics tends to suggest that inflation slightly increases the public's preference for monetary assets. Inflation certainly does not reduce the public's appetite for building society deposits.[1]

In Britain the provision of long-term fixed-interest capital had been one of the functions of the stock-market. The big banks had never been willing or indeed able to provide it. Under the British arrangement, while it lasted, it was stock-market investors who provided long-term fixed-interest capital for quoted companies. After 1965 the supply of such capital gradually evaporated, and did not return for nearly thirty years, and even then it was partly due to government compulsion directed at pension and insurance funds. The stock market had, of course, never been a prolific source of long-term loan capital for private companies, a major defect in the British capital market. Other sources of debenture and loan capital for private companies had also steadily dried up.

Interest rates rise

Following the introduction of Corporation Tax, the laws of supply and demand caused long-term interest rates on loans and debentures to rise. In the early days of Japan's surge of economic growth bank loans at nine per cent were common, but in the late 1960s when Associated Portland Cement Manufacturers Ltd. issued a debenture with a coupon of nine per cent, there was consternation that a blue-chip British company should have to pay such a high price for a loan. At lunchtime in Christ's College, Cambridge on the day of the announcement of the debenture issue, the eminent historian, Professor Sir John Plumb, who was very knowledgeable and interested in financial matters, asked for my comment. My answer was a forecast that if the pattern of equity yields remained as it then was, simple arithmetic showed that the interest rate on industrial company loan stocks would rise to 14 per cent. That forecast astonished many of those around the table, though not, if memory is accurate, Professor James Meade, later to be awarded the Nobel Prize for economics. He seemed to take the point with his usual calm. Corporation Tax's lack of neutrality no doubt inspired him to oppose it. My forecast was more than fulfilled.

The general rise in interest rates increased the government's own borrowing costs, making necessary an increase in taxation. Unbelievably, one of the taxes raised was Corporation Tax, a move which had the knock-on effect of increasing the rate of interest which a company would be willing to pay rather than resort to an equity issue. Only when equity yields were very low, such as in 1968, a year of stockmarket boom, was any substantial amount of new equity capital raised. In 1970 industrial and commercial companies raised only £39,000,000 in equity capital, compared with over £1,200,000,000 borrowed from banks. Naturally these borrowings by the business community gave rise to another large increase in the intermediated money supply.

The influence of Corporation Tax was most effective upon the longer end of the interest yield curve, but the shorter end of the curve was dragged up by the necessity, consequent upon rising inflation, to bolster the exchange rate. In a desperate attempt to avoid devaluation, the Bank of England raised Bank Rate to 6½ per cent on 8th November 1967, but devaluation nevertheless came on the 18th. It had to be supported by an increase in Bank Rate to eight per cent on the same day, a level which later would not seem high, but which caused a sensation at the time; it was three per cent higher than the rate imposed in 1925 to help return sterling to the Gold Standard at an excessive valuation. It was one per cent higher than the rate set in 1957 during the financial crisis following the Suez War. Such was the transformation in interest rates triggered by Chancellor Callaghan's Corporation Tax. There was never a satisfactory intellectual basis for Corporation Tax; nor had any been put forward publicly.

The 1960s provided no empirical evidence whatsoever to support that most cherished of academic economic myths, the belief that raising interest rates to a high level will reduce inflation without adverse effects on the economy.

The notion that high interest rates cure inflation rests on two arguments which have already been set out. The first, it will be recalled, is that high interest rates discourage borrowing and thus hold back the expansion of the supply of credit. The second is that high interest rates cause recession and unemployment, and that these act as a brake on high wage claims which are the root cause of cost inflation. The second process proved to be effective but undesirable. It works especially well when high interest rates cause the currency to be overvalued with the result that British exports of goods and services are inhibited, and imports are cheap.

Taxing capital gains

Corporation Tax was not the sole taxation blunder of Chancellor James Callaghan. Although one of the other taxes he introduced is not fully relevant to our main topic of study, the problem of the control of credit creation, it is worth mentioning as it exposes some more faulty thinking by his economic advisers.

At the same time as Corporation Tax was introduced (April 1965), he brought in a full-blooded Capital Gains Tax. This was a blow for the non-intermediated credit market. It is theoretically quite sound and justifiable to tax realised capital gains, but one must understand that for the community in the aggregate all capital taxes are really burdens on current income, even though they are computed by reference to capital values.

Taxes on capital stimulate the growth of a virulent cancer of the economy in the form of a strongly growing tax avoidance industry. Fine brains, which might be underemployed in a socialised system because they are unable to carry out important tasks in the expansion of the real economy, are instead attracted into this industry. Those who should be leading the drive towards the target of economic growth are tied up with defensive measures which have only a little relevance to the creation of real wealth.

A more anaemic form of Capital Gains Tax had been applied in 1962. The Conservative Government then introduced a short-term Capital Gains Tax levied on realised gains. Its short-term aspect was that it was assessed only on gains made by the sale of an asset within six months of purchase. Anything held longer than that was exempt. The logic behind it was that anyone who took a profit so quickly was a trader in assets, not a true investor. But in addition to the logical reason there was also the moralistic attitude that anyone who took a quick profit was a speculator. Speculation was commonly regarded as an evil. The short-term tax was an intentionally half-hearted attack on the problem of taxing capital gains. The Conservative Government had instincts which told it that such a tax was nothing but damaging, though they might not have known quite why. Nevertheless they pandered to popular pressure, which was in truth pressure from clever young people who were writers on such matters in the newspapers, but were not quite as clever as they thought. In 2005 similar writers are advocating an even more damaging tax, Land Value Tax.

The wider benefit of speculation

The main effect of the short-term gains tax was indeed to discourage speculation, as was intended. One odd result was a distortion in the market in new share issues. There tended to be a dearth of sellers for six months after a new issue as few investors wanted to incur tax on any profit. This created an artificial one-way market for a while: prices would rise for six months, then fall back. The tax was no more than a bureaucratic money-waster for the compliance cost to the taxpayer was greater than the revenue raised, and the administration cost was also high.

In 1965 James Callaghan decided to tax all capital gains which had been realised by the sale of assets. The rate of tax was a flat 30 per cent, regardless of the size of the gain. Its most damaging immediate effect was to destabilise the market for company shares, an effect which increased over a period of years. All markets can be stabilised by the operations of successful speculators. Unsuccessful speculators can damage a market, but they are, like butterflies, a short-lived species, as they quickly lose the wherewithal for financing their attempts at speculation. On the other hand speculators who are successful can go on indefinitely, though the more of them there are, the smaller are their profits. Successful speculators are people who buy when prices are low, and sell when they are high. They shore up a falling market, limiting its fall. They take the froth off a rising market, limiting its rise. The sounder their judgement, the freer is the market from erratic short-term movements, and the smaller is their profit. Good speculators can make only small profits in a free market: if they are operating in a market which the government is trying to manipulate (and the most frequent instance of that is in the foreign exchange market), speculators make colossal profits, a fact which good economists know very well.

The destabilising effect of introducing a full Capital Gains Tax in 1965 showed up in the movement of the stock-market index. In the five years before the introduction of the tax the FT Ordinary Share Index fluctuated in a band whose maximum was 40 per cent above its minimum. In the five years following its introduction, the band of fluctuation was twice as wide. In the subsequent five years it increased a further fourfold, the minimum point being well below that of the previous two periods. That was the effect of removing the moderating effect of speculators from the market. It has since continued to be volatile, but the fact that a large and growing percentage of company shares are held by tax-free funds, like pension funds, may have latterly somewhat improved stability. It has not eliminated instability completely, because there is a tendency for investment fund managers, a brotherhood which enjoys togetherness, to move like a stampeding herd, fast, furious, and unitedly in one direction. Their herd instinct is so well developed they keep in very close and frequent communication with one another, not in order to fix the market deliberately, but just to know what the other man is thinking, and thereby gain psychological support for making their own similar decisions.

Side effects of Capital Gains Tax

The stock market instability caused serious problems for those institutions which, because their reserves are invested in stock-market securities, depend on the stability of stock and share prices. The insurance companies especially faced difficulties. They were also suffering from the effect on share prices of the introduction of the classical Corporation Tax, which, by reducing the net of tax profits of companies, indirectly lowered the value of shares, whose prices are normally set at a multiple of the net of tax profits per share. The insurance industry was very important to the British economy, partly because it earned very great amounts of foreign exchange. Its welfare, and especially its competitive ability, should have been carefully fostered. It was very silly to weaken its financial reserves at a time when it was beginning to face intense competition from foreign insurers.

In the longer run Capital Gains Tax gave an odd kind of boost to life assurance companies, for, although they had to make reserves for a contingent Capital Gains Tax liability, little of that liability had to be paid immediately. The tax is payable only on realised gains. But when investment values rise, even if it is only as a result of inflation, it is necessary to reserve for the contingent tax liability, however remote. When a with-profits life assurance policy matures, the payment made to the beneficiary of the policy suffers a deduction which reflects at least a part of the tax that might some day have to be paid in respect of known capital gains which have not been realised. Calculating the correct amount to deduct from the maturity value is an impossible exercise because there are three assumptions which have to be made, (I) when will the tax be payable, (ii) at what rate will it be levied, and (iii) what profit will the investment representing the tax earn in the meantime? Faced with such an impossible calculation how can an assurance company decide what premiums to charge?

The reserves for tax made by the insurance companies remain with them to earn income and further capital appreciation, but they belong to no-one. They do not belong to the Inland Revenue, because the tax is not yet payable. They do not belong to the policyholders; they do not belong to the insurance company's shareholders, though the policyholders and the shareholders can benefit from the income and the capital profits earned by these reserves. Within a very few years of the introduction of the tax, old-established assurance companies had reserves for contingent tax which may have been greater than their shareholders' funds. As the old-established companies benefited most, competition was distorted. Industrial companies too had huge contingent capital tax liabilities, almost wholly as a result of inflation. They made no reserves against the liability to tax as in practice it would only be payable in the event of the winding-up of a company. This fact could cause declining companies to continue to trade longer than they should, prolonging their death throes.

Between 1965 and 1982 there was no provision for adjusting for inflation when a capital gain was calculated, nor has there been one since 1997. One commonly found that Capital Gains Tax was payable even though, because of inflation, the proceeds of sale of an asset had a lower current purchasing power than the original acquisition cost.

Inflation adjustment was introduced in 1982, and in 1985 Chancellor Nigel Lawson corrected some of the remaining mistakes which his predecessors had been persuaded to perpetrate. James Callaghan's version of Capital Gains Tax gave a government a strong financial incentive to encourage inflation. Inflation converted the tax into an arbitrary and harsh wealth tax, extremely erratic in its incidence. Capital Gains Tax is undoubtedly an extremely effective instrument for diverting attention from the real problems of an economy. It ensures that resources of skill and energy are wasted in dealing with the purely artificial problem of avoiding a tax which had been made, almost deliberately, irrational and destructive. A vast effort had to go into the study of the ways of reducing the impact of Capital Gains Tax. Superficially estate and inheritance taxes may seem to be more destructive of private wealth, but whenever one tried to tackle the problem of preserving a business from the ravages of the other capital taxes, one found that there was a preliminary difficulty, usually quite insurmountable, of avoiding Capital Gains Tax. As that meant that inheritance taxes could not be ameliorated, Capital Gains Tax was doubly destructive in its effect.[2]

Gordon Brown, Chancellor of the Exchequer in the Labour Government which came to power in 1997, abolished the inflation indexing of capital gains, but introduced a tapering of the rate of tax. This measure could further discourage the taking of short-term profits, and may further destabilize the stock-market. To make sure that even more chaos was caused in stock markets, he made the rate of Capital Gains Tax on business assets considerably lower than that on fully quoted stocks and shares, and the taper period was four years instead of ten. This caused a rush to move quotations from the main stock market to the 'AIM' list. The fact that the latter were free of Inheritance Tax was an additional incentive, and it soon ensured that the AIM quoted stocks were twice as dear, in terms of earnings yield, than stocks on the main market list. For directors who held large shareholdings in the companies which they directed, there was an even larger tax advantage to be achieved by taking their companies private through management buy-outs. Of course the buy-outs are often done with newly created credit, and the credit supply/money supply soars relentlessly upwards.

Tracking indices

But the practice which brought even more instability than had ever been known before, creating huge price bubbles, was the work of the investment institutions themselves. Having lost confidence in their ability to beat the market indices, they decided to be cautious and to promise nothing more than to equal chosen indices of stocks. The *'Tracker Fund'* was invented, with predictably disastrous results. The funds might not have been so dangerous if it had not been for the 'dot.com' boom, new companies in the Information Technology Industry which seemed to promise great growth. A small company, making no profits, would be launched, and a mad rush for the shares by super-optimists would raise the market price to the point that the company's capitalisation might be great enough to take it into the index of the top 350 shares. At that point every fund which tracked the 350 index had to buy it, driving the price up to the point where it qualified for the 250 index. Now every fund which tracked the 250 share index had to buy it, and the demand drove the share into the 100 index. So the funds which tracked that index had to buy it. The FTSE 100 Index reached a peak of 7,000 at the end of 1999. Then the bubbles starting violently bursting. At the beginning of 2003 the FTSE Index went under 4,000. The All-Share Index followed the same course. Those who avoided the dot.coms had not much difficulty in beating the indices by 100 per cent over a five year period.

If the regulators of the Financial Services Authority had any understanding of how stock markets work, they would instantly ban tracker funds. All mechanistic methods of fund management should be discouraged. In October 1987 there was a very sharp fall in share values, and I suspected that it was caused by the adoption by a large number of fund managers of the same computer program to detect market movements, a program which they all left on its default settings. If every fund manager is using a program which signals that, say, a ten per cent fall in the market has occurred and that has been chosen as the level to start stop-loss selling, it is inevitable that a market crash will take place, and continue until either some sensible person trashes the computer, or the cleverer managers step in to buy on the cheap. I have heard that academic research has since confirmed my suspicion. I admit that in October 1987 the market had reached an unjustifiable level, supported only by the reluctance of investors to pay Capital Gains Tax at 40 per cent on their profits, but the reaction was greater than was justified by fundamentals.

The boom in share prices in the late 1990s had created the illusion that pension funds were over-funded. It is, of course, totally wrong in principle that the viability of a long-term pension or life assurance fund should be measured by its capital profits, for if ever the pension funds found themselves in a net selling phase, prices of their assets would plummet. The high stock-market prices of the last fifty years have been a function of the strong growth of such funds. Too much saving chased too few investments. The viability of a pension fund should be measured by its income potential. Dividends are self-liquidating; capital profits are not.

The illusion of overfunding, enhanced by the Inland Revenue's rules on funding adequacy, caused many companies to take contribution holidays, itself a factor which weakened the rise in share prices.

To make matters worse, the regulators panicked, and demonstrated that they did not understand stock-markets. *'Those who can invest cleverly do so, and those who cannot become regulators,'* may be the reason for their incredibly dangerous behaviour. They put pressure on the funds to divest from equities, and re-invest in bonds. Falling interest rates had caused bonds to appreciate dramatically since 1990, but by the time the regulators started their campaign of harassment, that effect was almost played out. Standard Life Assurance, the largest mutual assurance fund, was forced, it was reported in 2004, to sell £7.5 billion of equities. Why that did not cause an immediate fall in the market is a mystery one would like to solve. In the last quarter of 1974, when for the first time the pension and assurance funds became net sellers of equities to the extent of £62 million (perhaps £800 million in 2004 values), there was a three-fifths fall in the index. Perhaps disaster was avoided in 2004 because the funds had had to end their contribution holidays, and become net investors again.

At the time of writing press commentators are reporting that it has been calculated that the action by Standard Life Assurance cost the policy-holders on average £482 each.

But many pension funds had switched to bonds from equities, just at the wrong time, of course. The herd instinct of fund managers was displayed once again. The problem for a fund manager is that if he or she does the opposite to the herd, and gets it wrong, then he or she is for the high jump, but if one does the same as the herd and the herd gets it wrong, no-one seems to mind. Back in the 1970s, for some time I occupied a desk next to our company head of investment research. Every morning he began the day by phoning his opposite numbers in rival institutions to find out what their attitude was to the market, and no way could he be persuaded to judge differently. The odd thing was that this co-operation transcended the barrier of competition.

Corporation Tax continues to damage

In 1970 a Conservative Government was elected, and it decided to ameliorate the effects of Corporation Tax. They did not return to the earlier system, but they allowed the income tax payable by investors to be 'franked' against Corporation Tax, thus eliminating some, but not all, of the double taxation of dividends. The United States retained the classical Corporation Tax system, and it was not until the election of George W. Bush as President that there was any attempt to end the double taxation of company profits belonging to private investors. In both countries the incentive to capitalise companies with loan capital remained very strong.

As at 2005, in the United Kingdom £100 of loan interest paid by a company is worth £80 for a basic rate tax-payer, and £60 for a maximum rate tax-payer. £100 of profits is normally worth £70 for a basic rate tax-payer and £45.50 for a higher rate tax-payer. It is not possible to give an accurate figure for the United States, as income tax is payable not only to the Federal Government, but also to a resident's State and City governments. In the highest taxed states a maximum rate tax-payer might get a bit over $50 from $100 of interest paid by a company, and about $26 from $100 of profits.

The different treatment of interest and profits must be a special annoyance to the members of religious groups who are not allowed to receive interest payments.

If a company is taken over by another which pays for the purchase with bonds, not shares, the government loses out significantly. When the British government allowed Wal-Mart to purchase the ASDA supermarket chain with borrowed money, it automatically reduced the tax paid by ASDA by a third. In any sane system of Corporation Tax, it would be levied on the pre-interest profits in order to avoid this effect. In the United States, faced with a far bigger anomaly, companies followed more drastic policies. Many ceased paying dividends altogether, instead using profits to buy back shares. For many investors the rate of Capital Gains Tax is less than the income tax rate, so this makes very good sense. Often the buy-backs were paid for with borrowed money, and if that was newly created credit, the potential inflationary effects are obvious.

The 'mergers and acquisitions' business is promoted strongly by banks as part of their search for remunerative uses for the credit whose creation they can assist.

Nor are capital adequacy ratios any longer much of a problem. Banks now fully understand the Basel Capital Accord, and how to work around it. They have learned how to 'securitise' their loans, a process which transfers them to the direct credit market and therefore off the bank's balance sheet. That reduces capital adequacy needs.

The scene would appear to be set for a gigantic increase in inflation, but it has not happened. Why not? There are several reasons. Firstly there is the fact that many industries are working well below capacity, so inflation is not demand driven. Secondly, interest rates have remained low, so the pressure by employees for higher pay to cover higher mortgage payments no longer exists. Thirdly, the banks have managed to double the average indebtedness of workers, and they dare not strike for fear of going bankrupt. Fourthly, the banks are perhaps a little more prudent, though at any time competition could drive them to act foolishly again. The fight for market share is often won by the player who takes the most risks. Fifthly, competition in the retail sector is high, and that is keeping a large range of prices down. Sixthly one must not forget that nearly everywhere unemployment is still high.

But perhaps we are forgetting one point: domestic inflation in truth is high but is hidden by the falling cost of imports. There is domestic cost inflation, but its effect is hidden by import price deflation.

12

Savings, Investment and Debt

*Saving is a very fine thing, especially
if your parents have done it for you.*
SIR WINSTON CHURCHILL (*attributed*)

IN CHAPTER SIXTEEN of his book *The General Theory of Employment, Interest and Money* Lord Keynes analysed the nature and effects of saving. He pointed out that when a person saves he or she is postponing consumption, possibly, but not necessarily, with a view to consuming later. The consequence of this, Keynes suggested, is that saving reduces the immediate demand for goods and services. The first conclusion the reader is led to draw from his analysis is that saving must cause unemployment.

He also suggested, however, that if the saving were for the purpose of some future consumption, the entrepreneur might think it worthwhile to invest capital immediately in order to be ready to supply the future demand when it appears. This would counter the tendency for unemployment to rise as a result of an increased propensity to save. But he seems to expect that the normal knock-on effect of the reduction in the demand for goods for immediate consumption would be to reduce, not increase, the demand for capital equipment such as machine tools.

Keynes' remarks must have had great influence on political economists and politicians. Some have favoured the second of the alternative results of saving, and have used his analysis as a reason to inhibit saving during a recession. Others have chosen the more optimistic version, and have encouraged saving on the principle that it will artificially stimulate investment, and therefore the expansion of the economy. An extreme example of the latter policy would be to adopt an Expenditure Tax as the sole method of taxation. Such a tax would have the effect of making all savings an allowable deduction from income for tax purposes.

Throughout Keynes' book, *The Treatise on Money*, he appears to be under the impression that savings always finances investment. Presumably he means by investment what the Office for National

Statistics much more sensibly calls *fixed capital formation*. Moreover he also appears to believe that savings have to precede investment. It is this mistake which makes a very large part of his *Treatise on Money* wrong and misleading. An act of true investment can *precede* an act of true saving in the same way that borrowing must *precede* an increase in money deposits. A further principle is that an attempt to save which is not matched by some act of real capital formation must end up financing some form of consumer expenditure; that is a logical necessity.

Keynes got himself deeply confused over the definition of saving. On no other aspect of economics does he seem to have failed so completely in his analysis. Five years later, in Chapter Six of *The General Theory of Employment Interest and Money*, he has another go at clarification and writes,

> *So far as I know, everyone is agreed that saving means the excess of income over expenditure on consumption.*

But everyone does not agree. For the ordinary citizen saving is the failure to exercise a right to consume to the limit of one's current income, and the acquisition with the unspent income of financial assets. As all financial assets are other peoples' debts, whatever the citizen has not spent is lent to someone else for whatever purchase that person prefers. Keynes' definition of saving is the aggregate expenditure of the whole community on non-consumption goods – whatever they may be. He sets out his proof on page 63 in a syllogism of three equations:–

Income   = value of output = consumption plus investment.
Saving   = income minus consumption.
Therefore:– Saving = investment.

Keynes has neatly fudged the discussion by defining saving in terms of real investment. Government statisticians have done the same ever since. He avoided examining what the ordinary man sees as savings, and instead looks at only that part of the net aggregate saving of the whole community which has been invested in a strictly defined set of assets, assets which in his mind have some common characteristic. Did he assume that that characteristic was that the assets were all productive investments? If so it is not apparent in the list of items which the ONS regards as fixed capital formation. He was aware there was some problem, for he returns to the issue in Chapter Seven. On page 75 he defined net investment as the net addition to all kinds of capital equipment. Then he had a cigarette, as was his wont, had a bright idea, and wrote the next sentence in which he expands the term *'capital equipment'* to include *'working capital or liquid capital'*. Yes, savings can also finance work-in-progress and stocks of consumption goods. How true indeed! It can also provide consumer finance, which has nothing at all to do with real investment.

The Treatise's other errors

The Treatise on Money, published by Keynes in 1930, contains two other mistakes. The first is the strange *'Widow's Cruse'* simile, postulating an eternal and inexhaustible supply of *profit*. The second is Keynes' definition of profit, and all the long reasoning derived from it. He seems to cherish the illusion that one person's profit is always some other person's loss. This is not true; profit is the entrepreneur's reward for his work and skill, or the return on his capital. It is perfectly possible for *all* entrepreneurs to make a profit at the same time. Perhaps Keynes' mistake is due to his personal preoccupation with financial speculation, through which he became very rich. In stock-market and currency speculation, in both of which he was active and successful, one man's profits may well reflect another man's losses. But gambling and productive industry are two totally different things. Gambling is always a zero-sum game, while productive industry is about positive gains to the economy.

The financing of real capital formation

In Britain it was most unusual in the post-1945 era for the savings of its ordinary citizens to help finance the creation of new productive resources, because for several decades British industry was, in the aggregate, more than self-financing. If we take one year, 1987, for example, industrial and commercial companies spent £28,411 million on fixed capital formation in Britain, yet their undistributed earnings amounted to £46,415 million. There was no need in 1987 for the personal sector of the economy to save in order to provide the finance for any of private industry's capital formation, and the same has been true in very nearly every year, before or since, for more than half a century. In the aggregate industry was well able to finance itself. However that is nothing to be proud of as it reflects a low level of industrial capital formation. Later this position changed dramatically, though briefly, but only because so many capital hungry utilities were transferred to the private sector from the public sector of the economy. In the first 11 years of privatisation the water supply industry alone spent £39 billion on its assets.

We assert firmly that there is no automatic association between a high level of individual saving and a high level of capital formation in production capacity. Saving can just as easily finance consumer credit as finance capital expenditure on production facilities. In an economy such as the United Kingdom's, which has regularly been internationally uncompetitive because of an overvalued currency, saving is much more likely to finance the consumer rather than the producer of goods and services. That process has continued and grown in recent decades. See *Credit and Savings in the UK: a More Indebted Society?* by Gordon Blunt, published 2004 by the Manchester Statistical Society.

To put it simply, we rewrite Keynes' definition to state that savings is always equal to borrowing: saving is not equal to investment, if by investment one means the creation of new real capital assets ('fixed capital formation').

Primary and secondary capital markets

A saver may not deposit his savings in a bank: he may use them to purchase other financial assets such as a life policy, an investment in stocks and shares, or a unit trust (mutual fund), or a host of other investment instruments. In such cases the money may find its way via the investment institution the saver has trusted with his savings into either the primary or secondary capital market; the saver does not know which it will be. If it is the primary capital market, it could finance the purchase of durable things which will become the real capital of future generations. But that will not necessarily be so, for as we have seen, the primary capital market can finance stock in trade, debtors, or consumer borrowing as readily as it can finance factories or machinery. If the saving finds its way into the secondary capital market, it may be buying an asset belonging to someone who is dis-saving, and who proposes to turn his financial asset into the wherewithal to purchase part of the current production of goods and services of the economy. In either case the saver finances demand which will completely replace his own deferred demand, the value of which is measured by his saving. That does not mean that there is a gap in demand which can cause unemployment, as Keynes so often suggested.

The principles restated

Let us restate the principles yet again. In a developed economy all positive saving, that is saving which takes place not merely for the repayment of existing debt, will be matched by an equivalent dis-saving. One man's postponement of the right to consume, which he has earned by his work, will normally be replaced by someone else's active anticipation of his expected future right to consume. The routine process of matching each act of saving with an act of borrowing, whether it is to finance consumption or to finance real capital formation, will be achieved through the financial system's capital markets.

All wealth is debt: one man's wealth is someone else's liability. Saving cannot exist without dis-saving; thrift cannot exist without profligacy.

Although Keynes' analysis was wholly misconceived, we could no doubt construct a scenario of events which do run an economy down. If an economy can expand, it can also contract. But it is most unlikely that the horrifying picture of a declining economy which Keynes paints in the third section of Chapter 16 of *The General Theory of Employment, Interest and Money* would result solely from the propensity to save without assistance from another factor. An increased propensity to repay debts is that other factor. So the problem activity is what may be called *negative saving,* the reduction of debt.

Investment, and the meaning of capital

Investment is therefore a much misused word, the misuse has led to the very mistaken, or very misleading statement, that *'savings equals investment'.* One can only avoid misunderstanding by the labourious process of redefining the word every time one uses it. Keynes should have been less general in his statement and content just to say, *'A certain kind of investment is equal to a certain kind of saving'.* The kind of investment is that which results in the creation of new structures which produce real wealth faster than did previous structures, and the kind of saving is that which finances such structures.

The word *investment* can in popular parlance include portfolio investment as well as referring to real investment. Portfolio investment is the purchase of existing productive assets, whereas real investment is the creation of new productive assets. To avoid confusing the two we should use the alternative expression *real capital formation* for the latter. Unfortunately not all real capital assets are productive: they are merely fixed, permanent. Thus we can go on refining our terms and perhaps arrive at *fixed real productive capital formation.*

Aristotelian classification always prompts further questions, and so does our refined term. Is a new road, which is obviously something real and fixed, a productive asset? *'Yes,'* one could say, *'if it assists the economy to be more productive.'* Is a school a productive asset? *'Yes, because it provides a service.'* Is a dwelling productive? *'No, because it is an object of production, one of the goods we desire.'* However it is capital, is it not, for it is real and fixed?

Then what is capital? We tend to feel that a house is capital but a washing machine is not. We therefore invent a new term, and the washing machine is consequently classified as a *durable consumer product*, as if that distinguishes it from true capital assets. Truly all it does is distinguish it from non-durable consumer products. Is not a house truly a durable consumer product too?

What is Income?

Let us approach from another direction. The opposite of capital can be income. Is not the aggregate income of a community the totality of all its current production of goods and services? Surely it is; in that we agree with Keynes. But that totality includes *all* of the current production of capital goods. Gradually we discover that the popular meaning of *capital* has no logical foundation. It is pure nonsense. It has a vague instinctive meaning, incapable of precise definition. Let us therefore drop the popular use, try to be more scientific, and, like Maynard Keynes, apply terms to definitions, not definitions to terms. Now the thought process becomes quite easy. Income is the current production of all goods and services, and capital must therefore be the surviving results of *past* production. If it exists, it is real capital. If it is being produced, it is income. Because creation can be a speedy process, the transformation from being part of income to being an item of capital can also be quick. So to measure income we take a fixed period and count up the value of all production in that period. The production of one day would be the ideal time period, but a year is more convenient. We have thus defined as income the gross domestic product for a year, exactly the definition used in the official statistics.

Some goods remain capital for only a brief period in time, as production and final consumption may be very close together, and the consumption may leave no residue. Food is consumed and thereby destroyed, but if we think of the purchase of a washing machine as consumption we must admit that it is consumption which certainly does not *consume* in the sense of *destroy*.

An individual's own production of goods and services has a value, and he is entitled to consume other goods and services to the same value. He may choose not to exercise all his proper entitlement. The difference between his entitlement and his actual consumption is his saving, and he will want his saving to be represented by some store of value, something of continuing value. As has already been demonstrated, for production and consumption to be in balance, some other person must borrow in order to finance the acquisition of the exact value of current production whose consumption the saver has deferred by his act of saving. That other person becomes a debtor for the value of his borrowing: the debt becomes the saver's store of wealth.

A vital purpose, indeed the basic purpose, of the financial system is to match the underconsumption of a saver to the overconsumption of a borrower. This statement should make it clear that savings can finance the production of *any* goods and services, whether of lasting nature or not.

Through positive investment the community tries to make a proportion of the current production of food, lighting, heating, clothing, lodging, etcetera, available to other workers who are producing no immediately consumable goods or services. Instead they are fully engaged in producing new capital structures, which may eventually enhance the production of goods and services. In return for their abstinence savers are rewarded by getting some of the new wealth generated by those new assets.

The gap

Between 1921 and 1939 there was persistent unemployment in Britain and other parts of the world, and its causes and cures were the subject of fierce discussions. One of those who thought he knew the cause and the solution was a Canadian, Major Clifford Douglas. From a study of company balance sheets he concluded that the value of the sales of a company was not matched by the amount of purchasing power their cost of production returned to the economy. I am sure I can claim to have studied far more balance sheets than ever Major Douglas saw, but I have never detected the gap which he claimed to have seen. There is a gap, nevertheless, a different one from that of Douglas, and it works as follows.

Assume that a bank agrees to advance £1,000,000 of newly created credit to a company to make some new widget or other. The one million pounds are paid out to suppliers and workers, and thus there is injected into the economy exactly the amount spent on producing the widgets. This is what is meant by supply creating it's own demand, *Say's Law*, though it would be better worded to say that the cost of producing something provides the wherewithal for its purchase. But there is a problem; if a worker does not spend all he earns from producing the widgets, but saves some of his income on a bank account, the amount injected into the economy is reduced by the amount of that saving, creating a gap between the cost of production and the amount of purchasing power available for its purchase. The worker who is saving is financing his own production. He is indirectly lending money to his employer to provide his own pay. Keynes expressed it in the words, *'One man's saving is another man's unemployment.'* To negate the effect there needs to be another creation of new credit to allow someone to buy the production. Major Douglas was correct in thinking there could be a gap between supply and demand, but he did not define it correctly.

There also needs to be additional new credit creation to provide the money which will enable the employer to make a profit. The bank has lent him enough to pay the costs of his suppliers and workers, but may not have lent him anything to pay himself. In that case his profit will depend on what is termed 'final credit inflation'. Profit must be financed by new credit creation.

But there is a prudential limit on credit creation, and eventually a period of excessive credit creation is followed by consolidation, an attempt to reduce debt, and a recession follows.

Promotion of productive investment

Maynard Keynes' old colleague, Professor James Meade, wanted to make the encouragement of saving the prime object of the taxation system, and in 1985 his views were adopted by the Confederation of British Industry. The instrument of the policy was an Expenditure Tax.

A taxation policy to promote saving is not the real need: we need a policy to promote productive real capital formation. Meade was on the wrong track. If the community decides to produce capital assets, the saving to finance them automatically takes place. It has to, because there arises a deficiency of goods to consume upon which to spend the money incomes earned. At any particular moment in time some persons or institutions must have on their bank accounts the money which was borrowed and paid to the workers who built the new productive asset. These bank balances may get passed from hand to hand, chasing an insufficient supply of consumer goods. Some inflation may ensue. However a successful project of productive real capital formation will result in the supply of goods at a lower price than before. So deflation then follows.

Even if the continued creation of real capital assets does cause some inflation, it is worth tolerating as the price of the expansion of the economy. However the inflationary effect of capital projects is in any event only marked if there is a dearth of resources, either of workers, skills or materials, so that demand for them exceeds supply. But if there is no deficiency, the inflationary effect will be slight, being limited to the difference between the workers' wages and what they would receive in unemployment benefit. If that difference increases demand, there will be a further reduction in unemployment.

The increased demand will almost certainly lower unit costs, with yet more benefit to the economy. Retail prices may therefore go down, not up. Oddly enough that is not entirely a blessing, because the truly dangerous side effect of real investment is deflation, rather than inflation.

The inflationary eventuality which one will prefer to prevent is the growth of an over-liberal credit supply, which *cannot* be applied to real investment, and which therefore merely pushes up the price of existing assets. Failure to prevent that was the tragic error of the late 1980s. The violent credit explosion of that era was primed, as already shown in Chapter Four, by high interest rates. If interest rates had been low, there would have been a much greater likelihood of the credit increase being absorbed by productive real investment. A lower exchange rate would have also helped that result. The exchange rate would have been lower if interest rates had been lower, a double benefit.

Capital taxation

When a government taxes its people, what it is trying to obtain, as with other kinds of taxation, is the power to use some of the current production of goods and services for its own purposes. For the most part, any existing goods, that is the community's capital assets, are of no use to it. It follows that the taxation of capital, except in kind, is impossible. A government wanting its taxes paid in cash can tax only income. What are called capital taxes are truly income taxes computed by reference to capital values. If a taxpayer has insufficient income to pay a tax on his capital he must sell an asset to someone who is saving. Then it is the *saver's* income which finances the tax. Those economists who have advocated increased capital taxation, and they are legion, have not clearly understood what they are about. Some proposals, such as those emanating from the Trades Union Congress, have envisaged tax revenues exceeding the net savings of the personal sector of the economy. Not only is that a logical impossibility, but it also has the effect, when attempted, of deflating capital values.

In 1974 J. S. Flemming and Professor I. M. D. Little published a pamphlet called *Why We Need a Wealth Tax*. The pamphlet avoids any discussion of the effect of such a capital tax on security values. Nor does it mention the natural limit which the aggregate net saving of the community places on capital taxation, a limit which their tax proposals came very near to breaching. There was room in the pamphlet to do so, but the authors preferred to use it for emotive pictures of people hunting, of an art auction, and of the Stock Exchange. Little was Oxford University Professor of the Economics of Undeveloped Countries. Flemming became economic adviser to the Bank of England, and, for a while, a director of the Bank.

Foreign investment

Foreign investment can take several forms, only some of which necessitate savings in the home country. Often it simply means borrowing money in a foreign country and using it to create new productive assets in that country. Sometimes it can mean the purchase of existing foreign assets with capital raised in the home country. In such cases the transfer of money abroad will of necessity be matched by a movement of bank funds in the reverse direction. Sometimes the purchase can be made with capital raised abroad so that no transfer of funds abroad is required.

But sometimes foreign investment is the production at home of goods and services for use in the creation of productive assets abroad. That production may be financed either by savings, or by newly created credit. It is inevitable that this last form of investment causes an export of goods and services. Keynes knew that, of course, but he preferred investment to be made at home. This was because he, and others, believed that there is no investment multiplier effect when investment is made abroad. That opinion must be wrong. Because the money invested in the production of the goods and services for export is spent in the country doing the exporting there *must* be a multiplier effect: the money will circulate *only* in the home country. Moreover, as there has been an export of goods and services, there must be a deficiency of the same in the home country relative to the total income of workers. The wages of the producers of the exports will therefore drive up demand for goods and services in exactly the same way as any other investment, unless it is balanced – coincidentally – by true saving (a postponement of a right to consume). Foreign investment of this kind is creating a demand for goods and services at home, but is not supplying it. If the finance for the investment is new credit, not savings, home demand will be enhanced.

Conversely a true disinvestment of assets abroad results in a real inward transfer of goods and services, which is financed by the proceeds of sale of foreign assets. It must cause an increase in imports. That too is axiomatic.

Nevertheless, in 1985 the Trades Union Congress and the Labour Party Conference both advocated government action to force a return of the investments made abroad by British investment funds. No government action was taken, but by coincidence a substantial disinvestment from foreign assets took place at the end of 1987. It was accompanied, as one might expect, by an increase in imports and the appearance of a trade deficit. It has already been mentioned earlier in this book that as the distribution of goods is about as expensive as their production, one of the paradoxical effects of a trade deficit, whether financed by a sale of foreign investments or by borrowing from abroad, is to increase the number of people employed in distributive trades in the importing country. Even though it may also tend to precipitate some reduction in employment in home manufacturing industries whose competitive position is eroded by the effect of the disinvestment or borrowing on the exchange rate, an overall fall in unemployment must inevitably follow the appearance of a trade deficit. In the three years after 1987 such a fall duly took place. The British government, failing to distinguish fact from fancy, deemed it a *recovery*. Presumably the work of distributing the increased quantity of imports was counted in the statistics as part of Gross Domestic Product, and the economy was deemed to have grown. Since then the trade deficit has grown to a frightening level, and has been accompanied, as this analysis would predict, by rising employment. Thus an appearance of a booming economy has been created.

The conclusion from this chapter must be that in reality no necessary connection exists between an act of saving and *real capital formation*, as the creation of physical capital assets is called. Whether savings are used to finance real capital formation or only consumer expenditure will depend on market forces in the overall capital market.

Richard Kahn

Maynard Keynes relied heavily on one associate, Richard Kahn, a Fellow, like Keynes, of King's College, Cambridge. Kahn is remembered by academic economists as the author of the *investment multiplier*, a theory which finds its way into every examination on economic theory. Kahn maintained that every act of investment, by which one presumes he meant an act of fixed capital formation, had a multiplier effect on the economy, leading to further investment. He backed up his theory with some mathematics which Keynes did not understand. As we have shown that new credit creation has a multiplier effect on Gross Domestic Product, can we accept that an act of fixed capital formation also has a multiplier effect? No, we cannot. Indeed the opposite is true: any act of investment which lowers costs has an automatic deflationary effect unless further new credit creation takes up the slack, and employs the resources made redundant by the act of investment.

One can illustrate this with a case study:–[1]

The Brunel Effect

Kahn's assumption, and that of most economists, is that 'investment,' by which is meant in this context the creation of new productive equipment, will automatically bring economic growth. But this assumption is invalid, as another case study will show.

In 1801 a Mr. Kingdom visited Mr. Samuel Taylor in Portsmouth. Taylor was one of the partners in the firm of Fox and Taylor whose business was the making of wooden rigging blocks for the Royal Navy. It employed 110 skilled men in the manufacture of the blocks, 100,000 of which were required by the Navy every year. Kingdom made the visit as a result of a meeting between his brother-in-law, Marc Isambard Brunel, and Brigadier General Sir Samuel Bentham, the Inspector General of Naval Works. Marc Brunel was born in France in 1769 and served as an officer in the French Navy, but the French Revolution had caused him to leave France and settle in America. He became an American citizen. In 1798 he went to England to marry Miss Sophia Kingdom. Her brother was Under-Secretary to the Navy Board.[2]

While still in America Marc Brunel had developed an interest in block-making machinery. In 1801 he took out British patent number 2478 for a suite of machines designed to make rigging blocks automatically. Bentham was very interested in Brunel's ideas but Samuel Taylor was not. A letter to Kingdom survives in which Samuel Taylor flatly refused the machinery. Bentham therefore persuaded the Royal Navy to set up its own block-making factory and to use Brunel's machines. By 1808 130,000 blocks were being made by just ten unskilled operatives. It is claimed that this was the first time that machine tools made entirely of metal were used for mass production. Brunel's reward was one year's savings in costs. That was calculated at £17,663.95. The cost of making the machines was three times as much.

One hundred skilled men had lost their jobs as a result of the invention, but before that happened perhaps three times as many got one year's work from the making of the machines. They were the employees of the engineer, Henry Maudslay. So there may have been a temporary increase in employment from 110 to 410, followed by a reduction to ten. The final effect was highly deflationary. The capital investment in new productive equipment had the effect of lowering the incomes of the factors of production. This must be a common result of capital investment in more cost-effective means of production. To celebrate the 300th anniversary of its foundation, the Bank of England produced in 1994 a graph of inflation covering the whole 300 years of its existence. From 1694 to 1938 the graph can be seen to show a slight long-term tendency to deflation in peacetime, though inflation was often very evident in wartime. The deflationary tendency appears to accelerate after 1801. It seems rational to assume that this was partly the result of the increased use of automatic machinery driven by steam power.

All the financial scenarios

It is most enlightening to speculate on the effects of all the possible scenarios in which the investment in the block-making machinery took place. There are several.

Let us assume as the first scenario that the government paid for Brunel's automatic machines by raising taxation. Taxation is a diversion of purchasing power from the public to the government. If increased government expenditure is balanced by increased taxation the effect on gross domestic product is nil. Some suppliers lose their market because public spending power is artificially reduced, but others who are supplying the government increase their sales.

The same effect would result if the government borrowed the money to purchase the machines and that borrowing was financed by saving by the public, using saving in the sense that the public has not spent all its income, but has placed some in financial assets, the financial asset in this case being a loan to the government.

If, however, the extra expenditure is financed by newly created credit and therefore does not in any way reduce existing demand, there is an increase in employment of resources. The savings which balance the loan come from the additional income arising from the expenditure. There is a rise in gross domestic product. Moreover the created money may circulate rapidly enough to generate further demand, over and above the original expenditure it was created to finance, so that gross domestic product goes up by more than the government's borrowing. The rate of circulation of created money is a vital factor in deciding the effect of a loan in expanding the economy.

All these scenarios concern the period during which Brunel's machines are under construction but not yet producing. Let us look at the succeeding scenarios once the machines are producing. They are extremely complex and varied. Not all bear out Richard Kahn's thesis.

Henry Maudslay's men who built the machines may have no further orders; therefore 300 of them are redundant. The machines come into use and all Fox and Taylor's 110 men are redundant. Ten men get work at the Navy Yard using the new machines. Four hundred men are without incomes, having been earning the previous year. Although the rigging blocks are cheaper, that does not increase demand for them to any great extent. In fact production went to 130,000 blocks in 1808 from 100,000 in 1800. That may have been due to the Battle of Trafalgar which damaged a lot of ships even on the winning side.

In nominal terms the gross domestic product has declined because rigging blocks are 90 per cent cheaper. It may also have gone down because 400 men have no income to spend. On the other hand the government is spending £17,663.95 less and may require that much less in taxation, or may borrow that much less from the public. If that were true, the public would have sufficient extra money to buy the product of 100 extra workmen. There would be disruption, but equilibrium should return to produce the same employment, except for Henry Maudslay's men. They had a year's temporary work producing capital items which will not need replacing for a long time. Indeed the machines still exist and could still work if wooden rigging blocks were needed. But although employment remains the same as before the investment, the output of physical goods and services is slightly increased.

A further scenario is that the government could have raised additional taxes to pay Maudslay's men to make the machines. In that scenario the additional taxation would have reduced demand (and thereby demand for labour) by exactly the amount by which it was raised at Maudslay's. The ending of the work at Maudslay's and the lowering of taxation in consequence would reverse relative demands.

It can be seen from these scenarios that it is only when a project is financed by newly created credit that employment is increased, and even in that case the effect can be temporary, and indeed even reduce employment in the long run. The extent of the increase in labour requirement will be determined by the speed with which the newly created money circulates. If it circulates not at all, the increase will be only that financed directly by the new credit. This might happen if the recipients of the payments financed by the credits used the money to pay off debts. In all other circumstances there is a multiplier effect. The machines are made and add to the wealth of the nation; the workers who made them spend their wages on goods and services; the producers of those goods and services do the same. The effects can be dramatic, but they come to an end the moment the circulation ceases, that is when someone 'saves' the money he has received, instead of spending it. No one can predict when that point will be reached. No computer programme could ever be devised to make an accurate estimate of the effect. Hopefully the knock-on effects will be great enough to raise the economy to a new equilibrium level in which a higher level of production, consumption and employment is sustained. But it can easily relapse. If it does, then another injection of credit into the system will be required to get things moving again.

But one cannot go on injecting credit into the system indefinitely. The public's borrowing capacity is finite, being a prudent multiple of its income. What happens when the public tries to repay its borrowing from its income? Demand is automatically reduced; so is production; so is the public's income. Also, the balances of money capable of circulating are reduced. A deflationary spiral is induced. It is made worse by psychological effects. Faced with recession the public tries harder to save, and the government is urged to reduce expenditure because its revenues are falling.

The lesson to be learned from the Brunel incident is that no new capital investment in labour-saving equipment will increase the overall demand for goods and services unless other new credit is created to finance the bringing back into production of the resources freed up by the earlier capital investment. The Brunel machines were financed by new credit. All new credit creation, for whatever purpose, has a multiplier effect. Richard Kahn's belief that 'real investment' alone had a multiplier effect is defective. He was some distance from a full understanding of how an economy works.

Postscript to Brunel

In fact there was a multiplier effect on this investment. Since first writing the above case study, I have discovered that even Brigadier-General Sir Samuel Bentham could not achieve a public sector contract at a modest price. Henry Maudslay made such a large profit that he was able to build a new factory. That further investment was an example of the credit multiplier at work, not Kahn's investment multiplier.

Savings structures

Having dealt with the principles and effects of real investment, we should now look at the savings structures which support portfolio investment. The ones that matter are Unit Trusts (Mutual Funds), Investment Trusts, Life Assurance Funds and public and private sector Pension Funds.

The first two enable the personal sector to invest with a spread of risk and get professional management. Investment trusts are a bit of a problem as their shares persistently sell at less than the net value of the investments the trusts hold. The moral of this is never to invest in a new trust, as it is almost certain to fall in price. Unit trusts are a great invention, first introduced to Britain in 1931 by the Late Ian Fairbairn, a great enthusiast for investment for the small investor right to the end of his life. Unfortunately the deregulation of management charges caused the charges to rocket upwards, as much as four times. It was an instance of competition not working to the advantage of the public. The reason for this is simple: the sales tend to go to the managers who pay the highest commission to intermediaries, not to the ones with the lowest charges. The same can apply to assurance funds too. There is a strong case for reverting to controls of charges. In the meantime, the charges are a very large proportion of the income of the underlying investments. What does work to the advantage of the public is the way Capital Gains Tax is applied to unit trusts. The managers can change investments without any charge to tax, a benefit a private investor does not enjoy. To create a level playing field, private investors should not have to pay Capital Gains Tax on proceeds which are reinvested, but should be charged tax on any proceeds which are spent on consumption, a sort of Expenditure Tax.

There is a serious problem with some specialist funds. The decision to invest in them is exogenous to the investment opportunities available. The result can be that too much money chases 'special situations', or some other objective, and the investors find that the trust becomes a Ponzi style scam, the profits of the early investors coming from the money brought in by later investors. These profits are therefore unrelated to the real worth of the underlying investments. The name 'Ponzi' comes from a swindler who in 1920 made fools of investors by declaring fictitious profits, and paying them from the money which later investors injected. For further information about Ponzi schemes see:–

http://home.nycap.rr.com/useless/ponzi/

But even closer approximations to Ponzi scams are Pension Funds, if the situation arises where the net aggregate contributions to the funds are greater than aggregate net new issues by companies. Whether this situation exists can be determined very readily by looking at the net asset value of leading stocks and comparing those figures with the share prices. If the latter is far above the former, then a false situation exists. So long as the pension and life assurance funds are net investors, prices will continue to rise, but if they become net sellers, there is no floor to the price fall.

This effect is very bad news for those who rely on pension funds for their income in old age, for if ever the funds became permanent net sellers, and with an ageing population that is not impossible, their pensions would be at risk. The situation would not be so dangerous if the viability of a pension fund were assessed on its ability to produce income, and not on its capital value, but at present that is not true. The defect of capital profits is that they are not self-liquidating. In order to spend them one has to sell the investment, and no-one knows in advance what the market level might be decades hence. On the other hand, dividends are self-liquidating.

The unreality of saving

But the whole concept of saving for old age is based on an unreality. The saver believes he is postponing spending to the distant future, and that when the time comes, he or she can claim what has been forgone many years before. The error in this thinking is that whatever we consume is produced around the time we consume it, not decades earlier. Whether the claims on value one has assiduously and prudently accumulated in one's working years will be honoured by the workers of some future era, is a matter that cannot be ascertained in advance. The majority of wealth owners are the elderly; the poor and indebted are on the whole those who are economically active. The young and indebted have not shown much enthusiasm to pay the taxes that fund the state pension, so why should they be any more eager that their efforts should produce dividends for the elderly to spend? The claims on value may be legal, but history shows that that does not guarantee they will be honoured.

Indeed the workers of the era from 1945 destroyed the savings of their predecessors by encouraging inflation. The earlier generation had been wary of investments which might give some protection against inflation, because in the 1930s such investment lost so much value as a result of the 1929 Stock Market crash, and the subsequent recession. They favoured fixed interest investments, such as government stocks, or fixed capital value holdings like deposits in building societies. When inflation came on the scene both fell gigantically in real terms, some by 98 per cent.

Will the next generation be equally ruthless about impoverishing the elderly? There are plenty of signs they would like to, but the elderly are now a much stronger political force, and that may save them. But if one looks at the views of the leaders of a trade union such as Amicus, one must have doubts. This union now represents many workers in the financial services industry who have traditionally enjoyed good pension provision. Amicus claims to look after the interest of pensioners, yet it is also striving to get higher wages for the current workers. It tends to have an old-fashioned socialist antipathy to profits, yet the retired members of the union rely on the taxes on profits for their state pensions, on dividends from profits for their company pensions and on the dividends from shares bought with the proceeds of commuting part of their pension entitlement. Can Amicus reconcile the potential conflict of interest between those it represents, or will its leaders prefer populist attitudes which benefit only its working members?

Popular capitalism

The growth of the pension funds represented an enormous change in the capitalist system, a change many anti-capitalists have not fully grasped. The huge private fortunes of a century ago were cut down by the high capital taxation of the period from 1949 to the early 1980s. A glance at the statistics for the last 60 years or so, shows clearly that the personal sector of the economy pays its capital taxes from the proceeds of sale of company securities. The sector has been a persistent net investor in all other financial assets, but a net seller of company shares in all but a very, very few years. The net buyers of shares have been the pension funds and life assurance funds. These funds are investing as trustees for over 30 million beneficial owners. Private ownership of shares fell from about 80 per cent in the 1960s to somewhere around ten per cent. The privatisation issues of the late 1980s briefly reversed the trend, and at the moment there may be a growth in private holdings, but nevertheless the latter half of the 20th century saw a change to what has been called 'Popular Capitalism', the beneficial ownership of industry by the masses. In the United States pension funds own 28 per cent of quoted stocks, and financial institutions in the aggregate own 68 per cent of all stocks.[3]

But the gross savings have been high enough to create a false market in shares. The effect is even more marked in the United States where price/earnings ratios, the indicators of whether a market is over-priced, have tended to be higher than for British shares. Whether this will matter in the long run cannot be known, but it is worrying.

It is essential that pension funds be more intelligently supervised. Current regulators seem to be intent on doing the opposite, and the government tends to see them as a source of cheap funds to cover its budget deficit. The principles on which the Government Actuary operates also seem to be less than fully scientific. There is concern that the expectation of life is growing fast, but some doctors are convinced that the current plague of mature onset diabetes mellitus will reduce life expectation. The disease afflicts the Asian population at six times the rate of the indigenous population, and its higher birthrate is making it a bigger proportion of the population, altering the mortality profile of the nation. The Government Actuary is confident that the profile will not change, because the birth rate of immigrant populations always trends to the same level as the existing population. (That contention could surely be disputed with regard to people of Irish Catholic origin.) When questioned as to whether his staff monitor all developments in medicine which might affect the rate of population increase, the answer was 'No'.

Endowment mortgages

The potential for the development of a false market in shares to grow received a very big boost in the early 1980s when endowment mortgages were promoted, ostensibly as a way of making the servicing of a mortgage cheaper, but they also happened to suit the purposes of mortgage lenders. Up to that time, endowment mortgages had been about one per cent of the mortgage market. The reason for the low take-up was that they were expensive, despite a useful tax advantage. The way the endowment mortgage works is that the mortgage loan remains undiminished until the maturity of an endowment life assurance policy pays it off in full. The mortgagor pays interest on the amount originally borrowed for the whole life of the mortgage, commonly 20 years. There used to be a tax relief in respect of life assurance premiums which reduced the cost of the premiums by around 15 per cent, depending on the marginal tax rate paid by the borrower. The special tax relief was abolished in respect of new life assurance policies at roughly the same time as lenders started to promote endowment mortgages. Inflation in the 1950s, 1960s, and 1970s had made the returns on a with-profit endowment life policy rise to an annual compound rate of 8 or 9 per cent net, and in some cases as high as 13 per cent. The amount paid on the policy when it matured could be many times the amount originally assured by the policy.

Mortgage lenders were beginning to find it difficult to get enough borrowers to take up all the loans they were able to finance. More money was pouring into building societies than they knew what to do with. Yet money placed in building societies was effectively ring-fenced from any other use. The flow of funds must have been much enhanced by the favourable tax rates given to building society investors, a discrepancy not abolished until the early 1990s. Mortgage lenders realised two things: one, they could collect commission from life assurance companies for introducing borrowers to them, and two, they could suggest to borrowers that the guaranteed return on the policy could be much less than the amount owed, because one could assume that the premiums would be invested by the life company to give a net return of 7½ per cent compound, and still leave a margin for error. This made the endowment mortgage, despite the abolition about that time of the tax relief on life policy premiums, seem cheaper than the normal subscription mortgage. The stage was set for an increase in the sale of endowment mortgages from one per cent to 80 per cent of the mortgage market.

Naturally there was a fallacy in all this, indeed several. The first was that investment conditions had changed, and the high returns of the equity boom of the post-1950 era might not be repeated. But another fallacy arose from a misunderstanding as to how life companies made some of the profits they shared with their policy holders. The common impression in the life assurance industry was that only a minority of life policies were held to redemption, the majority being surrendered before maturity to the assurers on terms highly disadvantageous to the holder. If true, the profits accruing to the assurance companies from these surrenders were shared with those policy holders who did stay the course to maturity. But once endowment mortgages became the main business of life companies, that source of profit dried up; policy holders had to stay the course to maturity if their mortgages were to be fully paid off. Another problem was that the vast increase in the amounts going into the stock market from life funds pushed share prices to levels which more than halved the dividend yield on shares, and as a result the compound rate of growth had to fall.

There were many reasons why endowment mortgages were not a good idea for most borrowers. Good advice to borrowers was that they should not take out an endowment mortgage unless they, 1) had a totally secure job, 2) could borrow at a fixed rate of interest, and 3) could afford to insure for the whole amount repayable. Few people could satisfy all those requirements.

Naturally it all ended in tears.

State pensions

The pensions payable under the United States Social Security Scheme are funded. That is effected by investing the contributions paid by workers in US Treasuries. What many workers do not understand is that that means that all their contributions are lent to the US Government which spends them immediately. Several trillion dollars have been used in this way. The debts of a government can only be redeemed by taxation. That means that the potential beneficiaries of the future pension will be dependent when the time comes to receive their pensions on the willingness of those who are working at that time to pay taxes. They will have no greater security than if their pensions were not funded at all but were a direct charge on taxation, as is the British State Pension. The funding exercise is no more than a psychological lever on tax-payers; they cannot escape the knowledge that there is a written obligation, a lawful promise, to the elderly.

Postscript

In early November 2005 several mutual funds whose sole purpose is to invest the savings of prospective pensioners in commercial property announced that for an indefinite period they were refusing all new investment because of the dearth of opportunities for the purchase of properties at sensible prices. The money which such funds accept has qualified the investors for substantial tax relief. Thus the tax system has encouraged more savings than there are new investment opportunities. This imbalance must cause asset price inflation. The level of savings has been forced by the government to become exogenous to the demands for finance from creators of new real assets.

13

Eruptions of Credit

Debt is the worst poverty.
THOMAS FULLER, MD.

I N THE SPRING of 1988 the Bank Of England lowered Minimum Lending Rate to 7½ per cent. The huge monetary explosion which followed is blamed by monetarists upon this reduction. There was the best of reasons for lowering interest rates, and that was the need to lower the exchange value of the pound which was then far too high, pulled up by the combination of high interest rates and sterling's status as a petro-currency.

The argument that the lowering of interest rates alone led to the credit explosion does not bear close examination: average interest rates were little different in 1988 from the rates in earlier years. According to the Office for National Statistics, average base rates and the percentage rises in M4 for five successive years were as follows:–

Year	1986	1987	1988	1989	1990
Average base rates (%)	10.90	9.74	10.09	13.85	14.77
Rise in M4 (%)	15.88	16.35	17.60	18.42	12.07

The lowest level for base rates was in the second quarter of 1988 when the average was 8.15 per cent. The increase in M4 in that quarter was at a rate about 10 per cent greater than in the previous two quarters. However in the third quarter the increase in the rate of expansion of deposits was 50 per cent, even though the average of base rates for that quarter at 11.08 per cent was 3 per cent higher than in the preceding quarter. One suspects, of course, that the sharp rise in the second half of the year was in part a consequence of the exploitation of the £920,000,000 which Barclays Bank had added to its capital base by way of a rights issue in May, 1988.

Lift off for M3

When added to other increased capital resources, this fresh capital enabled Barclays to expand its balance sheet by almost £17 billion (19 per cent) by the end of the year, to be responsible for 33 per cent of the increase in M3, to expand its UK lending by 32 per cent, and to increase its mortgage lending by 51 per cent. The following year, despite even higher interest rates, its balance sheet was expanded by a further £24 billion. This was done while high interest rates, the Treasury's favourite homeopathic remedy, were supposed to be discouraging borrowing and therefore controlling inflation. Surely they were promoting its growth? Although the rates of interest at the time of the rights issue were lower than for some years, they were higher than in other countries. Even at its lowest, Minimum Lending Rate was nearly five times the level of Bank Rate during the 1939–45 War.

Barclays Bank's performance in increasing lending was in no way exceptional; it was eventually matched both by the other clearing banks and by the big building societies. It was, however, exceeded by foreign banks operating in Britain by a factor of at least three.

These happenings exposed fully the fundamental error in monetary theory. In the 15 years between 1948 and 1963, when the lowest Bank Rate was two per cent, and the highest 7 per cent, the deposits of the clearing banks rose 34½ per cent; in the late 1980s, when the lowest Minimum Lending Rate was 7½ per cent and the highest 14 per cent, Barclays Bank needed just over two years to increase its deposits by the same percentage.

The Chancellor is disarmed

The Chancellor of the Exchequer had already abandoned the weapon for controlling the growth of credit. In March 1985 Chancellor Nigel Lawson announced that he was going to abolish an effective but idle instrument of control, the Control of Borrowing Order. Such an order, which could control both share issues and borrowing, had the statutory authority of the Borrowing (Control and Guarantees) Act 1946. That Act was a relic, no doubt, of the armoury of control procedures inspired by Maynard Keynes and his associates. A Statutory Instrument, SI 1958 No. 1208, later supplemented the Act. One oddity of the Statutory Instrument was that it exempted building societies from such orders. This no doubt reflected official opinion about the unimportance of building societies in 1958 as a force in the increase of the intermediated money supply. It was a long time before the authorities realised the error of that opinion.

Control of Borrowing Orders could have controlled credit creation directly, but possibly an even better course would have been to use their power also to limit, when necessary, issues of shares or other capital raising exercises by the banks. By such simple means the authorities could have kept under control the capital bases of the banks, and of all other licensed deposit takers and moneylenders. Once again the essential truth set out earlier is crucial: if lending institutions cannot increase their capital bases, they *cannot* increase their lendings, because total lendings may not be greater than a prescribed multiple of the capital base.

To be totally effective the limitation of the banks' power to raise capital must be accompanied by some power to restrict the non-intermediated credit market. The 1946 Act had sensibly envisaged the use of such restrictions. The credit market, intermediated and non-intermediated, is one market, and must be supervised as a totality; looking at only bits of it is illogical. For instance, the longstanding debates between academic economists about the relative importance of M0 and M3 as economic indicators is without rational foundation, and the tendency to dismiss the modern bond market as irrelevant to the control of the money supply is wholly unscientific. The attitude of 1946 was much wiser, and it was a strange development to abandon such wisdom. True, the 1946 controls were probably overused by busybodying and ignorant bureaucrats of that time, who still thought they were running a siege economy, but the principle was sound and its total abandonment was disastrous.

Competition and uncontrolled credit

What also helped precipitate the vast expansion in the money supply, which took place once the market was deregulated, was competition between banks for increased market share. It was alleged in the press that Barclays Bank intended to regain the status of being Britain's biggest bank. The bank's directors knew that extra capital would be required and, as mentioned earlier, in May 1988 raised £920 million by a rights issue. The report of their intentions would surely have been enough to goad the other banks into increasing their efforts to expand their business too. The result was that the British banks and building societies initially expanded their balance sheets at roughly the same rate, and Barclays won only a trivial advantage. A dangerous race had begun, a race to see who could reach Nemesis first. All the competitors finished the course, in the early 1990s.

They were also fighting intense competition from foreign banks. The Chairman of Barclays Bank complained about the low margins which Japanese banks were prepared to take, and foreign banks were successful in winning much of the lending business generated by the Channel Tunnel project. The increase in credit creation by foreign banks was for a while at a rate at least three times greater than the rate of increase of the United Kingdom banks' lendings.

Take-overs and buy-outs

Two other factors which played a large part were, firstly, a craze imported from America, the leveraged company buy-out, and, secondly, a spate of large cash take-overs of companies. Several teams of financial experts were formed whose sole purpose was to seek out or stimulate opportunities to lend money to companies for take-over purposes, or to provoke management teams to buy from holding companies the subsidiaries which they ran. The big accountancy practices and the merchant banks were active in forming such teams. Later the Labour Government which came to power in 1997 increased the tax incentives, originally initiated by the preceding Conservative Government, which stimulated the forces driving the tendency to take companies private, or to switch to the Alternative Investment Market (AIM).

The pressure generated was intense. It was strongly encouraged by the need for managements to show performance in order to protect themselves from being the victims of take-overs. Many managements also had share options which could become very valuable once profitable growth was achieved. The only thing lacking was the special taxation factor which in America made loan capital so much more attractive than equity. The United States had a tax upon company profits which was a classical Corporation Tax system. As has already been explained, that system encourages the use of loan capital in preference to equity capital. In Britain the classical Corporation Tax system had long been amended to reduce the incentive to capitalise with loan capital, though it had not been entirely eliminated. Besides 'gearing-up,' (as 'leverage' was termed in Britain,) was the best way of making the equity capital, and hence directors' share options, more valuable – given a rising tide – but worthless given an ebb tide!

The 'Merger and Acquisition' teams went into action with great success. Table 8.8 of the Financial Statistics for the period gives the details. In 1988 the cash used for acquisition of independent companies totalled £11,569 million. In 1989 it was higher at £17,052 million. Acquisitions of subsidiaries cost £4,421 million in cash in 1988 and £5,307 million in 1989. Despite very high interest rates, 1990 saw an expenditure of £6,175 million on acquisitions, raising the three year total to £44,524 million. Then the inevitable credit crunch came, and the figures dropped dramatically, the low of £5,941 million occurring in 1992. 1995 saw the figures leap again to £32,600 million.

Much of this money must have been borrowed from the banks, including foreign banks. Money lent to finance the purchase of an existing capital asset is certain to be newly created money. It cannot be money saved from the proceeds of current economic activity (that is, from income), for that has to be used to finance new production of real wealth, if the economy is not to run down. True savings, being an addition to capital, cannot finance the purchase of *existing* capital assets unless there is a compensating dis-saving by the vendor of those assets. In that case his saving is truly financing the vendor's profligacy, not real capital investment.

The loans made for the purchases of companies were a major constituent in the huge expansion of the credit supply which took place. During the first three years of the boom, the bulk of it may have come from foreign banks which were then subject to a less stringent requirement regarding capital adequacy ratios than the British banks. British banks were observing a capital adequacy ratio of around eight per cent; as mentioned earlier, Professor David Llewellyn observed that the equity to assets ratio of Dai-Ichi Kangyo Bank, the Japanese bank that was the largest in the world, was in 1988 2.4 per cent compared with a ratio of 6.1 per cent for National Westminster Bank.[1] A bank capitalised that much lower is able to charge a rate of interest perhaps half a percentage point lower than that charged by the bank with a larger capital adequacy ratio, and yet will still achieve the same return on shareholder's funds.

The floodgates opened in the late 1980s have remained firmly open ever since, but as interest rates fell, banks lost much of their long-term corporate lending to the bond market and had to find other outlets for the profitable use of their excess base capital. Even so, capital adequacy ratios remain stubbornly high, despite returns of capital to bank shareholders, and the buying in of shares to be cancelled.

Asset price inflation

Where the acquisitions were of quoted companies, the prices paid for the shares were much greater than the value previously placed upon them by the market. The purchases therefore caused inflation of asset values. Most of the increase in lending took place after base rates had begun to rise again from the low level of May 1988, indeed after they had reached 9½ per cent. Lending for take-overs and buy-outs tapered off briefly when base rates reached 13 per cent, but surged to its highest level in the third quarter of 1989, when base rates averaged 14 per cent. It still continued at a high rate even when base rates were 15 per cent. It was therefore quite wrong to suggest that it was the *fall* in interest rates in the Spring of 1988 which caused the credit explosion.

Why corporate borrowers were ready to pay well over asset value for shares, and also to pay very high rates of interest to borrow the money to do so, seems to be a question for psychologists, or even for psychiatrists, rather than for economists. It made no immediate business sense at all. By 1995 the short-term rate of interest was down to 5½ per cent, so the figure of acquisitions for that year, and subsequent ones, is much more understandable.

The personal sector is a net seller of company securities

It has long been the practice of the personal sector of the British economy to be a net seller of company securities, but the amount of the sales hugely increased in 1988 and 1989 to a two year total of £28,586 million. Sales of UK company securities totalled £30,631 million, the difference between the two figures being balanced by net purchases of overseas securities. Some of this cash no doubt came from selling privatisation issues, that is issues for cash made by the government of shares in former state industries, but a very large sum must have come from the cash used in take-overs. In 1990 sales of company securities by the personal sector were £8,694 million. Though still a very high figure, it was lower than in 1987. 1992 saw a net acquisition of company shares by the personal sector, but normality returned, and in 1998 sales reached £22.6 billion. The net sales continued until 2001, but then a curious thing happened. The acquisition of quoted company shares rose to a positive figure and stayed there, but disposals of unquoted shares, always erratic, varied between trivial figures and mighty ones. In 2004 the figure for net disposals of unquoted shares exceeded the net acquisition of quoted shares. Clearly some of those who had made successful management buy-outs with borrowed money had decided to cash in their profits by returning their companies to the publicly quoted list.

The inflation of asset prices did not stop with share prices. Once created, the money used for the purchases of shares could circulate, and the route of circulation of a considerable portion of it is easy to guess, for another habit of the personal sector is to use stock exchange profits to buy bigger and more expensive houses, partly as an anti-inflationary hedge. Finally, a third habit of the personal sector, and especially its older members, is to put any surplus cash into building societies deposits. Personal sector deposits in building societies and banks increased dramatically, and 1988 saw a huge surge in house prices as a result. The increased level was maintained throughout the following year.

The credit Krakatoa erupts

Asset price inflation also stimulated the public's willingness to borrow for the purchase of consumer goods, and the credit was available. The whole scenario is unusually clear for an event in economics, and it reveals a vivid example of a *multiplier* in action. Of course the money the banks had lent to finance acquisitions had to find its way to the liabilities side of their balance sheets, but its route thither must have gone through many banks, creating deposits and lendings along its way. It left a trail of asset price inflation and a huge increase in the credit supply. We have earlier explained the mechanism by which one act of credit creation can cause an increase in the money supply that is many times the amount of the lending which started the process.

The total for the three years 1988–90 was £171,700 million, an increase on December 1987 of 56½ per cent. The theories upon which the government's interest rate policy had been founded do not begin to explain this empirical evidence. The evidence supports the view that to contain the growth of credit at the right time, direct controls are needed; interest rates alone are not sufficient and, indeed, the evidence proves that a rise in interest rates in the short term aggravates the problem of control.

Of course the banks had to raise new capital to provide the base for the enormous increase in their lendings. So too did the building societies, but for the latter the task was made easier by the fact that high interest rates increased the speed of increase of their reserves. Building societies were then mostly mutual companies, and did not have their profits drained away by the need to pay dividends: if they were lending profitably they must accumulate the profit and all the interest earned by their reserves. The reserves increased exponentially through compounded interest. The exponential rate of growth of reserves is amplified by a high interest rate. Hitherto monetary theorists do not seem to have taken sufficient note of the fact that reserves earn interest.

Indeed the building societies were also allowed to join the banks in the raising of subordinated loan capital in order to enhance their capital bases. Later they added permanent interest-bearing shares (PIBS) to their methods of increasing their capital bases. Although one could not see a purpose for these increased capital resources, other than a further attempt to push up house prices, there was no indication that the supervising authority objected to the building societies' capital raising exercises. They were just as complacent about the effect of compounding interest on Building Society reserves as they were about its effect on money owed to oil-producers. The government appeared to be completely oblivious of the way in which it was steadily wrecking its own efforts to reduce inflationary pressures. Starting in 1989, most of the building societies converted to being true banks, quoted on the stock market, and another significant development of the time was that they also at last got direct access to the money market, and did not have to rely on increased deposits to increase lending; they could rely on acquiring the balances to fund any new loans they made via the automatic balancing effect of the money transfer system, of which they were at last full participants.

Neutral taxation: its effect

Prior to that change, building society deposits had effectively been ring-fenced from uses other than the financing of loans for house purchase. The societies also had a tax advantage. The interest they paid was taxed at a rate a fifth lower than interest paid by banks. Naturally the Building Societies therefore had a tax advantage in attracting deposits, compared with the commercial banks. Thus a very false saving market had been encouraged, one which could not have been better designed to boost house prices. The financial market was highly distorted, and it was not until the taxation anomaly was abolished by Chancellor Nigel Lawson that the banks could become true savings institutions. The banks then used their new competitiveness to expand. Part of their expansion was to move into the house mortgage market and their lending for house purchase increased sharply.

It was a paradoxical result. The taxation anomaly had led to an increase in house prices: yet its abolition increased house prices even further! The Chancellor of the Exchequer had made a classic error. It was now possible for banks to compete in the building societies' traditional area of lending, but not the reverse. The building societies could not lend heavily in the non-mortgage market. By ill-chance the change came at a time when the banks were enthused with the safety of lending to private individuals, who had on average been a good credit risk. The banks forgot that this good record had been a function of the severe restriction there had often been on borrowing by private sector consumers during most of the post-war era. The ordinary man and woman had been given few opportunities for a borrowing spree. That was all about to change.

Distortion in the capital market

One effect of distortion of the British capital market was that the needs of small industrial enterprises were poorly served. A major sector of the savings industry ignored them. But a gigantic lending juggernaut had been created to oversupply the house mortgage market. The building societies were not allowed the chance to provide for industry the resources which equivalent savings institutions in foreign countries were able to give to their industry, either directly or indirectly.

The expansion of lending in the United Kingdom had taken place without due regard for prudence. As a result the banks were announcing in 1991 large provisions for losses. In early 1990 two of the big clearing banks paid dividends out of capital reserves because profits were insufficient to cover them. Shareholders' funds were thereby reduced and with them the capital base for lending. When the shareholders approved the payment of a dividend to themselves they should have also been required to choose which of their banks' borrowers were to be forced to repay a total sum 20 times the amount of the dividends! The payment of dividends out of capital was repeated the following year. Between December 1988 and December 1991 the shareholders' funds of the big four commercial banks fell by £1,735,000,000. Theoretically that reduced their aggregate lending capacity by at least £21,000,000,000, and potentially by up to twice as much.

One way to resolve such a shortage of bank funds is to force creditworthy business customers to raise equity capital by rights issues, effectively a reversal of what happened in 1988. In principle this should free the banks' capital base for use as support for loans to small business customers who have no source of capital other than the banks. The actual outcome was that the lendings of the banks were cut back to such an extent that their capital adequacy ratios rose well above 8 per cent, indeed in one case to 10.3 per cent. They have remained high ever since.

Vandalising industry

The switch of £44,524 million from equity capital to loan capital in the three years 1988 to 1990 was a staggeringly large change in the form of the capitalisation of British industry. It should have stimulated some heart-searching at the Department of Trade and Industry (DTI). The Bank of England too should have taken worried note of what was happening and dreaded the likely consequences of an increase in interest rates in such a radically changed environment. Is there any evidence that anyone in the DTI, in the Bank of England, or in the

Treasury was alive to the dangers of this trend? Did *anyone* in those sophisticated institutions warn the Chancellor that in the circumstances a rise in interest rates would both vandalise British industry and bring untold suffering to those who had borrowed very excessively on mortgage in 1988 and subsequently? Or was the Chancellor so totally obsessed with an erroneous monetary theory that he ignored advice, if given, and continued to pursue a deflationary policy without giving proper thought to its terrible consequences for a host of over-borrowed citizens? Hundreds of thousands of mortgagors were dispossessed of their houses. Inflation would have saved them from that cruel experience. No wonder Keynes called those responsible for such an economic policy inhumane.

Some mortgage borrowers were hit two ways: their mortgage payments went up because of higher rates of interest, and they also found themselves unemployed because higher interest rates had put their over-borrowed employers out of business.

Were foreign banks to blame?

The total intermediated money supply, M4, rose by 57 per cent, but the lendings of the banks increased by 100 per cent. The accounts of the big British clearing banks do not reflect so great an increase. Although Barclays Bank had promised in 1988 a period of rapid growth, it achieved only a 53 per cent increase in its assets in the three years. One deduces therefore that foreign banks increased their lendings in the United Kingdom at a far greater rate than 100 per cent. They were reported to be responsible for much of the funding of the construction of the Channel Tunnel, and to be active in lending for company acquisitions and management buy-outs.

What constituted the capital base for their loans in Britain? Was it represented by sterling assets or by their overseas assets? Japanese banks had much lower capital adequacy ratios than British banks yet do not appear to have been restricted in their lending in Britain by the supervising authority.

It was during that period that the Basel Capital Accord on capital adequacy ratios was agreed internationally, though its full implementation was postponed until 1993. The effect on Japanese banks has been described in Chapter Eight.

The Law of Distribution of Wealth

The greater part of the personal wealth of the nation is held by those over the age of fifty; the bulk of the borrowing, especially for house purchase, is done by those under fifty. The *haves* therefore belong to the older generation, many of them retired, and the *have-nots* are the workers and their young families. An increase in interest rates effects a transfer of income from the have-nots to the haves, from the young to the old, from the workers to the retired, from those best able to cause inflation by high wage claims to those who cannot. The switch of gross income in 1990 from the young to the old could have amounted to as much as £15 billion. What greater incentive could there be to cause wage inflation, and therefore, because of the government's intransigent pursuit of its dis-inflationary and recessionary policies, to cause unemployment? The government said it was aiming to avoid unemployment by checking inflation. Truly it was causing both. Inflation is not, on its own, either an inevitable or a major cause of unemployment. Indeed experience suggests that it is much more likely to increase employment. As we have already stated, it is what is sometimes foolishly done both by governments and by ordinary people *in response* to inflation which increases unemployment.

The desire of young married people for wage rises was further aggravated by a factor which was not part of the monetarist philosophy, but of the government's attitude towards the welfare state. To demonstrate this point one must compare the relative financial positions of a young family man with a non-working wife and three young children in 1963, and his successor a generation later in 1990 with the same job, same family, same house, and same proportion of its value on mortgage. Although the salary for the job had increased 25 per cent more than the index of retail prices, the successor in 1990 would have had £4,000 (in 1990 money) less to spend than his 1963 predecessor. In practice this meant that he would not have been able to afford such a good house or the third child. This is a very significant change, but seemingly it was not understood by many of the experts who held the limelight on the fiscal studies scene.

Some of the difference between the two generations of parents was due to higher interest rates, plus the inflation of house prices at a rate higher than general inflation. But part was due to the reduction in family allowances, the ending of tax allowances for children, and the abolition of the lower rate bands of income tax. These last three factors strengthened the motivation to seek pay rises, which go to all workers, not merely the family men. The government did not seem to understand that generous family allowances, by subsidising the family wage-earner, make it possible to keep general wage rates down, thereby assisting international competitiveness. The government's policy on tax and national insurance benefits was therefore highly inflationary.

The arrival of the 21st century has seen some government attempts to alleviate the tax burden on those with young families, but the housing bubble has grown even larger, and the chances of a young couple being able to be decently housed and afford a family have diminished even further. The average house price in 2003 had increased at four times the figure for general inflation. The age at which women on average have their first child is higher than it was during the depression years of the 1930s. The average would be even higher if it were not for brave, or foolhardy, young girls who have children and live on the welfare benefits given to single parents. The pensioners of 30 years hence should be grateful to them. The children of today's young, and often single, mothers will be producing what they will consume. The events of 1990, the last fling of mad monetarism, so destroyed all social norms that there is no single standard of behaviour by which to characterise the nation.

The so-called trade cycle

Much academic effort has gone into the discussion of the origin of the trade cycle, but surely the cause is a simple one: it reflects booms and dearths in the demand for credit. The booms are periods when too many people simultaneously decide to borrow in anticipation of future income. The recessions are when too many people simultaneously attempt to reduce their accumulation of debt. If all these decisions were nicely phased over time there might be no trade cycle. In the absence of a steady, phased replacement process, a credit explosion must eventually be followed by a period of consolidation when people try to pay off their debts. Having consumed in advance of receipt of their income, they have to cease consuming while the income to repay debts comes in. But the cessation of consumption and the consequent reduction in economic activity reduces peoples' aggregate income and, therefore, their aggregate ability to repay. The banks become worried at their losses and reduce lendings, thereby further aggravating the problem. A downward spiral takes place. It is a very simple scenario. One wonders why so much academic ink has been wasted on the subject.

The problem is made worse still if the lending has been effective in inflating asset values. One recalls that the American stock-market crash of 1929 followed a period of rising share prices which had been stimulated by dealings 'on margin', that is, on credit. When the inevitable reaction came many banks were in trouble and a grievous recession followed. The banking failures reduced the credit supply. The credit available to

American stock-market investors more than halved. Stock-market values, and indeed all asset values, collapsed as an inevitable result.

Bankers at bay

In the expansionary boom period of the late 1980s the British banks reversed their traditional attitude and made much more credit available to the small business sector of the economy. Perhaps they were led to do this because the foreign banks had competed so successfully with them in the large corporate market for credit. The recession induced by the government's interest rate policy caused much of the lending to small businesses to go sour. The chairman of one large bank announced that his bank was losing a million pounds a day of its loans to small businesses, and that it was therefore going to reduce its lending to the small business sector.

The small business at the mercy of the banks

The bankers' decision to cut back lending to small businesses was an attack on the foundations of the economy. The smaller businesses have become dependent on bank loans for, on average, 31 per cent of their capital needs. Moreover most of this borrowing is at short-term interest rates. During the long period of high inflation one of its effects was to make the traditional forms of long-term fixed interest capital no longer available to smaller businesses, which were therefore very vulnerable to increases in interest rates. It was most unfortunate for them, therefore, that high interest rates had become the favourite tool of government in pursuance of its vain attempt to control the money supply.

High interest rates had another effect: they discouraged people from paying their bills on the due date. Many small businesses are suppliers of goods and services to large companies whose finance directors became ruthless in delaying payment. In 1991 a bill that was contracted to be paid at thirty days was on average paid after eighty-one days. There has been little improvement since then. As a result of this practice a large proportion of bank lending to small companies indirectly finances large companies. If 15 per cent of all the capital of small companies was absorbed in this way, and if bank borrowing is the marginal capital source of small businesses, it means that in the aggregate one half of all bank credit to small companies is indirectly financing the capital requirements of larger companies on an interest free basis. The true proportion could be higher.

Was the chairman of the bank referred to earlier aware of this fact? Was he happy to bankrupt many of the suppliers of his larger customers, or would he prefer to try to persuade his larger customers to pay their bills on time? Would he lend them the money to do so? To refuse would be an effective way of killing off British business from its most sensitive small roots upwards.

At the local branch level bank staff were well aware of this problem and marvelled at the lack of action by their superiors, and at the long failure of parliamentary lobbying promoted by business organisations such as the Forum of Private Business and the Federation of Small Businesses. Bank staff knew the problems of their small business customers because they faced them regularly across the counter; bank directors on the other hand faced only the finance directors of multi-nationals across the claret glasses in their lunch rooms.

To Civil Service mandarins small businessmen are a nuisance; to some Labour Party members of Parliament they are vermin fit only for elimination by destructive taxation. The minds of Conservative members of Parliament have been fuddled by simplistic monetary theories. What chance has the small businessman of getting funda-mental reforms of the financial system which might aid him and also make the banker's life less stressed? The only hope for small businesses is that the fall in interest rates at last to levels which are in line with the experiences of most generations before 1960 will not be reversed by the Monetary Policy Committee of the Bank of England, or, in the United States, by the chairman of the Federal Reserve Bank.

Where are we on the credit cycle?

At the time of writing this text, we have experienced a decade at least of boom, and a decade or more of sharply rising debt. Will the borrowers try to consolidate? Between 1987 and 2003 total lending increased about five times. This is far faster than the increase in Gross Domestic Product, and much faster than general inflation. We should be on the verge of a recession, caused by the wish to reduce debt. Will it happen, or will the boom continue? The worst will happen only if expectations of a recession grow. Psychology is the essence of economics.

A little general inflation is the right prophylactic, so it should be a great relief to citizens to know that governments no longer plan to eliminate inflation entirely. The current monetary consensus is that the inflation target should between two and three per cent, and should not be allowed to fall below that target. How different from, say, the 1950s, when many politicians regarded such a level of inflation as a national disaster. However the monetary consensus still envisages the possible use of extremely high interest rates, as in the period 1979 to 1992. It has not abandoned the theory behind the actions taken then. This book has concentrated on the period 1979 to 1992, the era of the worst monetarist crimes, for although those years may sound like ancient history to younger readers, the lessons to be learnt from them are vital. Monetarists must never again be allowed to do what was done then.

14
Planning or the Market

This very remarkable man
Commends a most practical plan:
You can do what you want
If you don't think you can't,
So don't think you can't if you can.

CHARLES INGE

BESIDES BEING MONETARIST most modern governments pretend to be strongly committed to market economics. There was an inter-action between the two policies: indeed the government would have seen them as being just two facets of one policy. It is appropriate, therefore, that we should discuss the merits of the market economy and its rival, the planned economy.

There is a deep ideological division in the acrimonious politics of economics between those who support a state-planned economy, and those who believe in a free market economy. There are also those who support a compromise between the two, the mixed economy. The fully planned economy implies that the allocation and use of all economic resources must be controlled by the state's planners; nothing is left to private enterprise and private choice. In the market economy market forces are left to operate and react with one another without government intervention; each individual is left to make his own economic decisions. The expectation is that as a result the optimum allocation of resources will come about of itself, and far more efficiently than could be achieved by the decisions of any government planner, however knowledgeable, experienced, and prescient.

Faced with these two very strong philosophies, each claiming to have absolute truth, those who doubt them both, and maintain that an economy must be a mixture of the two, are regarded as weak compromisers and fudgers, which indeed some may be.

Yet it is truly inevitable that all economies will be mixed, first, because in a planned economy it is quite impossible to suppress all private enterprise and individual initiative, and second, because in a market economy the sticky-fingered government bureaucracy cannot resist the temptation to exercise its power to interfere in the economy, even if it were not under constant pressure from members of the public, and the tabloid press, to do so. It is also necessary, for reasons given below.

1. THE MARKET ECONOMY

The philosophy behind the market economy is a strong one, as it is rooted deeply in economic theory going back at least to Adam Smith, the author of *The Wealth of Nations*. It is based on economists' assumptions about the behaviour of economic man. The belief is that man's natural greed will always lead him to attempt to provide what the consumer wants, because, in doing so, he will profit. It is further believed that in order to maximise his profit he will do whatever is necessary to lower his production costs. To this end the cheapest resources will always be used. With a host of *economic men* reacting quickly, efficiently, and uninhibitedly to each other's actions and decisions the economy is strongly propelled to ever greater efficiency, and growth. Any attempt to interfere with this mechanism must damage it. Planning will fail because of the complexity of the plans required, and because of the lack of incentive to achieve efficiency. There is also the lack of any accurate mechanism to ascertain the true needs and wants of the populace, with the consequence that the planner's own bias dominates decisions. The market economy is therefore based on the belief that if market forces are allowed to operate without artificial hindrance or restraint, the best compromise solution to all economic problems will arise spontaneously and naturally.

But one must be careful: the market economy can be confused with the unplanned economy, which some might assume to be the natural economic system. In fact it differs considerably from it. There are strong natural and corrupting forces within the unplanned economy which will prevent it growing into a true market economy. These forces may easily predominate, and prevent the beneficent market forces working properly. Therefore there has to be some state interference in order to enable market forces to work benignly. Even the market economy has to be planned to the extent that action must be taken to prevent the growth of restrictive practices, such as cartels, monopolies and associations. The true market economy is a tough environment, and the weaker citizens find peace preferable to profit. They are, as Adam Smith warned, quite naturally motivated to seek the safety of monopolies, or of markets neatly regulated and allocated by an association. They fear the effect of competition on themselves and refuse to embrace it. The fear is so strong that despite the legislation against restrictive practices all sorts of dodges still survive to keep rivals out of a market. It is this fear which drives the policies of public sector trade unions.

An example of a protective marketing ploy is the loyalty bonus, which is a discount allowed to a retailer by a manufacturer if the retailer agrees to stock only that manufacturer's product. To prevent this sort of thing occurring, and to make the market economy work at maximum efficiency, requires constant vigilance and interference by the state, even though the popular cry of the zealous but imperceptive supporter of the market economy is, *'No state interference!'*[1]

The market has no foresight

In ideal conditions the market economy might be able to bring about the perfect allocation of resources which is appropriate for a particular moment in time. But the market economy has little or no foresight. It will tend to do what is advantageous for today, even though that same action could bring disaster tomorrow. The market economy is unable to plan what is best for the future because its natural drive is towards what is best for today. It cannot sufficiently consider the future, especially the more distant future beyond the lives of the current population of the Earth. The market economy, therefore, has no fourth dimension, that is no dimension in time. If there exists a finite resource which is very easily won, the market economy will ensure that that resource is used wastefully right up to the moment of its exhaustion, regardless of the resultant damage to mankind. An example is found in coal mining. A coal mine will often contain several seams of different thicknesses, and market economics would cause the miner to mine the coal from the thickest seam and leave the rest. But one can never return to a mine, so the thinner seams are lost for ever.

The free market also tends to be blind to growing pollution. On the other hand a nation which takes anti-pollution measures may lose its market to rivals which are not pollution conscious. Therefore the protection of the environment needs international agreement and therefore planning on an international scale.

Although the arrangements arrived at by the market economy should be a natural compromise dictated by the interaction of the forces generated by the whole variety of human needs, not merely the economic ones, the forces seeking quiet, comfort, clean air, healthy environment, and generally pleasant social conditions, seem to be submerged by purely economic forces to an extent which may not reflect the true balance of the needs and wants of society. Perhaps this is because those who are most strongly motivated by the acquisitive instinct are the driving force which determines the direction of an economy. One cannot be sure that the influence of the economic pressure from a small group is not over-amplified in the decision-making process. Judgements on this point are inevitably subjective, and one has to bear in mind the possibility, even though one may be appalled by it, that what happens may reflect the general democratic wish. Certainly, in a poor society the economic pressures are much more likely to predominate, unless it is a very unusual society which is poor only because it is not motivated by greed.

In both the unplanned economy and the market economy the disparity of wealth is likely to grow. If the disparity is great, there may be slow economic growth, and a low average wealth. This may arise from the tendency of the rich to spend their large incomes on menial domestic services, causing the expansion of the tertiary sector of the economy at the expense of the secondary. In the past, the greatest economic growth has taken place where there was a strong demand for manufactures, the products of the secondary sector of the economy. (This may be changing.) Such demand is highest when buying power is evenly spread. On the other hand, if there is no disparity of wealth at all, a condition desired by theoretical socialists, but which cannot occur in a market economy, there may be poor economic growth because the requisite motivation for effort is lacking.

Five propositions about the market economy

1. The market economy cannot be a totally unplanned or an uncontrolled economy.

2. The market economy will prejudice the distant future in favour of the present and the near future. It will waste some resources, even non-renewable ones.

3. State interference with the market economy will reduce its immediate efficiency.

4. Egalitarianism will prevent it operating at anywhere near full efficiency, but excessive disparity of wealth will also damage it.

5. The market economy is capable of providing the highest rates of economic growth.

2. THE PLANNED ECONOMY

The advocates of the planned economy insist that it is the only way to ensure there is no waste, that the basic needs of the people are supplied, and that the enhancement of the spiritual and mental well-being of the populace is not sacrificed to its material well-being. The basic philosophical justification is, however, that what is planned must logically, and therefore necessarily, be better than what is unplanned. Although the planned economy is always contrasted with the market economy, it was the evils of the unplanned economy which first motivated the advocates of the planned economy. It is very common for them to confuse the unplanned economy with the market economy.

To succeed, a planned economy needs people who are capable of doing the planning. They must have unerring benevolence, total omniscience, and perfect prescience, and must be absolutely incorruptible. Such qualities necessitate vast experience, and must be coupled with complete objectivity in ascertaining the wishes of society. The planners need a total understanding of economics, a quality which has never existed. It is also doubtful whether a person having the other qualities exists, or would rise to a position of authority if he did exist. However, there is no lack of people who are fully convinced of their possession of all these qualities. They are to be found in quantity at every gathering of politicians, and they are abundant in universities.

The likelihood of an economically able political leader getting power is fairly small. Those who propose to use political power to plan the economy usually make known which of the people's economic needs it is their intention to target for satisfaction. Unfortunately the voters do not have the technical knowledge to enable them to know which are the best policies for the achievement of their needs, so they put their trust in politicians with the simple answers, or in those who promise the most. Moreover, even on the rare occasions when they make their choice with something approaching correctness, they, as individuals, will continue to pursue their own well-being, and thus will give impetus to the market economy. Their instinctive behaviour will hinder the operation of the planned economy.

The planned economy is notorious for causing shortages, which in turn create large windfall profits for traders, for the enterprising trader who attempts to defeat the planners in order to provide what the public really needs will find his profits amplified. It is for this reason that in a planned economy there is always a prosperous black market. Revelations in eastern Europe after the fall of the communist rulers tend to confirm the suspicion that corruption and planning are inseparable. India, too has been a victim of the over-optimistic attachment of its leaders at the time of independence to the planned economy. With a market economy the great talent of its businessmen would surely have made it an industrial power of the first rank within twenty years of achieving independence.

A British National Plan

Parliamentary enthusiasm for planning was at its height in Britain in 1965. In that year the Labour Government produced its National Plan, running to about 700 pages. It is not really one plan but an aggregation of dozens of plans stitched together. Each group of planners no doubt worked in ignorance of what the others were doing.

An economic plan has certain basic requirements. The first would to some appear to be unrelated to economics: it is the legal structure. Nineteenth century economic growth was given an enormous forward thrust when the lawyers invented the joint stock company. The economic importance of that development cannot be exaggerated. There was no mention of legal matters in the 1965 National Plan. One desirable change in the law, a new form of incorporation for small businesses, was not achieved until the beginning of the 21st century, despite the appearance of a government discussion paper on the subject in the 1970s, and much subsequent lobbying.

A second important requirement is the taxation system. The National Plan had one sentence about fiscal policy but no actual proposals. Five months before the publication of the Plan the government had introduced the classical form of Corporation Tax with damaging effect. There had been no prior discussion of it.

A third requirement is a good primary capital market. Britain has long had a very good secondary capital market for certain investments, but a primary capital market, such as the French and Japanese industrialists enjoyed, hardly existed in Britain in 1965. The National Plan did not mention primary capital markets.

Nor was there a mention of exchange rate policy. As the economies which experienced spectacular success in the post-war era all enjoyed the benefit of undervalued currencies it was a remarkable omission. Instead a policy of overvaluation for sterling was continued until devaluation was eventually forced by market pressures on an unwilling government on 18th November 1967. The Prime Minister blamed *The Gnomes of Zürich* for speculating against the pound, but some of the speculators were much closer to home.[2]

Finally, there was no mention of interest rate policy, probably because there was none. It was impossible to take seriously any planning document without one.

Seven propositions about the fully planned economy

1.   A planned economy ought to be an improvement upon a totally unplanned economy, but only because the unplanned economy will have in it those defects which prevent it from functioning as a true market economy.

2.   Despite what it ought to be, the fully planned economy in practice is rarely a substantial improvement on anything.

3.   To plan an economy totally is not within human capability.

4.   The politicians who find themselves in charge of a planned economy are likely to be less than fully competent at planning.

5.   Career politicians will hand over the real work of planning to civil servants who will be subject to few of the influences which motivate human beings to perform well, and will have no worthwhile incentive to improve the economy. In addition they may well become corrupt, though Britain seems to have been generally spared that trauma.

6.   A fully planned economy will never expand the economy of a modern industrialised country as fast as a market-oriented, but mixed economy.

7.   The engines of the economy are run by bureaucrats whose motivation is not profits, but the desire to maximise their bureaux.[3]

Perhaps the fundamental reason for the failure of economic planning was best summed up by a sentence in an anthology of quotations. It was taken from a book by Edward Noyes Westcott. A character in the book says:–

> *I guess there's about as much human nature in some folks as there's in others, if not more.*

The advocates of planning seem to share two characteristics to excess: they have too much faith in their own ability to plan, and too little understanding of the essential natures of their fellow human beings or, indeed, of their own.

3. THE MIXED ECONOMY

It must be obvious that the economy has to be mixed; nothing else is possible. But market forces must be allowed to have their way wherever they can achieve a benefit. Planning has a place, but its most important purpose is to eliminate any hindrances to the proper functioning of the market economy where that has an established record of success. Its main objective should be to add, preferably with full international agreement, that fourth dimension, which the market economy lacks, in order to prevent wastage of non-renewable resources and eliminate pollution in circumstances where such important objectives necessitate that people should forego some immediate profit.

Governments must ensure that they do not develop the kind of mixed economy which possesses few of the virtues of either of its components.

The mixed economy will always be the battleground of two ideologies, the planners versus the market economists. To build a mixed economy requires knowledge, skill, understanding, and level-headed commonsense, all of the highest order. But what happens in practice is that doctrinaire ideologues pursue utopian dreams while they are mentally divorced from the realities of the community around them. Of course there will be peacemakers between the two battling groups of ideologues, but the would-be peacemakers will tend to be those who always flee from any controversy, and are convinced that the answer to any dispute lies in compromise and fudge.

The post-1979 Conservative Government was right to try to make the economy much more market-oriented, but it was too doctrinaire about it, and it failed to exercise the standard of supervision which was necessary to avoid pitfalls. The subsequent 'New' Labour Government has tended to go the other way, the route of excessive and often incompetent regulation.

There are certain areas of economic activity where close state supervision is necessary. Banks, for instance, cannot be allowed to expand the money supply at their whim. An unregulated banking system leads to disaster.[4] It is also desirable to have minimum standards of prudence in lending agreed nationally, and indeed internationally.

Success in marketing

The realm of financial services provides an instructive example of the fact that market forces do not always tend to ensure the success of the institution which provides the best deal to the consumer. Rather, it is the institution paying the highest commission to intermediaries which thrives. Before letting market forces rip, one must ascertain whether their natural direction is towards support for the objectives of better choice and service for the consumer. In Margaret Thatcher's government, the ideological advocates of market forces made the unwarranted assumption that by oiling the engines of the economy, market forces *invariably* act for the public good. Every ideology has some weaknesses to which its advocates tend to blind themselves. Although the basic assumptions of the philosophy of the market economy are much sounder than those of doctrinaire socialism, which ignore the facts of human nature, every economic doctrine is no more than a rule of thumb which may fail on occasions. Blind adherence to doctrine is a proven route to the wrecking of the economy. For this reason earlier Conservative governments seemed to pride themselves on being pragmatic, but after 1979 the Conservative Party became subject to doctrinal intransigence. A good radical programme of reform was thereby damaged.

State control of credit

Market economists will find unwelcome the suggestion that the system for creating credit should be controlled by the state. It is a suggestion which is made with the greatest reluctance, as there is the utmost likelihood that the control will be badly exercised. Unfortunately it is now crystal clear that one cannot allow credit institutions to compete freely in the creation of credit, or in the creation of money, if people insist on referring to the other side of the balance sheet. Sadly one must accept that although the greatest possible freedom should remain, the final decision as to the rate of expansion of each bank must, when there is risk to the economy, be a state decision, not a result of free market competition.

This does not imply that one might as well go to the logical extreme and have only one bank, a state bank. There are good reasons why there must be many competing banks. Let potential borrowers have plenty of choice. Let the banks be rivals on quality of service. The potential borrower should continue to be able to hawk a lending proposition around until he finds a sympathetic or understanding ear. It would be totally wrong for one person alone to have both the first and the final say as to whether a borrowing proposition succeeds or fails. Nothing written in this book should be taken as an argument in favour of detailed state planning. Let us accept the humane philosophy of socialism which advocates social justice, but not the methods which have been used to try to enforce it, and which have usually attenuated the freedom of the individual and slowed the process of wealth creation.

This subject was, of course, brilliantly discussed by F. A. Hayek, in his book, *Road to Serfdom*, which was published in 1944 at the height of the popularity of communism and the national socialist method.

15
Creditary Economics

I think that money is on the way out.
Anita Loos

THE PURPOSE of this book has been to switch attention from the deposits side of the banking balance sheet, to the assets side, the loans. The old monetarist approach rests on the assumption that the only money likely to be spent is that which already exists as deposits, whereas the potential to create hitherto unused spending power is ignored. As the latter advances at a rate of six to seven per cent per year, it is clearly of vital importance.

Thus money spent can be of two kinds, completely new money, and old money. Let us term them primary and secondary credit. A newly advanced credit ends up in many cases as new deposits, the exception being when the new money merely reduces the balance on some overdrawn account. The new deposits can be spent or lent, not once, but many times, or can remain as a permanent investment, financing only the original lending. There is no way of determining for certain which of these variations will happen. What is clearly significant is that a new lending can have a multiplier effect, and expand the economy. But equally significant is that a recession will assuredly ensue if the nation in the aggregate ceases to increase borrowing, and tries to reduce it. A downward spiral with no obvious end can be created.

A second aim has been to establish the importance of the capital base of the banks, for it has some potential to be a limiting factor on new credit creation. This powerful effect was ignored by all economists until about 1990. Before the Basel Capital Accord was mooted, those who advocated the virtue of regulating and supervising the capital base of the banks were not understood. The advent of the Basel Capital Accord should at last have helped focus some attention where it is needed. It highlights an economic mechanism which must be far more effective than the succession of irrational, ineffective and counterproductive controls used by governments in the past to limit the money supply. One must admit that it is possible that varying capital adequacy ratios might not affect the aggregate credit supply, as the indirect credit supply could take up the slack in the indirect supply, but the experience of Japan in adjusting to higher CARs also indicates that varying them unwisely could be disastrous.

Our first aim causes us to argue that it is variations in the total credit supply – not just in one small component, the money supply – which govern the progress of an economy and the trade cycle. The credit aggregate to watch includes both intermediated and disintermediated credit supplies. Studies confined to bits of the intermediated credit supply, which have been the bread and butter pursuit of academic economists at least since Keynes published his *Treatise on Money*, if not before, are minor irrelevancies by comparison.

Monetary theory has been devoted to the study, analysis and classification of the money supply rather than its much larger counterpart, the supply of credit. Writers on economics have been obsessed with the people who have currency in their pockets or in their strong boxes, who have deposits of cash in banks or in building societies. They have been far less interested in those people who own bonds, debentures or other forms of securitised loans. They have ignored trade credit completely. They have ignored all the potential for new credit creation. The time has surely come to switch emphasis from the money supply back to the credit supply in its entirety and the immediate potential increase in the credit supply.

Deflation the rule

Deflation is the natural order of things in a society which continually improves its production techniques, and it is a disaster for all debtors. History is full of instances of farmers getting into debt, and being unable to repay bankers because of a fall in prices. It is a recurrent theme even in ancient history, and must be the origin of the anathemas of religious leaders against the lending of money. Debt often reduced peasants to the condition of serfs or worse. There may be some surprise at the farmer getting into trouble, not because of a crop failure, but because of an overabundant harvest. A novelist would have chosen the former scenario. Although a complete crop failure may be a disaster for a community, a partial failure can be a bonanza for its farmers. In 1976, when fourteen months of unusually low rainfall in East Anglia reduced the potato harvest dramatically, many potato farmers made fortunes. Yet when new insecticides increased fruit crops in the Vale of Evesham in the 1950s, a local producer was heard to say, *'There is a fortune awaiting the man who can make one apple grow where two do now.'* Price deflation is the enemy of the farmer as it is of all debtors.

Because of the need for farming in the aggregate always to aim at a surplus, covering the risk that nature will cause a poor harvest, the farmer is invariably in a weak position in the market. Realising this, most governments, even those which favour the principles of market economics, have decided that there are always exceptions to every rule and that the farming industry has to be protected from the more extreme free-market forces. This assessment is assuredly correct, for the alternative is to risk starvation. It must be admitted, however, that the protection given is often too great.

Ancient history is full of accounts of farmers descending into debt slavery. Rulers found this very inconvenient because debt-slaves were not interested in serving as soldiers to defend their country, and indeed could not afford to equip themselves. Rulers therefore often acted to wipe away those debts over which they had jurisdiction, the debts to the state. In those days the state was more likely to be a creditor than a debtor, so the wiping clean of the slates on which debts to the state were recorded was effective. The earliest recorded example took place in the city of Lagash in Mesopotamia in about 2,400 BC.[1]

Ancient kings also indulged in price maintenance. The first known legislation to maintain prices is Law 51 of Hammurapi the Great of Assyria, 1760 BC. It gives a debtor the right to pay his debts to a merchant in corn or sesame (instead of silver, presumably) at a price determined by the King. This law was doubtless designed to help farmers who could not sell their crops at a viable price because of poor demand when there was a glut. The pricing problems which afflict modern agriculture date right back to the invention of commercial agriculture.

The formal theory of credit

The invention of credit must have preceded the invention of money for two reasons. The first is that money, as we have already seen, is created by the creation of debt. A system of giving credit and incurring debt must have existed long before someone found a way of measuring it in a common unit, or of making it transferable. The second is that by definition money is transferable debt (or negotiable debt), and the invention of money had to await the invention of legal processes for the assignment of debts, and for their enforcement. What the populace thinks of first as money, notes and coins, are portable credit. In a modern society all money is just some form of transferable credit. The twin innovations of enforceable debt and portable credit completed the invention of money. Thus credit requires a legal structure, and the quality of the legal system will have a profound effect on the ability of an economy to grow. The other important structure every society must have is, of course, an effective taxation system so that the state can also be a trustworthy debtor.

In a modern society, where precious metals are not used as a medium of exchange, it is easy to perceive the identity of money and negotiable debt, but currencies made of precious metals seem to confuse the concept of money as debt. It is time to root out that confusion. As our account has shown, the invention of metallic currencies was merely an early way of making debt assignable and portable. By convention, that is by an unspoken common agreement, everyone who held gold or silver, or any other form of portable money, was held to be a creditor of society for goods and services to a value based on the value given by consensus or decree to those metals. Gold itself is a fairly useless commodity, being needed for filling teeth, plating electrical terminals, durable ornamentation and little else. It became more useful, and therefore more valuable, by substituting, especially in an illiterate society, for transferable credits. However the use of gold as money was always rare; silver was the preferred choice from times before the reach of written history.

Gold and silver were unnecessary in a system of bills of exchange and cheques as instruments for assigning debts. Such a system preceded the use of precious metals by thousands of years. There was already a silver standard in use by the time writing was invented, but it need not be actual silver which changed hands, but virtual silver represented by documents or symbols. In the mediaeval era the fairs which took place across Europe were the events when merchants netted out their debts to one another, only the balance, if any, being settled in silver or gold, if required, but it is more than likely that in most cases any balance was carried forward, not settled. If a balance was paid, it is most likely it would be by the handing over of a bill of exchange, not silver. The fairs were seen to be so important that even in times of war they took place, and the travelling merchants were protected by the ruler even when they came from enemy territory. Each fair had its own weight standards for precious metals, but that of Troyes in France eventually became the world standard for gold and silver. Gold is priced daily in Troy(es) ounces.

Classifying the credit supply

If it is accepted that the credit supply is more significant than the money supply alone, let us make some suggestions for its classification. Credit deserves scientific study, and since Aristotle an essential feature of scientific study has been the process of classification: it helps to elucidate the truth.

We have already seen that credit falls into two important broad classes, intermediated and disintermediated (or non-intermediated). If we use C for credit, in the same way that economists use M for money, we can name three classes of credit, C_{int}, C_{disint}, for the intermediated and disintermediated categories, and C_{total} for the total of all credit. But there is a further breakdown of credit which gives a second classification.

C0 could, for instance, be the counterpart of M0. It consists of the investments held by the Issue Department of the Bank of England.

C4 would be the counterpart of M4. C4 consists of the investments which originate from the lending of all bank deposits, including of course those of the building societies and other lending institutions, but also the loans which represent the investment of the banks capital bases. So C4 is slightly larger than M4, but there is a correspondence between M4 and C4.

Before further Cs are allocated for other classes of credit a general discussion of the subject among economists would be desirable. One question to be answered is whether it is possible, or desirable, to make all the other possible Cs cumulative in the way that the Ms are cumulative up to the final one, which currently is M4, (the former M5 and M6 having been abandoned). There are many more Cs than Ms, and there may be no benefit from progressively cumulating them together before one gets to C_{total}. Further Cs may therefore be individual. They will be needed for the following categories, at the very least:–

- Shareholders funds of all incorporated businesses.
- All bond issues. Bonds can also be subcategorised, – possibly by the level of security, and also by maturity.
- All trade credit. This will be a very large category.
- All government borrowing, whether central or local.
- All lending abroad.

Some of these figures are currently gathered by the statisticians.

There are many possible and useful subcategories, the figures for some of which are already published by the ONS, but which have never been given identifying numbers by economists as have the categories of money. The ONS gives all its statistical categories identifying codes, each being a group of letters. One cannot, however, expect that these codes will become popular identifiers among students of monetary theory as they are not mnemonics.

Finally we would need to identify the total of all forms of credit which are readily transferable, and can therefore serve as a medium of exchange. Perhaps in this class we shall arrive at a far more useful figure for true money than is given presently by M4, for many of the components of M4 are not readily assignable. A Treasury Bill (not included in M4), for instance, is much more readily transferable than some items which are included in M4, such as a fixed term deposit in a building society or a bank. A subcategory, if not, indeed, a separate category, would be those investments or deposits which are readily liquidated because of the existence of an efficient secondary capital market.

An essential step

The more one thinks about the classification of the components of the credit supply, the less satisfactory is the emphasis hitherto given by economists to the liabilities side of the balance sheets of the lending institutions, that is to their deposits. The change of viewpoint to the assets side reveals in very sharp focus the importance for the economy of the total credit supply (C_{total}). How could economists go on so long without any knowledge of C_{total}, or any apparent wish to know it? Why was C4 not calculated until 1990? Even now no figures are published for C4 before 1985.

A hundred-headed monster

Control of the entire credit supply should be the very essence of a true monetary theory, though I prefer to use the wider term, creditary theory. The arguments put forward in this book have surely shown that the government must seek to observe, and even on occasions control, the whole credit supply in all its many forms. That is the way to understand the relationship of the credit supply to the functioning of the economic system and to economic growth.

Creditary Economics is the overall name for our study, and that term is now established and understood. We can abandon the discredited term 'monetarism'.

So many are the forms of credit, the task of controlling the whole credit supply is one worthy of Hercules. Perhaps that is why the British government, among others, has gradually backed away from doing so since the death of Maynard Keynes. The abandoned Borrowing (Control and Guarantees) Act was dated 12th July 1946. Section one of the Act gave the Treasury full power over almost the whole credit supply, for the borrowing of any sum over £10,000 in any single year was subject to control. Trade credit was not exempted, but one must suspect that the draftsmen did not contemplate the exercise of restrictions over it. Trade credit can be very important, as it often involves new credit creation.

One of Hercules' tasks was to slay the Hydra, a dog with nine serpent heads. When one head was cut off, two more grew in its place. The total credit supply is a hundred-headed Hydra. When one source of credit is suppressed, others are invented to take its place, or other existing sources are expanded. In Greek mythology the duplication of the Hydras head could be prevented by cauterising the wound. Analogous measures to deal with the sources of credit would doubtless destroy the economy as effectively as Hercules destroyed the Hydra.

The powers given by the Act of 1946, and which were dispensed with in 1985, should be studied with a view to reinstatement in a modern form. They should however be used with the greatest possible discretion, equal to that with which the flowers of the foxglove were used to treat heart disease. Three flowers are a remedy, four are a poison. Perhaps a supervising commission of businessmen would be a good creation.

Credit guidelines

Applying control to the growth of credit overall is a daunting task. One suspects that the attraction of the theories of the monetarists was that they appeared to provide an easy way out of the many difficulties. Lazy-mindedness is a widespread human failing, even among those with the brain to win first-class academic honours. It was a characteristic of the twentieth century to look for easy ways of doing things. One can but hope that a characteristic of the twenty-first century will be recognition that economic causes and effects are not linked in a simple, unchanging mechanical way.

The economic situation shifts and changes with a myriad varying details making up the whole. Any one of a vast number of factors may be different from the last similar scenario, and yet quite a small variation may warrant a different decision from that in the last apparently similar situation. Consequently no firm rules can be promulgated as to what should be the automatic responses of the supervising authority to any future event. Only guidelines can be formulated, and even those must carry a severe health warning. Governments must also recognise that the course of economic events is changed not only by actions they deliberately initiate themselves. As earlier chapters have shown, the course of events can be transformed by apparently innocent little taxes, and by detailed tax regulations which look even less significant. One need only compare the provision of housing finance in Britain, Germany and the USA to see how small differences in regulation and practice can cause huge differences in the housing market. If British politicians were sincere in what they say about supporting small businesses, they would give Japanese-style trust banks, as the providers of capital to business, a very warm welcome.[2] Yet attempts to foster trust banks would instinctively veer towards some cumbersome and impotent bureaucratic structure. Nor is every structure of credit shaped only by government action. The rules and conventions of auditors and accountants can also be a major influence; so can the fashions, requirements and practices of the Stock Market. Enthusiasm can lead to danger as can be seen from what Venture Capital Funds are doing. these funds were created to allow small investors to participate in the ownership of small but growing business, but the amount the investors put into the funds is not automatically related to needs. As already mentioned on page 194, the funds have more money than there are opportunities for its use. The result is that silly prices are being paid, and the managers of the businesses will be unable to meet the expectations of the investors. The supply of investment funds is being over-stimulated by tax advantages in the form of exemption from Inheritance Tax and a fast tapering of Capital Gains Tax rates.

Funding real assets

One guideline might be that a supply of new credit should preferably expand the stock of real assets. One would be cautious about any provision of credit to finance a take-over or a buy-out, especially if the price reflects an inflation of asset values above intrinsic cost. Any supply of credit which tends to inflate asset values should be restrained, or neutralised, and especially those which suddenly inflate house prices in the manner experienced in Britain at least four times in 35 years.

Recognition of the full subtlety of the economic mechanism is long overdue: proper study of the credit supply in all its manifestations would help force economists to do this. The way forward for monetarists is to study the effects of proposed guidelines, and refine them. The immense effort hitherto wasted on spurious computerised models of the economy should be directed to these studies instead. A new generation of economists is needed who fully understand bookkeeping and, above all, cost-accounting. Better still they should have had real hands-on experience in industry. Number-crunching mathematical economists, abusing the techniques invented by Professor Sir Ronald Aylmer Fisher, inevitably remote from the real action, are dispensable.

The purpose

The primary purpose of credit control should be to attempt to iron out the trade cycle. An excessive supply of credit creates an unsustainable boom, which goes into reverse when the borrowers try to reduce their debts. The proper phasing of credit creation and credit destruction is the goal. Lacking the correct mechanisms, some people have abandoned all faith in the possibility of eliminating the trade/credit cycle. An air of resignation seems to permeate finance ministries around the world. They even think that it has a mystical and inevitable regularity about it. There is a psychological element in the cycle with the result that the more lunatic trade-cycle theories are like fairies: they happen if you believe in them! The true creditary theorist will continue to strive to reduce the cycle. He or she will not accept that it is beyond human control. He or she will also observe that many measures, supposed to be anti-inflationary, have had the effect of deepening the troughs of the trade cycle.

Out of the frictions and uncertainties of the trade cycle springs unemployment, the cruellest of all economic faults. From 1939 until 1971 there was little apparent unemployment, and no real depression. One reason for this was the gentle inflation which reduced the burden of debt associated with boom conditions, and thereby avoided recessionary effects. The house-price boom of 1979 was not followed by bankruptcies or house-repossessions because the subsequent 50 per cent inflation kept the nominal value of houses stable, even though real values fell substantially. Inflation is the debtor's friend. In the next house-price boom it was a very different experience, and that must never be forgotten. The adverse consequences of curing inflation can be far worse than the consequences of letting it continue. Bankruptcy has a domino effect, taking sound businessmen down with the unsound.

There are those who insist that unemployment is inevitable, a price we pay for technological advance. They say this despite the obvious need for more goods and services for the poor, the sick, and the aged. It is a feeble and defeatist philosophy. Eliminating the extremes of the trade cycle will be an important step forward, allowing economies to move towards a beneficent equilibrium over much longer periods of time. It is a starting point, but the solution of the unemployment problem in its entirety almost certainly embraces many other structures and habits in society. That challenge lies beyond the scope of this book, which seeks only to reveal and if possible remove some of the crass economic errors of present day governments and the International Monetary Fund. The employment problem is several times larger still. One powerful element is the willingness of people in different countries to do the same task for less money, and manufacturing industry especially loves to chase low wage rates around the world. As the techniques and knowledge of manufacturing industry spread around the globe to the poorer countries, the challenge to employment in rich countries grows larger. Global free trade, carried to its fullest extent, must ultimately eliminate global differences in standards of living. That is bad news for complacent Europeans and Americans.

Surely human ingenuity can find a way of marrying the need for work with the unsatisfied need for goods and services. This was the same problem that stirred the consciences of those whom Keynes called the 'Brave Heretics', such as Gesell, Douglas and Marx. Though they might seem somewhat muddled and wrong in their analyses, their hearts were in the right place, so Keynes was kind to their ideas. But one must be wary: there are few more dangerous beings than well-meaning but mistaken do-gooders. Karl Marx is no doubt the most notorious example, but there are legions of others alive and active.

The humanitarian dimension

We see them in the European Community which is a hotbed for humanitarian attitudes. It is still fundamentally socialist, in both the better and worse senses of that adjective. Unfortunately it is difficult for a Community with a social conscience to compete with systems in other countries which are ruthless sweat shops. Free movement of labour, of goods, and of capital cannot coexist with differing standards of living. Some protection of the western economies is inevitable in order to negate the effect of their loading of high social costs onto industry. Despite the fashionable liberal theory to the contrary, the philosophy of free competition will not make everyone rich and happy. If like is not competing with like, victory and riches go to the nations which are less tender-hearted, not to those which make generous provisions for the protection of workers. That is a paradox of economics. The standard British view is that mercantilism, the protection of one's own industry by discrimination, is both immoral and, in the long run, prejudicial to the growth of one's own economy. Other countries of the European

Community seem less convinced of its eternal truth. Nor can their enthusiasm for the so-called Social Chapter be reconciled with success in a competitive world. Socialist ideals are too often the Achilles heel of an economic community's competitive strength. There is therefore a massive dilemma.

Despite strong British opposition, the European Community's attitude to farming is still strongly protectionist. The consequences for several European countries of a market economy in food are too horrifying for them to contemplate. Millions more would become unemployed to no good purpose. It is not a problem for Britain, which exposed its farming to free competition in the days when farm-workers had no votes, and eventually found different employment for them in urban conditions. A technological revolution in farming methods happened after the 1939–45 War, but the further surplus of labour it created was too small in number to carry any political weight, and anyway the majority were readily able to find alternative work during the post-war boom.

A free market in food could be a bonanza to the eastern Europeans, some of whom now have a market economy in agriculture, and also have grossly undervalued currencies. It could also cause them to be short of food, and indeed already the demand from Western Europe for meat is causing a shortage in Poland.[3] At the time of writing, Polish food prices are one fifth the British level, the effect not of comparative efficiencies but of a false exchange rate. As has been made clear earlier, efficiency cannot of itself enable one country to compete with another which has an undervalued currency. The exchange rate, not industrial efficiency is the dominant factor in international competition. Future historians, free of current prejudices, will recognise that monetarist policies which ignored the way high interest rates overpriced the currency were destructive in the extreme.

A computerised model is not a Deus ex Machina

A different management of economies will require a different kind of economist. One practice which richly deserves to be treated with scepticism is their worship of applied algebra in an attempt to model the workings of an entire economy. It helps breed a mechanistic approach to economic management which is wholly at odds with every observable human trait; Goodhart's famous law has many fresh applications yet. The true division in schools of economists is that between the practical observers, and the idealistic seekers of mechanical repeatability. By comparison the distinction between monetarists and Keynesians is a mere shading of emphasis: they are much more similar than they like to think.

Some monetary theorists have raised mere possibilities to the category of necessities. They have turned probabilities into compulsions. Their study of the infinitely complex science of economics has been made to deduce very simple, indeed simplistic, principles. To protect their intellectual status they have sought to make those principles part of an unchallengeable Law, no longer for consideration by the logical part of the human mind, but to be protected in that area of the brain which is not amenable to reason, the area ruled by the obsessive neuroses of human beings. The mechanistic approach to economic planning which economic modelling encourages is a handicap to correct decision making. This book has argued that it is the whole credit supply, not the money supply alone, which affects the progress of the economy, but it must be emphasised that this does not mean that there is any mechanistic, unaltering relationship between the credit supply and GDP which can be modelled in a computer program. The relationship will always be different at different times. The task of the economist is to observe carefully what the differences are, and in what ways they are important.

Future generations of economists may liken their twentieth-century predecessors to the alchemists of old who used pseudo-scientific techniques in vain pursuit of the philosopher's stone. The pestles and mortars of the alchemists were used with misdirected skill, and so were the computers of the mathematical economists. Another analogy of a profession which misled itself is the doctors whose leeches killed patients as effectively as the economists' high interest rates have killed businesses.

True economists will in future be more flexible, more clearly scientific, less dogmatic and far less mechanistic. They will also understand that they can expect no final truth in a human science such as economics. The search for truth will for ever be a continuing process.

Creditary economics and the Less Developed Countries

A set of credit institutions and an effective tax system are the essentials for any economic development. If a country does not have both, it is very likely, if not indeed certain, that one will also find it is a country with a large and unserviceable foreign debt problem. That does not mean that the population in the aggregate has a net debt to foreign institutions; what it does mean is that its citizens prefer to have their savings of claims on value denominated in some currency other than their own. Those savings are often concentrated in the ownership of a small, very wealthy elite, but not in all cases.

The leaders of the *'Make Poverty History'* campaign would like to clean the slates of poorer debtor countries, but do not propose that the cleansing of the slates should be, in the first stage, at the expense of the elites of those countries. Thus the elites would remain creditors of the countries in whose currencies their assets are denominated, and the workers of those countries would bear the full burden of the debt relief.

What is the full extent of this problem? Accurate information is difficult to ascertain, for although national statistical offices try to assess the total of the foreign liabilities of their banks, the possibilities for double counting, or for not counting at all, are considerable. One way in which double counting occurs is that the initial deposit of money may be into an account in a tax haven, but as there is usually no way that very large sums of money can be deployed in a small tax haven, the deposits are passed on to the parent or correspondent bank in a major world financial centre.

This situation needs remedying but how can one do it? The best one can suggest is that heavily indebted countries be assisted in setting up their own banks, and be encouraged to create credit in their own currencies, not to borrow in US dollars, GB pounds or Euros. Many of these countries do not need foreign loans. They often have the workers, the resources and the skills, and the money to finance development in such countries could be created by their own creditary structures, if they had them. One would also like to see sensible interest rates. Many inflation-prone debtor countries allow huge rates of interest, and as we have shown, high interest rates are of themselves the major cause of inflation. They therefore weaken the currency, the opposite of what is intended.

The real debtors

The Office for National Statistics publishes a 'Pink Book', which is a record of the United Kingdom's trading position with the rest of the world. The latest figure at time of writing shows a substantial overall deficit. A map of the world included in the Pink Book shows those countries with which the UK has a deficit in pink, and those with which it has a surplus in grey. It may surprise many that the whole of Africa is pink. Thus those heavily indebted countries in Africa are in reality lending the UK the money to buy their produce. There is nothing the UK can do to help clear the debts of these countries, for to do that the UK would have to have a trade surplus. Luckily the UK has a surplus with most of the Americas, but it has a deficit with Russia and most of Asia.

The US is in a similar situation, and its debts are gigantic and unpayable. So why do Africans look poor and Britons and Americans look rich? The reason is that borrowed wealth can be used to buy things that make one look rich. The late Robert Maxwell had the ultimate symbol of wealth, an ocean-going yacht, yet at his death he was totally insolvent.

The British, European and United States governments are asked to open up their market for food to poor African countries. But the exchange rates between Europe and these poor countries are so false that they get next to nothing in return value from their exports to First World countries. They would get far better value for their exports from other poor countries, so the first priority should be for the trade between poorer countries to be increased, and to discourage them from lending First World countries the money to buy their produce. The situation is in danger of resembling that between Great Britain and Ireland in the 1840s. Then a starving Ireland was sending wheat and meat to a rich England, and the profits of the sales were recycled by the landowners back to England to support their rich lifestyles. Effectively the impoverished Irish were lending the English the wherewithal to buy their produce. The same phenomenon exists all across the modern world.

This is a very big subject, and one which demands a separate book. We must now leave it, but with the warning that the campaign to make poverty history must not be allowed to make poverty universal.

Some good news

A country which appeared to be in dire financial condition in the 1990s is now becoming a success story. That is Russia. Its national currency looked worthless, the tax take was tiny, and the main currency of the people was US dollar bills, more it was said than circulated in the United States itself. The monetarist ghouls were hovering around the body, eager to thrust upon it dollar loans to tide it over. A few economists in the West urged Russia to have nothing to do with these remedies. The prescription of their lead speakers was, firstly, a moratorium on foreign debt repayment, secondly, no loans from the International Monetary Fund or any foreign bank or government, and thirdly to monetise the inter-company debts of Russia's large utilities and other big businesses, thus making them the basis of its money system. The latter means doing what we have shown was happening in the 1830s in Britain. The first would gain time for the huge export industries of Russia to get going on a sounder basis. It was obvious that Russia would soon have a large trade surplus from its primary products, and that has proved true; it is now one of the ten largest surpluses in the world. It needs a debt moratorium no longer.

The adjustment from inept communist ideology to effective creditary structures has slowly been taking place, but one can guess that it was not easy in a country where the idea of charging depreciation on capital equipment did not exist, and where even double-entry bookkeeping had been regarded as a false capitalistic doctrine. Because industry was not charged for its capital assets, the Russians tended to throw capital at all production problems, whereas the Japanese threw management expertise at them. To make matters even worse for the Russians, after 1989 they were assaulted by an invasion of western free-market theorists who saw the opportunity to create, in one great leap forward, a free market economy such as has never existed in the whole history of the world.

This book may make the way forward a little clearer for those who wish to have a better understanding of creditary structures and how to control them.

16
101 Principles of Creditary Economics

If you tell the truth you don't have to remember anything.
MARK TWAIN

1   The drawing down of a loan facility granted by a bank increases both the total of credit in use (the credit supply), and the total of deposits (the money supply).

2   In most circumstances a government can administer short-term interest rates.

3   A government can strongly influence but not in all environments control long-term interest rates.

4   A Central Bank can fix interest rates because it controls the flow of money between banks.

5   A bank can lend money for which it has no balancing deposit in the sure expectation that one will become available.

6   The level of notes and coin required in an economy is decided by market forces. Any attempt to restrict the amount of currency in issue will cause the public to invent alternatives.

7   If interest rates are raised, the ability of a business to survive may depend more on its capital structure, and especially its level of gearing, than on its efficiency.

8   Charging taxes on unused (but usable) buildings during a recession causes the unnecessary destruction of industrial capacity. At such a time mothballing or set-aside should be facilitated.

9   With a fixed capital adequacy ratio, the capital base of the banks determines the size of the intermediated credit supply and its counterpart, the money supply.

10   The rate of growth of the total credit supply should be the prime concern of monetarists.

11   Money represents only a small part of the total credit supply.

12   Money is created by the granting of credit. Credit therefore comes before money in the causal process.

13   All things used as money are negotiable debts.

14   An increase in the money supply can arise only from an increase in the level of intermediated debt.

15   Savings equal borrowings (broadly defined to include equity capital).

16   Savings are not equal to investment unless one redefines savings to mean something quite different from the normal meaning.

17   The credit supply should be under governmental supervision.

18   Falling prices, even though they are not deflationary in origin, can precipitate a deflationary spiral, especially if there is an overhang of existing debt.

19   Deflation of prices is the normal result of technical innovation and high investment. Unfortunately deflation can bring growth to a halt.

20   Economists must not abuse statistical techniques.

21   Rising prices and inflation are not always the same thing. Unavoidable real cost increases due to technical problems may raise prices. It is preferable to restrict the term inflation to price rises resulting from the debasement of the currency.

22   Falling prices and deflation are not the same thing. A true reduction in costs achieved by investment leads to lower prices. One may prefer not to call this deflation, which could be defined as any appreciation in the purchasing power of the currency which is not the result of technology.

23   An oversupply of credit assists the growth of inflation, but it is not normally a first cause except when it is used to inflate asset values.

24   Low long-term interest rates encourage investment which leads to lower costs and therefore lower prices.

25   High long-term interest rates discourage investment, and the consequent running down of the economy will lead to higher prices.

26   The expectation that high interest rates will discourage the demand for credit can be frustrated by marketing pressure by lenders.

27   Standard monetary theory fails to explain Gibson's Paradox, which correlates high interest rates with rising prices, and low interest rates with falling prices.

28   The credit supply and demand functions are not independent of one another.

29   The assumed capacity to service debt is the factor which is the ultimate limitation on the total credit supply.

30   A properly thought out system of reserve assets might be successful in controlling the intermediated credit supply. Such a system has never yet been invented or applied in Britain, and is probably impossible to implement.

31   The practice of British financial institutions of mismatching the maturity of assets and liabilities should be discouraged.

32   In economic systems exogenous variables are as rare as the Hydra and the Yeti. The whole economic system of the world is subject to dynamic interactions.

33   Special deposits do not restrict the intermediated credit supply; they merely transfer part of it to the Central Bank.

34   Special deposits can in certain circumstances assist the growth of inflation.

35   Overfunding makes possible the expansion of the overall credit supply. It therefore assists the growth of inflation, except when it is used to reduce government short-term borrowing which has been granted zero risk-weighting by the Central Bank. In the latter case it is neutral in its effect.

36   Under-funding increases the supply of credit to the private sector only if there is also an increase in the capital base of the banks.

37   Unless all government borrowing from banks is zero risk-weighted, under-funding will squeeze out private sector borrowers and cause a credit crunch. They will be forced to resort to the disintermediated sector of the credit supply. Private companies and individuals will not find that easy.

38   High interest rates can only cure inflation by causing high unemployment. It does not always work as unemployment and high inflation can continue together.

39   If a currency is put into a fixed exchange system at an overvaluation, the deflation which must follow will have its effects amplified if there is a serious overhang of existing debt. A deflationary spiral and a deep recession will be the result.

40   An overvalued currency will eventually ruin the economy of a trading country, but it may take a long time to do so.

41   Deflation will not be cured by lowering the interest rate if there is no mechanism for applying a negative nominal interest rate.

42   Deflation is self-perpetuating, in the absence of drastic remedial measures.

43   Deflation is the worst enemy of economic progress, and it is coupled with the worst social evil – unemployment.

44   The limitations of the science of economics must be fully recognised.

45   Although algebraic equations can be devised to illustrate functional relationships, it does not mean that any constant values can be substituted for the algebraic symbols in the equations. Economic forces are too numerous, too frequent in occurrence, too variable, and too erratic in motivation and application for any fully stable relationships to exist. Moreover the data variables on which the functions are supposed to operate are unstable, inconsistently observed, unreliable, or just inaccurate.

46   The endowment effect can cause rising interest rates to increase bank profits which in turn attract capital. With the help of the increased capital base, the banks increase the intermediated credit supply.

47   Rising interest rates cause inflation in the short term, firstly because they increase costs, secondly because they motivate wage claims, and thirdly because they indirectly inspire inflationary expectations.

48   A classical Corporation Tax system can be inflationary as it can cause long-term interest rates to rise.

49   A classical Corporation Tax system may encourage debt capitalisation beyond a prudent level.

50   By encouraging excessive borrowing, a classical Corporation Tax system will ensure that any subsequent recession is more damaging than it need be as companies are forced into liquidation at an earlier point than would be the case if they were entirely financed by equity capital.

51   Equity capitalisation should be encouraged, or at least not discouraged, by the tax system, as businesses financed by equity can more easily survive a recession.

52   The tax rate on profits of corporations must be no more than the standard rate of income tax.

53   If a profits tax is applied to company profits, it must relate to profits calculated *before* the charge for interest. This would keep the tax fiscally neutral in its effect on the choice of equity or loan capitalisation.

54   Capital taxation can destabilise securities markets and thereby damage the capital base of insurance companies.

55   The results of econometric studies can be interesting, but should not be readily accepted as persuasive unless the physical connection of cause and effect which underlies the functional relationships is totally

apparent. (This would bring the science of economics into line with other human sciences.)

56   Taxation should be planned to be neutral. It should not be levied in ways which harm international competitiveness.

57   Direct controls are necessary to limit credit expansion satisfactorily. (But the controls will doubtless be misapplied!)

58   Credit created to finance the purchase of existing assets, such as houses, will inflate their value, and will then leak through to general inflation.

59   The trade cycle is caused by the overexpansion of credit followed by an attempt to reduce it.

60   Attempts to repay an overhang of existing debt will cause a recessionary spiral.

61   Mild inflation is the least painful cure for an overhang of debt. It acts as an arbitrary form of wealth redistribution, taking from those with monetary assets for the benefit of those with monetary liabilities.

62   To raise interest rates after a credit explosion is economic vandalism.

63   Foreign banks must be made to observe the same prudence and capital ratios as domestic banks.

64   Credit institutions should be discouraged from over-specialisation in lending or there will be distortions in the supply of credit to differing sectors of the economy.

65   Particular care should be taken to make sure that the housing market is not oversupplied with credit. The warning sign is when the price of the site rises to more than about 15 per cent of the price of the finished house. High land prices constitute a form of taxation of the young for the benefit not of the state, but of the landowner.

66   Any shortage of intermediated credit especially injures the small business sector because it has no access to the alternative, the disintermediated credit supply.

67   Anti-inflationary measures have done more damage to the British economy (and others) than inflation itself.

68   High interest rates transfer buying power from the young, the have-nots, to the elderly, the haves.

69   Take-overs and management buy-outs of companies must not be allowed to cause asset price inflation, or to increase imprudently the proportion of loan capitalisation of industry.

70   Take-overs and management buy-outs paid for with borrowed cash must be limited, possibly eliminated. A management which thinks

that it can do better than another should offer shares as the consideration for the acquisition of another company.

71   The decision to make or accept a take-over bid must be agreed at a general meeting. The hope is that this might prevent individual shareholders in target companies being picked off separately.

72   It is impossible to tax capital except in specie. Capital taxes are normally taxes on the nation's income which have been computed by reference to capital values.

73   The only logical definition of capital is that it is the surviving product of past economic activity.

74   Income is equal to the product of current economic activity during a prescribed period of time.

75   Thrift and debt are two faces of the same thing. Neither can exist without the other. Let all moralists, as well as economists, note and understand that one man's saving is another man's debt. Moralists who preach both the virtue of saving and the evil of usury are being illogical. (That does not mean that debt should be encouraged!)

76   Net negative saving (which means the repayment of debt from savings) is deflationary. Net positive saving does not have to be deflationary, though in certain circumstances it will be.

77   Saving can assist real capital formation only if it goes into the primary capital market, and even there it will not necessarily do so.

78   Saving fed to the secondary capital market finances an equivalent dissaving, and nothing else.

79   The absolute limit on capital taxation (taxation by reference to capital values) is the aggregate net annual saving of the personal sector of the economy. It is unlikely that such a limit could ever be approached. A collapse in all asset values is the consequence of trying to approach or exceed that limit.

80   Money does not have a constant frequency of circulation.

81   Money cannot be transferred from one country to another unless there is a concomitant flow of goods and services in the same direction. The laws of double entry bookkeeping ensure that any flow which is not so accompanied has to be balanced by a transfer of money in the opposite direction.

82   An entrepreneur cannot ignore nominal rates of interest and observe only real rates of interest.

83   Nominal interest rate expectations are probably more influential than inflationary expectations.

84   The true real rate of interest experienced by an entrepreneur is specific to his business; it may differ wildly from the average real rate of interest.

85   The RPI is not a significant index for the businessman. There are other more appropriate deflators.

86   Different individuals in the community experience very different rates of retail price inflation. For instance an inflation of house prices mostly affects young workers.

87   The Third World debt problem would not have become so bad if banks in developed countries had paid lower interest rates.

88   A trade deficit can create the illusion of reduced unemployment by causing the creation of jobs in distribution.

89   The foreign business of United Kingdom banks, both deposit taking and loan granting, should be hived off to subsidiaries, and no bank may assume the liabilities of a defaulting subsidiary without the consent of the supervising authority. This is a reversal of existing policy.

90   Attempts to regulate an economy will always be counteracted, at least in part, by the public's response.

91   A market economy has no fourth dimension; it cannot plan forward to any worthwhile extent. Only planning can provide the necessary fourth dimension.

92   Market forces cannot control the money supply.

93   Market economics should be allowed as much scope as possible, despite the obvious deficiencies.

94   Market economics can never be allowed full control over the farming industry. It is a special case because it cannot control its production closely enough, nor can it be allowed to produce less than the minimum needs of the people.

95   Market economics cannot determine correctly the amount of power generating equipment that is needed.

96   As high interest rates precipitate firstly credit creation sprees, and then credit crunches, and as very low interest rates may stifle economic growth, the proper rates of interest are likely to be the low to intermediate ones; 5–7% may be achievable for industries' borrowing.

97   The historic real rate of interest paid by the British government has tended to be 3 per cent.

98   Moderate inflation is not wholly evil. Like the poison digitalis it can have a curative effect in small quantities.

99   The need for governments to use inflation as a crude method of taxation may diminish as more and more state enterprises, and their capital funding, are transferred to the private sector. The root of the problem hitherto has been the near impossibility of setting tax rates at such a level as will finance all public expenditure, and yet not damage private initiative. If the public wants high spending it must be prepared to tolerate inflation, hopefully at a modest rate.

100   The accumulation of wealth cannot be prevented, but if those with money spend, rather than save, those with lesser resources can thereby earn the money with which to purchase what they desire, and will not have the same need to borrow. A reduction in interest rates, by reducing the propensity to hold deposits, encourages depositors to spend their money. A multiplier effect follows.

101   Laws of economics are rarely, if ever, absolute. One must be prepared to recognise exceptions in specific circumstances.

Appendix A:
The Currency Principle

Chapter Six of Henry Tooke's book of 1844

Bills of Exchange

That transactions to a very large amount are adjusted by bills of exchange has long been known and admitted in general terms; but the vastness of the amount was not brought distinctly under the notice of the public till the appearance of a pamphlet by the late Mr. Leatham, an eminent banker at Wakefield. According to a computation, which he seems to have made with great care, founded upon official returns of bill stamps issued, the following are the results:–

RETURN OF BILL STAMPS, FOR 1832 TO 1839 INCLUSIVE

	Bills created in Great Britain and Ireland, founded on returns of Stamps issued from the Stamp Office.	Bill Average amount in circulation, at one time in each year
1832	356,153,409	59,038,852
1833	383,659,585	95,914,896
1834	379,155,052	94,788,763
1835	405,403,051	101,350,762
1836	485,943,473	121,485,868
1837	455,084,445	113,771,111
1838	465,504,041	116,316,010
1839	528,493,842	132,123,460

Mr. Leatham gives the process by which, upon the data furnished by the returns of stamps, he arrives at these results; and I am disposed to think that they are as near an approximation to the truth as the nature of the materials admits of arriving at. And some corroboration of the vastness of the amounts is afforded by a reference to the adjustments at the clearing house in London, which in the year 1839 amounted to £954,401,600, making an average amount of payments of upwards of £3,000,000 of bills of exchange and cheques daily effected through the medium of little more than £200,000 of bank notes.

As illustrative of the position for which Mr. Leatham contends, and conclusively, as I think, that bills of exchange perform the functions of money, he observes,

> For a great number of years, it had been the custom of merchants to pay the clothiers in small bills of £10, £15, £20, and so up to £100, drawn at two months after date on London bankers. I have always considered this the best part of our paper currency, ranking next to gold; the bills existing only for limited periods, and acquiring increased security as they pass from hand to hand by endorsement. From the unreasonably high stamp laid on small bills in 1815, the merchants have ceased to pay in bills, but pay notes instead, requiring 2d. in the pound for cash from the receiver; and I find the revenue has much decreased in consequence in this class of stamps.' (pp. 44, 45)

Mr. Lewis Loyd, when examined by the House of Lords' Committee on the Resumption of Cash Payments in 1819, gave the following evidence:–

Qu. 9. At the time when you began business in Manchester, in 1792, were there any country banks which issued notes in that town, or in any other part of Lancashire?

None, I believe.

10. Have there never been, at any time, country banks issuing notes in Lancashire?

None within my recollection. I began to reside in Manchester in 1789. There had been, before that period, notes issued there about the year 1787 or 1788; I think by a bank which failed. I believe that was the only attempt ever made in Lancashire till lately, except that there was lately, and is now, an attempt made to issue them at Blackburn.

11. How has the circulation of Lancashire been carried on since the period to which you refer?

Wholly in Bank of England notes and bills of exchange.

12. Is the proportion of Bank of England notes very considerable as compared with bills of exchange?

About one-tenth, I think, in Bank of England notes, and nine-tenths, at least, in bills of exchange. These bills of exchange circulate from band to hand, till they are covered with endorsements.

13. Is any inconvenience felt from this mode of circulation by bills of exchange?

None whatever.

14. Has the circulation of Bank of England notes increased or decreased of late years in proportion to bills of exchange?

I think the proportion of bank notes has increased.

15. To what do you attribute that increase?

Partly to the great increase of the stamp duties. It is within my knowledge, from the transactions of my own house, that the supplies of provisions, which are drawn from the neighbouring counties, used to be paid for in small bills of exchange, mostly of £10, or lower; but now the persons going to the neighbouring localities for supplies of provisions take with them bank notes and bank post bills, stating that the stamp is too serious an object to them to be paid on such small sums. There is scarcely a day when I do not send £2000 in bank post bills for that purpose to Manchester, which we hardly ever used to do before the last addition to the stamp duty.

16. Were these bills of exchange drawn for specific loans previous to their employment, or were they bills resulting from antecedent transactions?

Those who purchased provisions used to go to fairs and markets with bills ready drawn in their favour, very often for specific sums, as for the round sum of £10, just as they now take £10 in Bank of England notes and bank post bills. There was this peculiar circumstance attending them, that the bills were usually drawn at two months' date, and were considered as cash payment; they were bills drawn on London by country bankers, and remitted to London as suited the convenience of the parties who received them. Now, in consequence of having bank post bills and Bank of England notes, the persons who receive the bills make an allowance to those who pay them of two months' interest. My answer applies to the supply of the town with provisions. Nearly all the other transactions of Manchester, except the payment of labourers, are still carried on in bills of exchange, and the payment of labourers is mostly made in £1 Bank of England notes.

If by an alteration in an opposite direction, the stamp duty on bills of exchange were reduced or abolished, while that on promissory notes on demand remained the same, and still more, if it were raised, there would be a considerable change in practice, by making the smaller payments among dealers in bills of exchange as a substitute for bank notes.

In a work by the late Mr. Henry Thornton, which attracted considerable attention at the time, and which formed the subject of an article by Mr. Homer, in the first Number of the Edinburgh Review in 1802, there is a distinct and full description of the manner in which bills of exchange performed in his time the function of money; a description which is strictly applicable at the present day. He observes with reference to bills of exchange,

Bills, since they circulate chiefly among the trading world, come little under the observation of the public. The amount of bills in existence may yet, perhaps, be at all times greater than the amount of all the bank notes of every kind, and of all the circulating guineas. Liverpool and Manchester effect the whole of their larger mercantile payments, not by country bank notes, of which none are issued by the banks of those places, but by bills at one or two months' date, drawn on London. The bills annually drawn by the banks of each of those towns amount to many millions.

They not only spare the use of ready money, they also occupy its place in many cases. Let us imagine a farmer in the country to discharge a debt of £10 to his neighbouring grocer, by giving to him a bill for that sum, drawn on his corn-factor in London, for grain sold in the metropolis; and the grocer to transmit the bill, he having previously endorsed it to a neighbouring sugar baker, in the discharge of a like debt, and the sugar baker to send it, when again endorsed, to a West India merchant in an out-port, and the West India merchant to deliver it to his country banker, who also endorses it, and sends it into further circulation. The bill, in this case, will have effected five payments, exactly as if it were a £10 note payable to bearer on demand. It will, however, have circulated in consequence chiefly of the confidence placed by each receiver of it in the last endorser, his own correspondent in trade; whereas the circulation of a bank note is rather owing to the circumstance of the name of the issuer being so well known as to give to it an universal credit. A multitude of bills pass between trader and trader in the country in the manner which has been described; and they evidently form, in the strictest sense, a part of the circulating medium of the kingdom.

The late Sir Francis Baring, writing at a still earlier period (1797), and of a state of things within his immediate experience, refers, in the following passage, to the practice prevalent among country bankers, of issuing notes payable after date or after sight,

In the beginning of the year 1793, and of the present year, 1797, the banks of Newcastle stopped payment, while those of Exeter and of the West of England stood their ground. The partners in the banks at Newcastle were far more opulent, but their private fortunes being invested could not be realised in time to answer a run on their banks. Their notes allowed interest to commence some months after date, and were then payable on demand; by which means they had not an hour to prepare for their discharge. The banks of Exeter issued notes payable twenty days after sight with interest, to commence from the date of the note, and to cease on the day of acceptance. There can be no doubt that the practice of the banks at Newcastle is more lucrative, whilst it must for ever, be more liable to a return of what has happened. The twenty days received at Exeter furnishes ample time to communicate with London, and receive every degree of assistance which may be required.

If, according to the currency theory, the circumstance that written promises to pay being after date or sight, and to order, and therefore requiring an endorsement, are disqualified from being considered as performing the functions of money, on what ground is it that bank post bills, which are after sight and to order, have been always included in the returns of the circulation of the Bank of England? They are by their form strictly bills of exchange, being not only after sight and to order, but commonly used for transmission by post; and if these are considered to be part of the circulation, on what ground are the bills of the Bank of Ireland, and of the chartered Banks of Scotland, and of such banks throughout the United Kingdom as are of undoubted credit, not included in the return of the country circulation? This applies indeed only to short-dated bills of the most unquestioned credit; longer-dated bills, of more doubtful security, seem to have been alone in the view of those persons who assert the exclusive title of bank notes to be considered as money. Bills of this description, that is long-dated bills, are sometimes not used for purposes of circulation, they are simply written evidence of a debt which is discharged at maturity, without passing into third hands. I will not stop now to enter into the distinction between long and short-dated bills in the comparison with bank notes, and between bills drawn by bankers, and bills by merchants or dealers on dealers. It is a sufficient negative of the main proposition on which the currency theory rests, to have shown that short-dated bills of exchange are substitutes not only for coin, but for bank notes.

If, as a last resort in the argument, it be said that bills of exchange require the intervention of bank notes for the ultimate payment, the answer is, that this is a mere fiction, for that in fact the adjustment takes place by settlement, and that a small amount of bank notes for the balance effects the liquidation, which might equally be effected by drafts on the Bank of England; or, as is done in Scotland, by exchequer bills. An alteration in the stamp duties has, as stated by Mr. Lewis Loyd and Mr. Leatham, operated against the employment of the smaller bills of exchange instead of bank notes. If the case were reversed, the stamps lowered on bills and raised on notes, we should see an immense increase in the former, and a great diminution in the latter, in other words, bank notes would be withdrawn, and bills of exchange supply their place.

It is hardly perhaps necessary to advert to the latter part of the proposition quoted at page 20, viz., that the abolition of any or of all the contrivances for dispensing with the use of money, will not necessitate the introduction in their place of an equal amount of coin or bank notes. There surely can be little doubt but that the abolition of such contrivances would necessitate the substitute of an equal amount of bank notes or coin.

Sufficient grounds have, as I venture to think, been stated for establishing the claim in behalf of cheques on bankers, and of bills of exchange, to be considered as performing, concurrently with bank notes, the functions of money for the purposes for which they are respectively used.

If the propounders of the currency theory would confine their distinction in favour of bank notes to the lowest denominations, namely, the £1 notes wholly, and the £5 and £10 notes partially, it might, as I have already observed, be conceded; but then what becomes of the dogma or the axiom of Mr. Norman and Mr. Loyd, on which the currency theory is made to rest? and what becomes of the inferences which they have drawn as to the management of banks, from a view exclusively to the whole of the circulation, large notes as well as small? In truth, their tests of good and bad management, and their views of the purposes and properties of the whole of the circulating medium and of its component parts, are essentially defective and erroneous. They draw distinctions which are not real or substantial, as, for instance, of the higher denomination of bank notes compared with bills of exchange and cheques; while they totally overlook and confound the distinctive character of the instruments of interchange which are used in the distribution and expenditure of incomes, as compared with that of the instruments which are used in the distribution and employment of capital.

Appendix B:
Gibson Graphs

A. H. Gibson graphed long-term interest rates against an index of commodity prices. The fourth graph in this appendix is a facsimile of the graph which accompanied his 1926 paper. The one he first published, in 1923, covered a few years fewer. The first three graphs in this appendix follow his example but correlate the Three Month Libor rate of interest with the Retail Prices Index. The data is at monthly intervals. Libor is the London interbank rate of interest, that is the rate which banks operating in the London money market lend to each other. Libor was chosen because the data is readily available.

The graph by itself proves nothing because it cannot prove there is a physical relationship between the two variables. Readers are referred to page 60 for a discussion some of the issues raised by such graphs, and for an idea as to how one could research whether there is a physical relationship, and if there is, whether it is a lagged one. The graph is an indicator for research, not a proof of anything.

How valid is the inflation index? Today it tends to be taken for granted by the general public, and even by some economists, that the figures are valid. The great debates about validity of indexing which took place in the 1920s are forgotten. A. H. Gibson himself wrote as follows:–

> *Wholesale commodity prices have necessarily to be taken as representative of the cost of living for the purposes of this article, in the absence of an available and reliable index number based on a consumption standard. The difficulties in compiling such an index number have generally been considered insurmountable. Very little value can be attached to the index number of the cost of living published monthly in the Labour Gazette, for it only applies to working-class household expenditure, and even in this restricted capacity rests on a very rough basis.*

In one respect the present RPI is mischievously unsound. It gives no guide to the amount of inflation of domestic costs alone. During the period of the accompanying graphs, the price of imported manufactured goods fell dramatically, and the price of some domestic services rose equally dramatically. In the process of compiling the indices, these two influences at least partially cancel each other out, and the index of domestic costs alone remains a mystery.

The other great problem with the compilation of an informative retail price index is how to reflect house price inflation, which has risen at a rate far greater than other prices. But house price inflation affects substantially only first-time buyers or those trading up. For most people the purchase of a house insulates them from all rent inflation and any further house price inflation for their lifetime. If they have a long-term mortgage, it does not insulate them from interest rises. Therefore the current RPI reflects interest rates on mortgages, but not house prices. Yet it is the price of a house which motivates the young and economically active to seek wage rises, and, as in the final analysis it is wage rises which drive domestic cost inflation, it is the motivation for wage claims which is the most important factor to be considered in any anti-inflationary policy. As a rise in interest rates is bound to stimulate wage claims, one can see why the policy of fighting inflation with high interest rates was bound to fail, and fail badly. House prices are strange in that they are not determined solely by the effects of supply and demand for houses. Most houses are bought with borrowed money, so in areas where there is a tight housing supply the final determining factor for house prices is how much money the purchaser can borrow. The high rate of house price inflation exactly mirrors the increased availability of mortgages. That availability arises from several causes, some of which readers will deduce for themselves from earlier chapters, but lower prudence of lenders is a major factor. Competition for market share, or the search for greater economies of scale, are motives for lower prudence. But prudence has also been attacked by do-gooders, who assume quite wrongly that the housing problems of young, first-time buyers will be resolved if only they were allowed to borrow more.

Two large mortgage lenders construct indices of house prices. Many lenders employ economists to try to forecast the trend of house prices. Why should they want to do this? One has a nasty fear that the reason is this: the economist forecasts that prices will rise in the next year by eight per cent, and therefore the general managers of the mortgage lender instruct staff to take this forecast into account in setting prudential levels. For instance, if a house is being bought for £200, 000, and the loan limit is 90 per cent of the price, the staff are told they may lend 90 per cent of the anticipated value in a year's time, that is 90 per cent of £216,000. Naturally such an action fulfils the forecast automatically. The economist says, *'Wasn' t I clever to get it right?'*, and the management give him a bonus, and a bonus goes also to all the other staff who have been enabled by the decision to exceed their lending targets. Happiest of all is the general manager who gets the biggest bonus of all.

The sane reader will ask, *'But surely managements in the financial services industry know these factors are at work and guard against them?'* I wish they did.

The fourth graph is that of A. H. Gibson. The correlation it so clearly demonstrates of wholesale prices and the yield on 2½ per cent Consols is remarkable.

Gibson's sole purpose is to predict the future price of gilts.

> *The yield of high-class fixed interest-bearing stocks at market prices is mainly indirectly determined by the cost of living, a fall in the latter being usually accompanied or followed by a fall in the former, and a rise in the latter by a rise in the former.*

He explains inconsistencies in the graph

> *The rise in the yield of Consols for the years 1830 and 1831 was due to a Revolution in France in 1830 and the introduction of the Reform Bill into the English Parliament in 1831, which caused considerable political disturbances, though it passed both Houses the following year. Both these important factors temporarily severely depressed the price of Consols.*

He also explains the anomalies for the 1830s (revolution), the early 1870s (Franco-Prussian War), and 1914–20 (war in Europe). Then comes the surprise: commodity prices go up before interest rates. They are not driven by interest costs as seems often to be the case with consumer prices.

> *It will be observed from the chart that, generally speaking, the curve representing the course of the yield of Consols and the curve representing the course of commodity prices, generally either both rise together or fall together, a lead of any change in direction usually being given one year in advance by commodity prices.*

The next argument is one which might not appeal today.

> *The general sympathetic movement between the two curves representing commodity prices and the yield of Consols is obviously due*

*to the fact that the less the cost of living the greater must necessarily be the margin available for investment, and, conversely, the greater the cost of living the less such margin. The correctness of this opinion is strongly supported by the fact that the chart discloses that changes in the direction of the curve representing the yield of Consols have usually been preceded by like changes in the direction of the curve representing commodity prices. It is evident that some little time must elapse before falling or rising wholesale commodity prices can affect the margin of income available for investment, for one thing it is well known that retail prices do not change **immediately** after a change in wholesale prices, particularly if the latter be falling.*

The following selected paragraphs may be of interest. The first (partly quoted earlier) is no longer true in developed countries.

All economic history proves that the cost of foodstuffs, for man and beast, regulates, directly or indirectly, the ultimate cost of commodities in general consumption. The cost of foodstuffs is the basic cost of almost everything, unless a commodity rises in price on account of unusual scarcity. A considerable fall in the gold prices of foodstuffs since 1920 has already taken place almost throughout the world, and a further fall is to be expected in the near future. Excellent new harvests are already reported in several countries abroad.

Though the cost of living is undoubtedly the basic factor determining the course of first-class investment prices, yet changing trade conditions accelerate a fall or rise in such prices. During periods of trade activity, particularly in boom periods, when prices of commodities are rising and larger profits or dividends are, in consequence, being declared by industrial companies, there usually takes place a lesser demand for Government and other first-class stocks and an increased demand for industrial shares. In a period of falling prices, particularly if the fall be severe, when profits generally diminish, the converse takes place, an increased demand for first-class investments and a lesser demand for industrial shares. In this latter case financial embarrassment of some trading firms will first cause some liquidation of first-class investments, and, consequently, an initial fall in prices to be followed later by a material rise. The public have short memories, and the above-stated cycle of transfer of savings seeking investment has taken place during and after every marked period of trade activity in the past. Rising commodity prices, trade activity, greater trading profits, rising prices of industrial shares, and rising interest rates; falling commodity prices, trade depression, diminishing trading profits, often considerable losses, reconstructions, increased demand for Government and other first-class stocks, and falling interest rates. Such are, in brief, the events in sequence of the usual trade cycle.

Owing to the enormous amounts of capital attracted during 1907–1913, in particular from the United Kingdom, to food and raw material producing countries, there must have necessarily followed, under normal conditions of peace, a considerable increase, for many years to come, in the world's production of foodstuffs and raw materials. Consequently, a fall in commodity prices appeared to be inevitable sooner or later.

From 1897 to 1913, with the exception of two breaks, there was a considerable rise in commodity prices, the index number for 1913 being 85, as against 61 for 1896. This natural rise in commodity prices once more attracted enormous sums of capital to the food and raw material producing countries. From the United Kingdom alone, over £1,000,000,000 were attracted into foreign and Colonial investments during 1907-13, a period of but seven years, one-half of which capital was devoted to productive railway construction. That this newly invested capital was not able to make itself fully felt in net increased production during the war is obvious, on account of scarcity of labour in many countries. In the case of the British Colonies, a scarcity of labour was experienced owing to the large number of Colonials who fought for the British Empire.

Another factor that will inevitably force commodity prices materially below the present level in the future, and tend to keep them down, will be deflation of credit and currency by action of the banks. This influence has hardly yet commenced to operate. The fall in prices that has taken place since April, 1920, has been mainly due to economic and psychological causes. It is interesting to note, however, that a prolonged period of falling prices effects, of itself, part deflation of credit and currency, for a lower level of prices eventually reduces the demand for bank credit (as measured by the aggregate amount), and impels a return of currency from internal circulation.

Monetarists will take comfort from the fact that he accepted that cheap money could cause inflation of prices. He wrote, '*The cheapness of money* in 1824 led to inflation in 1825.' But his long-term expectation is clear. Low interest rates will encourage real investment which will lower costs, and the empirical evidence shows that lower prices will cause even lower interest rates, causing the price of 2½ per cent Consolidated Stock (a government loan with no final redemption date) to rise. His predictions for that price were uncannily accurate. His long-term expectation was that the price would rise to 77 between 1930 to 1934. It reached that price in 1932. But I have to admit that it needed a government decision to lower Bank Rate to 2 per cent to make it happen. He ends:–

> *Should gilt-edged investments appreciate to such an extent during the next ten years that Consols reach the predicted price of 77 by the end of the period, it is to be noted that the present amount of investments now held by the banks of the United Kingdom will have appreciated in market value by an amount more than sufficient to pay the total dividends of the banks (as a whole) for the next ten years, assuming no material alteration in dividend percentages meanwhile, and the banks to hold the investments for the full period, or, if sales be effected, then to re-invest the proceeds in Government securities.*

Gibson Graph 1.   Interest and inflation from 1983 to 1989

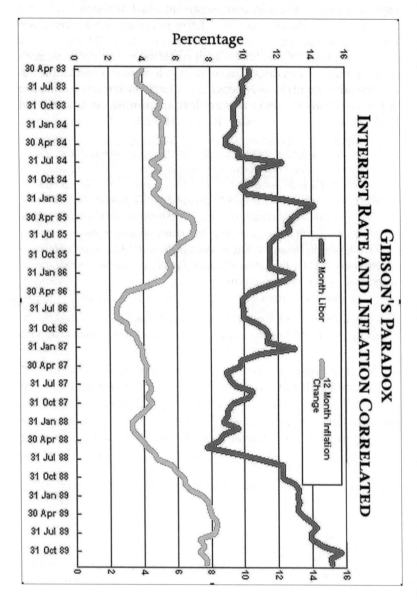

Gibson Graph 2.   Interest and inflation from 1990 to 1997

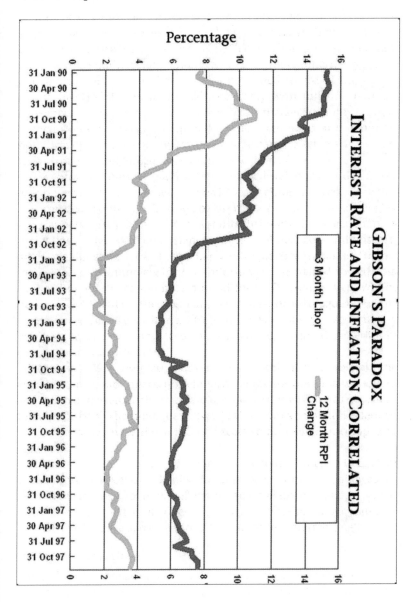

Gibson Graph 3. **Interest and inflation from 1998 to July 2005**

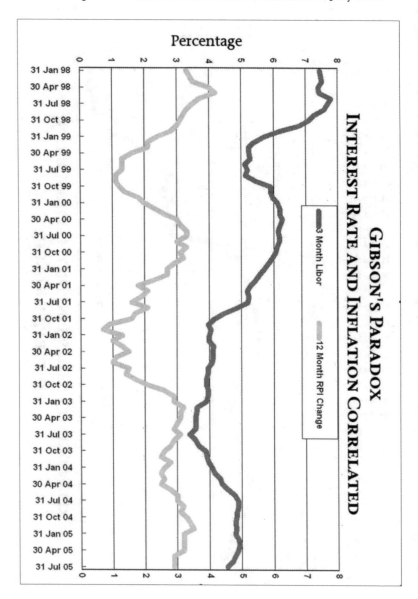

Gibson **Graph 4.** **A. H. Gibson's own graph**

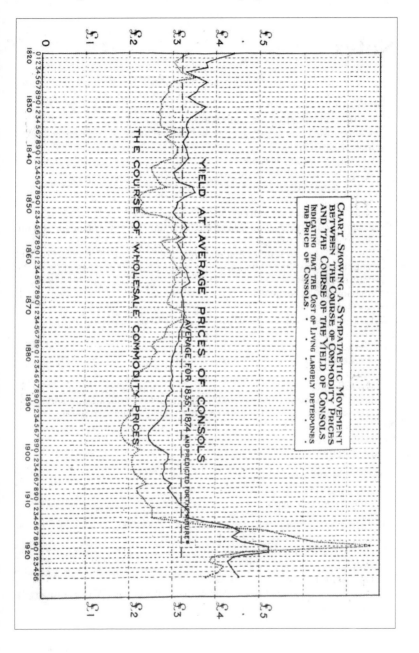

Notes

1 Suppositions and Truths

1 Smith (1776), Book One, Chapter One.
2 Schmandt-Besserat (1992).
3 Ifrah (1998), Chapter Five.
4 Hudson (2002), at page 23.
5 Wray (2004).
6 Arrian (c. 130 AD).
7 Stein (1912).
8 Fennel (1931) and Megrah (1945).
9 I thank Dr. John S. M. Botterill, an amateur numismatist for guidance on the history of British coinage.
10 The two papers of Alfred Mitchell Innes, published in 1913 and 1914, and republished in Wray (2004) are vital reading for an understanding of the nature of money.
11 Ingham (2004), pages 184-7.
12 Say (1803).
13 I am grateful to Gunnar Tómasson for this analysis.
14 Mills (2002).
15 Werner (2005).
16 Werner (2003).
17 Smith (1776).
18 Boswell (1785).
19 Rat (1964). See also Schama (1989), Chapter 3, for a brilliant summary of the effects the American Revolution had on the French financial system.
20 Smith (1776).
21 Glubb (1978).
22 Arnon (1991).

2 Modern Monetarism

1 Disraeli (1845).
2 Mills (1998), at page 34.

3 The Theory Of Monetarism

1 Walters (1977), at page 11.
2 Holloway (1986).
3 Holloway (1986), at page 45.
4 Quoted in Holloway (1986), at page 69.
5 Lacking the experience of working in the Bank of England, I have to rely on the statements of Professor Charles Goodhart (1989).

4 Credit Control By Interest Rates

1 For the standard theories see Kettel (1985).
2 Schumpeter(1986), at page 698.
3 Tooke (1844).
4 Skidelsky (1992), pages 36 et seq.
5 It was in 1920 that Keynes became Second Bursar of King's College, Cambridge, and in 1924 First Bursar. He had remarkable success with the College investments. See Harrod (1951) pp. 336, 352, 454–9.
6 How many computerised emulations (models) of the economy accord with Keynes' view? An error in this functional relationship might perhaps act like a Lorenz Attractor in any equation which included it and cause totally spurious results. Lorenz had only three equations in his original model of the weather system, yet a tiny difference in a figure altered his long-term results completely. Mathematical models of the economy contain hundreds of equations and therefore an infinite ability to produce errors. Surely an economy is almost as much a chaotic system as is the weather. Chaos theory must be applicable to all mathematical economics, and so-called *Butterfly Effects* must abound.
7 Barth and Ramey (2001).

5 Credit Control By Reserve Assets

1 Friedman (1991).
2 Kettel (1985).
3 The details of the legislation covering lending institutions were very complicated. Few bank officials knew them, and those who did were not senior directors but back-room advisers. My recollections of those details may not be fully accurate. I decided not to repeat the research I had to do in 1973–74 as it took a great deal of time, and the legislation is now of academic interest only.
4 I frequently saw the list of investments made by the treasury manager of Barclays Bank Trust Company Ltd during the period 1971–74.
5 The system of currency boards used in British Colonies seems to have had the effect of draining colonial capital to the London money market, and it was therefore essential for the colonies that the London market should recycle funds back to them. For a full explanation see *Do Currency Boards Have a Future?*, the twenty-second Harold Wincott Memorial Lecture given by Dr. Anna J. Schwarz in October 1992 and published by The Institute of Economic Affairs (ISBN 0-255 36312-5).
6 A week spent in discussion with Civil Service and Bank of England officials at the Civil Service College left me with an impression of unfocused prolixity and lack of professionalism. The Civil Service had a policy of discouraging its staff from studying for professional examinations (unlike the Armed Services, whose policy is exactly the opposite), as it relied on its own internal courses at the College. My impression was that the reliance was somewhat misplaced. Because I was then a member of the Council of the Institute of Chartered Secretaries and Administrators, an examining and qualifying body for high level executives, I may be accused of prejudice. My opinion was, however, shared by others with experience both inside and outside the Civil Service.
7 Day, A. C. L. (1957).

8   Wray (1998).
9   Schwarz (1992). At page 19.

7 Credit Control By Overfunding
1   Goodhart (1989), at page 232.

8 The Basel Capital Accord
1   For a detailed discussion of bank capital see *Bank Capital and Risk* by Bernard Wesson, Institute of Bankers, 1985, ISBN 0-85297-134-6. This is a very useful source book for information which illustrates our arguments, but it covers only the period 1976–83. Mr. Wesson's study, which was undertaken as the Centenary Research Fellow of the Institute, needs to be extended to cover the period from 1920 to the present.
2   Collins (1985).
3   Kapstein (1991).
4   Keynes (1930).
5   Kettel (1985), at page 69.
6   Goodhart (1989).
7   Goodhart (1984).
8   Llewellyn, Professor David (1992).
9   Werner (2002) at page 300.
10   Llewellyn, Professor David (1992).
11   Werner (2005).
12   Personal communication.

9 The Currency Principle
1   Ferguson (1998). At page 127. One wonders what the reaction of the Financial Services Authority would be if in 2005 N. M. Rothschild put all its capital into an undated gilt.
2   Malthus (1814).
3   My great-grand parents were among those who were eventually impoverished. They had to migrate from Crowle in Worcestershire to the industrial centre of Birmingham in the 1880s. They lived in Fazeley Street, one of the most densely populated areas.
4   Blake (1966), at page 231.
5   Disraeli (1845). *Sybil* was published in the same year in France and Germany.
6   Desmond and Moore (1991), at page 127.
7   Milner II, Clyde A., O'Connor, Carol A., Sandweiss, Martha A. eds. (1994).
8   Skidelsky (1992), page 36 et seq.
9   Smith (1776) Book II, Chapter II, at page 321 of Volume One of the University of Chicago 1976 edition.
10   Op. cit., at page 51.
11   Conversation with Dr. Christopher Walker.
12   I heard Sir Richard Hopkins lecture in Cambridge in 1947. He was impressive. Unknown to him he was the reason I was persuaded at school to study Classics not Natural Sciences. He was one of our 'old boys', and we were encouraged to follow his example.
13   The difference between the rewards to those in sheltered industries and those in industries exposed to foreign competition became enormous, as the following examples demonstrate. In the 1930s a bank clerk reached the top

scale for those without managerial responsibilities at age 31. The salary was £400 a year, with income tax paid by the bank, childrens' allowances, and a non-contributory pension of two thirds final salary. In 1936 The Birmingham Small Arms Company (BSA), then a producer of motor cycles, bicycles, cars &c., started producing guns again for the first time in 17 years, including the Browning machine gun with which the Spitfire was armed. In 1937 a company plan was prepared. One of its proposals was to set up a materials order department to control the purchase of materials for all its factories, probably about 28 in number and eventually employing 30,000 people. My father was appointed head of the department with a staff of 279. His basic pay was under £300 a year, and he received none of the extras the bank clerk got. His deputy earned £3.75 (£3. 15s. 0d.) a week.

14 Trade union shop stewards not only sought higher rewards for less output, but they also often prevented the better workers from getting their just rewards out of the piece-work system. When I studied for three months in the Cost Office of the Birmingham Small Arms Group, I saw at first hand the problems the unions caused. Yet the worker-management tensions in that Group were far from the worst in the country.

15 Personal communication.

16 It was Keynes' practice of demonstrating economic functions by algebraic equations which convinced Professor A. V. Hill, and other great scientists with a mathematical background, that economics was now a science. I pointed out to Hill that in the physical sciences one could deduce arithmetical constants to replace the algebraic symbols in the functions, but that in economics there are no demonstrable constants, and therefore no functions which are valid over time. The symbols in the functions can never be replaced by absolute values. Hill did not reply and after a brief silence changed the subject. Unfortunately I was not then aware of Hayek's similar criticism. Friedman's defensive attitude regarding economists' techniques also came to my notice much later.

10 Irving Fisher's Equation

1 The 1993 figure were collated by myself from bank balance sheets which I no longer have, so I cannot prove its reliability.

2 Laidler (1982).

3 Peacock (1976).
   The whole paragraph from which this quotation is taken, and the one which follows it, are a savage attack on the remoteness of young researchers from reality, even though Peacock prefaces his remarks with the words, *'I do not wish to promote knocking copy for those who would jeer at the developments...'*

11 The Unintended Consequences of Taxes

1 The inability of the general public to understand inflation was shared at the highest intellectual levels. The philosopher Bertrand Russell, perhaps the cleverest man of his era, sold a house in Cambridge for the same nominal price as he had paid for it, because his socialist principles forbade him to make a profit. But in real terms he was certainly making a loss. The purchaser, who had no intellectual pretensions, was delighted with the bargain and 25 years later told me the story with great glee. Trying to persuade holders of large cash

balances to invest in a way which might hedge against inflation was a frustrating task. They included close relatives, as well as friends and clients.

2   Comments made here on taxation are based on direct experience of the principles and practice of tax planning.

Many taxes at that time were introduced as political window-dressing, and legal loopholes were provided to avoid wrecking the economy completely. Many businessmen were uneasy about using loopholes; they were less cynical than the politicians. Eventually the Judicial Committee of the House of Lords refused to play along with the politicians' devious game, and schemes whose sole purpose was tax avoidance were declared void.

Would-be tax-avoiders were frequently deceived by fraudulent advisers.

12 Savings, Investment And Debt

1   As it is a case study I have used in another book, *The Credit and State Theories of Money*, I repeat what I wrote there, with the permission of the publisher, Edward Elgar Publishing Ltd.

2   Gilbert (1965).

3   Figures given by John C. Bogle in an article in the Wall Street Journal of October 3rd, 2995, page A16.

13 Eruptions of Credit

1   See Llewellyn (1992).

Chapter 14: Planning or the Market

1   The market economy does not always obey the economists' rules of behaviour for economic man. For instance, when food prices fall, small farmers try to increase production, often in a vain attempt to get the income needed to service their debts. This is not the response which market economists predict.

2   In June 1967 a member of an investment committee in Cambridge on which Professor James Meade served told me they had moved heavily into gold, gold related shares and dollar stocks. Other Cambridge committees almost certainly did the same.

3   I understand it was Karl Marx who stated that the purpose of an entrepreneur was to maximise his profit. I thank Christopher Meakin for the corresponding comment about bureaucrats.

4   Financial services, such as pensions and life assurance, involve the customer in taking decisions which will mature up to forty years later. The customer can take a decision only on an act of faith. The sole comfort is that the government will supervise properly the providers of the services so that a fair deal is given. Unfortunately the state failed those whom it encouraged to take out private pensions, and it ignored the growing pressure put by mortgagees upon house buyers to use endowment mortgages in a way which was risky.

15 Creditary Economics

1   Van De Mieroop (2002), at page 63.

2   In 1974 I instigated a project study by Barclays Bank, the purpose of which was to see if we could set up a British form of Loan Trusts, the main product of Japanese Trust Banks. We were defeated by two technical factors. Firstly, the fact that a unit trust of loans, which is what a loan trust is, was liable to Corporation Tax and could not therefore compete with Building Society

deposits, which had a very light tax regime. Secondly, why should investors tie up their funds for five years when the Building Societies were allowed to take what was effectively call money and lend it for 25 years?

3 Communication from a diplomatic source.

Bibliography

Arnon, Arie (1991), *Thomas Tooke*, Michigan, University of Michigan Press.

Arrian, (c. 140 AD), *The Campaigns of Alexander*, translated Aubrey de Sélincourt, London, Penguin Books.

Bank of England (1984), *Panel Paper 23*, London, Bank of England.

Barth III, Martin J. and Ramey, Valerie (2001), *The Cost Channel of Monetary Transmission*, Washington, Federal Reserve Board.

Blake, Robert (1966), *Disraeli*, London, Methuen.

Blunt, Gordon (2004),*Credit and Savings in the UK: a More Indebted Society?*, Manchester, The Statistical Society of Manchester.

Boswell, James (1785) *The Journal of a Tour to the Hebrides with Samuel Johnson*, London, Dent (1909).

Brittan, Samuel (1981), *How to End the Monetarist Controversy*, Hobart Paper 90, London, Institute of Economic Affairs.

Confederation of British Industry (1985), *Tax – time for change*, London, CBI.

Collins, Michael (1988), *Money and Banking in the UK: A History*, London, Beckenham Croome Helm.

Day, A. C. L. (1957), *Outline of Monetary Economics*, Oxford, Clarendon Press.

Desmond, Adrian and Moore, James (1991), *Darwin*, London, Penguin Books.

Disraeli, Benjamin (Lord Beaconsfield) (1845), *Sybil: Or The Two Nations*, London, Henry Colburn. (Many editions since, including Oxford University Press: World Classics.)

Douglas, Major Clifford H. Douglas (1931), *Warning Democracy: Addresses and Articles, 1920-1931*, London, C. M. Grieve.

Fennel, Cecil H. H. (1931), *A Practical Examination of the Bills of Exchange Acts*, London, Pitman.

Ferguson, Niall (1998), *The World's Banker*, London, Weidenfeld and Nicholson.

Flemming, Johns S. and Little, I. M. D. (1974), *Why We Need a Wealth Tax*, London, Methuen & Co Ltd.

Friedman, Milton (1991), *Monetarist Economics*, Basil Blackwell.

Gesell, Silvio, (1916), *Die Natürliche Wirtshaftsordnung durch Freiland und Freigeld*, Bern and Berlin.

Gibson, A. H. (1923), 'The Future Course of High-Class Investment Values', pages 15–34 in Vol. CXV January 1923 of *The Bankers' Magazine*, London.

Gibson, A. H. (1926), 'The Road To Economic Recovery', pages 595–612 in November 1926 issue of *The Bankers Magazine*, London.

Gilbert, K. R. (1965),*The Portsmouth Blockmaking Machinery*, London, HMSO.

Glubb, John (1978), *A Short History of the Arab Peoples*, London, Quartet Books Ltd (Namara Group).

Goodhart, Charles A. E. (1989) *Money, Information and Uncertainty*, Basingstoke, Macmillan (1975).

Goodhart, Charles A. E. (1984), *Monetary Theory and Practice,* Basingstoke, Macmillan (1975).

Grayling, Christopher (1987), *A Land Fit for Heroes,* London, Buchan and Enright.

Harrod, Sir Henry Roy Forbes (1958), *Policy Against Inflation,* London, Macmillan.

Harrod, Sir Henry Roy Forbes (1951), *John Maynard Keynes,* London, Macmillan. (In the opinion of Professor A. V. Hill, Keynes' brother-in-law, this was *'a very bad book'.*)

Hayek, F. A. (1944), *The Road to Serfdom,* Abingdon, Routledge.

Holloway, Edward (1986), *Money Matters,* London, Sherwood Press.

Hudson, Michael, *Trade Development and Foreign Debt,* London, Pluto Press.

Hudson, Michael (2002), 'Reconstructing the Origins of Interest-Bearing Debt and the Logic of Clean Slates', in *Debt and Economic Renewal in the Ancient Near East,* edited Michael Hudson and Marc Van De Mieroop, Bethesda, Maryland, USA, CDI.

Ifrah, George (1998), *The Universal History of Number,* English edition, London, Harvill Press (1994).

Ingham, Geoffrey *Nature of Money,* Oxford, Polity/Blackwells.

Innes, A. Mitchell (1913), 'The Nature of Money,' in *The Credit and State Theories of Money,* ed. L. Randall Wray, Cheltenham, Edward Elgar (2004).

Innes, A. Mitchell (1913), 'The Credit Theory of Money,' in *The Credit and State Theories of Money,* ed. L. Randall Wray, Cheltenham, Edward Elgar (2004).

Kapstein, Ethan B. (1991), *Supervising International Banks: Origins and Implications of the Basle Accord,* Princeton NJ, USA, Department of Economics, Princeton University.

Kettel, B. (1985), *Monetary Economics,* London, Graham and Trotman.

Keynes, John Maynard (1930), *The Treatise on Money,* London, Macmillan.

Keynes, John Maynard (1935), *The General Theory of Employment, Interest and Money,* London, Macmillan.

Knapp, Georg Friedrich (1924), translation from German edition of 1905), *The State Theory of Money,* Clifton, Augustus M. Kelley (1973).

Laidler, David, (1982), *Monetarist Perspectives,* Oxford, Philip Allan.

Locke, John (1691), *Considerations of the Consequences of the Lowering of Interest and the Raising the Value of Money,* London, Awnsham and John Churchill.

Macmillan, Lord (1931) *Report on the Committee of Finance and Industry,* [Macmillan Committee], Cmd 2897, 1931. Minutes of Evidence, Two Vols. The Treasury.

Malthus, Professor the Reverend Thomas R. (1814), *The Corn Laws,* London, J. Johnson and Co.

Megrah, Maurice (1945), *The Bills of Exchange Act 1882,* London, Pitman.

Mills, John (1998), *Europe's Economic Dilemma,* Basingstoke, Macmillan.

Mills, John (2002), *A Critical History of Economics,* Basingstoke, UK, and New York, USA, Palgrave.

Milner II, Clyde A., O'Connor, Carol A., Sandweiss, Martha A. eds. (1994), *The Oxford history of the American West,* Oxford, Oxford University Press.

Peacock, Professor Alan, (1976) *Seventh Wincott Memorial Lecture,* Occasional Paper 50, London, Institute of Economic Affairs.

Radcliffe, Lord (1959), *Report of the Committee on the Working of the Monetary System,* CMND 827, London, HMSO.

Rat, Maurice (1964), *Théatre de Beaumarchais,* Paris, Garnier.

Say, Jean Baptiste (1803), *Traité d'économie politique*, Paris. Also an English edition, Boston, C. R. Prinsep, 1821.

Schama, Professor Simon (1989), *Citizens*, London, Penguin Books.

Schmand-Bessarat, Denise, *Before Writing, from Counting to Cuneiform*, Volume One, University of Texas Press, 1992.

Schumpeter, Joseph A. (1986), *History of Economic Analysis*, London, Routledge, (Allen and Unwin 1954).

Schwarz, Anna J. (1992), *Monetarism and Monetary Policy*, Institute of Economic Affairs, Occasional Paper 86.

Selgin, Professor George (2003), *Good Money*, Draft book on web site http://www.terry.uga.edu/people/selgin/

Skidelsky, Robert (1992), *John Maynard Keynes*, Vol. 2, London, Macmillan.

Smith, Adam (1976) *The Wealth of Nations*, edited Edwin Cannan, Chicago, University of Chicago Press (1776).

Stein, M. Aurel (1912), *Ruins of Desert Cathay*, London, Macmillan. Reprinted by Asian Educational Services, New Delhi (1996).

Tooke, Henry (1844), *An Enquiry Into the Currency Principle*, London, Longman, Brown, Green, and Longmans.

Van De Mieroop, Marc (2002), 'A History of Near Eastern Debt', in *Debt and Economic Renewal in the Ancient Near East*, edited Michael Hudson and Marc Van De Mieroop, Bethesda, Maryland, CDI.

Walters, Sir Alan (1975), 'In Thrall to Creditors', in *Crisis 75*, London, Institute of Economic Affairs.

Walters, Sir Alan (1969), *Money in Boom and Slump*, London, Institute of Economic Affairs.

Walters, Sir Alan (1977), *Eighth Wincott Memorial Lecture, Occasional Paper 54*, London, Institute of Economic Affairs.

Werner, Richard A. (2005), *New Paradigm in Macro-Economics*, Basingstoke, UK, and New York, USA, Palgrave Macmillan.

Werner, Richard A. (2003), *Princes of the Yen*, Armonk, NY, USA, and London, UK, M. E. Sharpe.

Wesson, Bernard (1985), *Bank Capital and Risk*, London, Institute of Bankers.

Wray, L. Randall (1998), *Understanding Modern Money*, Edward Elgar, Cheltenham, England and Northampton MA, USA.

Index

Abbey National Bank 75
Acceptance Houses 23
Acceptances 23
Accounting
  accounting for inflation 26, 69, 160
  current cost accounting 68
  historic cost accounting 26, 66
Aggregate demand function for credit
  153
Agriculture 32
  antiquity of its problems 222
  economic policy toward 31
  effect of gold standard on 115
  low point of British farming 118
Alternative Investment Market 169
Althorp Committee of 1832 51
American Monetary Institute 11
American Revolution
  caused by Currency Act 1764 14
Anti-Corn Law League
  lies of 116
Arestis, Professor Philip xi
Aristotle 1-2, 10, 20, 22
Asset price inflation 67, 78, 156-157,
  199, 201
  leads to general inflation 157-158
Babylonia xii, 6, 21
Bank of England 5, 18, 20, 22, 26,
  39-40, 42-46, 50-51, 54-58, 61,
  69-70, 72-74, 79-80, 83, 87-90, 94,
  102, 104, 106, 115, 119-122, 125,
  158, 165, 186, 203, 245, 247-248,
  266
  Banking Department of 88
  gold holdings in 1830s 123
  Issue Department of 88, 224
  its caution 103
Bank Rate 53, 124, 133-135, 165, 196
  lowest practical level 128
Bankers Law Journal of New York 13

Banks
  See Capital base of banks
Barclays Bank 20, 26-27, 44, 66, 77, 82,
  107, 109, 195-197, 204
  buys back its shares 97
  gilt holdings 99
  rights issue by 104
Barter, limited usefulness 1
Barth, Marvin J. Barth III 61
Base rates 30, 46, 195
Basel Capital Accord 11, 96, 100, 102,
  104, 204, 220
  has pro-cyclical effect 110
Basel Capital Accord Mark II
  complexity of 111
Beaumarchais (Pierre-Augustin Caron)
  16
Bevin, Ernest
  reason for calling General Strike 125
Bills of exchange 6, 14, 18-19, 21, 39,
  42, 57, 81, 90, 121-122, 243-249
  business of Bank of England 103
  fall in discount rate on 99
  replace gold and silver 223
  use as popular currency killed by
    taxation 122
Black economy
  uses M0 151
Blair, Tony 29
Borrowing
  encouraged by tax system 162
Borrowing (Control and Guarantees)
  Act 1946 67, 226
Boswell, James 15
Bottomley, Horatio
  a swindler's example 132
Boulton, Matthew 7
Brash, Dr. Don 61, 112
Bretton Woods 123
British National Plan 215

British State Pension 194
Brittan, Sir Samuel 46
Brown, Gordon 29
Brunel, Marc I. 185-186
Buccleugh, Duke of 15
  owner of copper mine 16
Building Societies 192
  reserves of 202
Building Societies Association 45
Bundesbank, central bank of German
  Federal Republic 87
Buy-outs 198
Calendrical systems
  purpose of 3
Callaghan, James 160, 162, 165-166,
  169
Capital
  equity capital 32
  meaning of 178-179
Capital adequacy ratio 11, 67-68,
  95-96, 102, 106, 119, 134, 173, 199,
  203-204
  a weapon of control 112
  level of 103
  of Japanese banks 96
  of National Westminster Bank 108
  re derivatives trading 111
  rise of in 1990s 97
  tier one 96
  varying ratio a method of control
  221
  views of Goodhart 106
Capital base of banks 10, 26, 38, 65,
  68, 91, 95, 101-102, 106, 119, 152,
  195, 197, 201, 203-204, 224
  components of 96
  history of 97
  importance of 220
  lack of growth in 134
  of Japanese banks 102
  profitability of 96
  tier one 102
  tier two 102
Capital Gains Tax 157, 165, 167, 169,
  189
  adjustment for inflation 169
  anaemic form of 166
  effects on investment 227
  often less than income tax rate 172

Capital Issues Committee 67
Capital markets
  non-intermediated 83
  primary and secondary 177
Capital taxation 182
  dire effects of 137
Capitalism
  popular capitalism 191
Case tablet 5
Central bank 31, 38, 42, 44, 46, 52,
  71-72, 80, 82, 88, 94
  can it control HPM? 72
  independence of 87
Christian Council for Monetary Justice
  11
Churchill, Winston xiii, 135
  abject confession 131
  as Chancellor of Exchequer 123
Clean slates
  City of Lagash 222
  for indebted countries 232
Coinage 4
Collins, Michael 43, 104
Competition
  trade unions fear 211
Confederation of British Industry
  32-33, 181, 266
Conservative Government
  post-1979 217
Conservative Party 29, 218
The Continental Currency, of United
  States of America 16
Control (Borrowing and Guarantees)
  Act 1946 75
Controls on credit vii
Corn Laws 31, 115-117
  effect at home of repeal 117
  effects abroad of repeal 116
Corporation Tax 11, 65, 68, 70, 160,
  162, 164, 198, 215
  alleged to be a more modern tax 160
  influence of 165
  interest allowed in respect of 69
  lowered share values 168
  still causes damage 172
Cost Channel of Monetary
  Transmission 61
Cowrie shells 4
Credit

control of bank credit 11
credit control 26, 59, 73-74, 76, 141, 228
  bank losses 68
credit control by overfunding 94
credit multiplier 188
credit supply 12, 38, 40, 48, 54, 59, 71, 84, 95, 135, 182, 201
  Bank of England loans are part of 90
credit supply in 1922-5 119
credit system 8
demand for 49
final credit inflation 181
formal theory of 222
guidelines for 226
intermediated credit supply 10
new credit creation has a multiplier effect 188
state control of credit creation level 218
Credit card
  prehistoric 3
Credit supply
  classifying 224
  control of 8
  control of the whole 225
  disaggregating the intermediated supply 156
  intermediated 151
  what happens when limited 72
Credit systems vii
Credit Theory of Money 13, 19
Creditary Economics xii, 157
  for Less Developed Countries 231
  to replace monetary economics 225
Creditary structures vii
Crime
  raises M0 151
Cripps, Francis 26
Crisis 75 161
Culpeper, Sir Thomas 50
Currency
  debasement of 114
Currency Act of 1764 14
Current cost accounting 68
Cycle of boom and recession 41
Dai-Ichi Kangyo Bank 199
  capital adequacy ratio of 108

Debt
  accounting for debts 3
  state debt redeemed by taxation 19
Debt overhang 154
Debtors
  their aim 114
Defaults
  by governments 7
Deflation 56, 58, 130, 133, 141, 163, 181
  aim of monetarism 114
  cause of recession 115
  in 1920s 118
  is the norm 221
  makes debts harder to repay 132
  not understood 116
  of import prices 173
  self-perpetuating 128
  the enemy of the farmer 222
Deflationary spiral
  how created 188
Derivatives trading 111
Devaluation
  a consequence of inflation, not a cause of 161
  in 1967 215
Discount Houses 43, 82
Discount rate 51, 55, 125
  See Also Bank Rate
Domestic inflation
  negated by low import prices 158
Double-entry bookkeeping 39-41, 234
Douglas, Major C. H. 128-129, 180-181, 229
The Economic Consequences of Mr. Churchill, by J. M. Keynes xiii, 123, 130-131
Economic modelling
  dangers of 231
Economic Research Council 37
Economic treason 113
Economics
  Creditary Economics 13
  market economics 12
Economies of scale
  best in secondary industry 117
Economy
  planned 25
Egibi Archive 21

Elizabeth I, Queen
   debts of 115
Empiricism, the need for 150
Endogenous money 83
Engledow, Professor Sir Frank 27
Equities
   banks' investment in 107
Equity boom 193
Equity capital 32
Equity swapped for loan capital 203
European Central Bank 113
European Monetary System 123
Euro-system 113
   central banks 113
   reserves of 113
Evolution of creditary structures,
   sources for vii
Exchange
   system of 1
Exchange Rate Mechanism 112, 123,
   125
Exchange rates
   false 230, 233
Exogenous money 83
Expenditure Tax 174, 189
Federal Reserve Bank 5, 64, 72, 86-87,
   104
Financial services xi, 1, 77
   reaction to market forces 217
Financial Services Authority 44, 46,
   86-87, 149, 170
Fisher, Professor Irving 142
   Fisher's Equation 155-156
Fisher, Professor Malcolm 28
Fisher, Professor Sir R. A.
   abuse of his statistical techniques
   228
Foreign exchange 52
Foreign investment 183
Foreign loans 68
Fractional Reserve Banking 86
Franklin, Benjamin 14
Free market 3
   blind to pollution 212
Free market economy 210
Free trade 117
Frequency of circulation 75, 79, 84,
   95, 119, 129, 144, 156
   can it be a constant? 145

is it regular? 150
Friedman, Professor Milton 12, 30, 71,
   79, 84, 141, 145, 150
Friedman-Schwarz theory collapses
   148
Fringe banks 75-77, 79
Futures trading
   is gambling 110
*The General Theory of Employment,
   Interest and Money,* by J. M. Keynes
   174-175, 178
German Federal Republic 87
Germany 13, 25, 30, 46, 131
   level of home ownership 65
Gesell, Silvio 128, 229
Gibson, A. H. 57-59, 92
   prophecy by 134
Gilts 132
Gold
   bills of exchange made its use
      unnecessary 223
   mythological power of 120
Gold standard 122
   1925 version 123
   abandoned in 1797 115
   not the base of the credit system
      123
   restored in 1821 115
   restored in 1925 120
Goodenough, F. Roger 27
Goodhart, Professor Charles 43, 79,
   81, 98-99, 106, 145, 230
Goodhart's Law 145-146
Government Actuary 191
Governor of the Bank of England
   paper by in 1975 106
Greeks, Ancient 1, 4-5
The Greenbacker Movement 11, 18
Gresham, Sir Thomas
   achieves deflation 114
Gresham's Law 115
Gross Domestic Product 9, 25, 143
   of USA 17
Gross National Product 49, 141, 146
   a function of M 144
Harrod, Sir Roy 128
Hayek, Friedrich von 219
High Power Money 44, 71-72, 81
Highland Clearances 15

Hill, Professor A. V. 138, 140
Holloway, Edward 37
Hopkins, Sir Richard 125
House price inflation 93
Howe, Sir Geoffrey 28-29, 31, 35, 46, 49, 56
Hudson, Professor Michael vii, xi-xii, 22, 117
Hyper-inflation
   in Germany in 1923 120
Income
   meaning of 179
Income tax
   high rates of tax 137
Incomes policy 27
Index tracking
   should be banned 170
Inflation 35, 58, 173
   asset price inflation 78
   can be a function of taxation 159
   easy way out 133
   final demand inflation 11
   from 1940 to 1945 135
   the debtor's friend 228
Inflation accounting xi, 26
   See Also Accounting
Ingham, Dr. Geoffrey xii, 8
Inheritance Tax
   AIM stocks exempt 169
   effects on investment 227
Innes, Alfred Mitchell xii, 4, 7, 13, 19, 22
Institute for the Study of Long-term Economic Trends 12
Institute of Chartered Secretaries and Administrators xi
Institute of Economic Affairs 46, 84, 105, 141, 148, 150, 154, 161, 266
Institute of Fiscal Studies x
Interest rates
   effects of high interest rates 62
   effects of ultra-low rates 133
   formalised 45
   from 1940 to 1945 58
   real rates 69
Intermediated credit supply 100, 135
International Monetary Fund 30, 126, 140, 229

International Scholars Conference on Ancient Near Eastern Economies 12
Investment
   investment multiplier 183-184
Investment structures 189
Italy 25
Japan 13, 55, 138, 204
   effect of Basel Accord on 106
Japanese banking crisis 109, 111
Japanese Real Estate Institute 109
Johnson, Dr. Samuel 15
Kahn, Richard 184-185, 187-188
Kaldor, Professor Nicholas x, 162
Kaletsky, Anatole 67
Kelvin, Lord 139
Kettel, Brian 72, 105
Keynes, J. M. x-xi, xiii, 12, 56-59, 64, 78, 105, 118-119, 122-123, 126-127, 130-131, 135, 138, 140-141, 174-179, 181, 183-184, 196, 204, 221, 226, 230
Keynesian establishment 140
Keynesianism 85
Knapp, G. F. 13
   proposer of The State Theory of Money 13
Labour
   differentiation of 1
Labour Government 25, 29, 87, 169, 198, 215
   New Labour 217
Labour Party 66, 88, 93, 184, 208
   old-fashioned attitudes 33
Laidler, Professor David 151-152
Law vii
Lawson, Nigel 68, 169, 196, 202
Leasing
   tax problems with 68
Legal systems
   effect of vii
Less Developed Countries
   their needs 231
Life assurance 168, 171, 190-193
Llewellyn, Professor David
   on the Basel Capital Accord 106
Lloyds Bank 44, 95
   once had uncalled liability on shares 104

Loans
  to stock market speculators 75
Local Exchange Trading Schemes 8-9
Locke, John 51
London Money Market 76
Loyalty bonus
  anti-competitive ploy 212
M0 134, 143, 147, 150-151, 197, 224
M3 72, 75, 79-80, 134, 145, 150-151,
  196-197
M4 40, 49, 79-80, 143, 195, 204,
  224-225
M5 80, 224
MacDonald, Sir Alexander 15
Macmillan Committee 78, 125
Malthus, Professor The Reverend
  Thomas
  comment on Corn Laws 115
Market economics 15, 31
  must be exceptions to rules 222
Market economy 3, 24, 84-85, 234
  has no foresight 212
  in food 230
  rationale of 211
  virtues and faults of 211
Marx, Karl 129, 229
Mathematics
  use of 140
Maudslay, Henry 187
Maynard, Professor Geoffrey 26
Meade, Professor James x, 28, 141, 164,
  181
Meakin, Christopher xi-xii, 19
Means of exchange 4-5, 122
Mercantilism 229
Mesolithic Age 2
Mesopotamia 3-4
Metallic currencies
  make debt portable 223
Mina
  ancient weight 4
Minimum Lending Rate 46, 195-196
Mixed economy 210
  virtues of 217
Models, economic 153
The Monetary Consensus 208
Monetarism 7-8, 12, 27, 29, 141, 151
  causes unemployment 41
  not just a modern theory 114

Monetary policy
  targeted by Harold Wincott 140
Monetary Policy Committee 61, 208
Monetary reformers
  their mistakes 37
Monetary theorists 86, 201
Monetary theory xi, 28, 38, 57, 135
  books on by Charles Goodhart 106
  defects in 35
  erroneous 59
  fundamental error in 196
  its underlying problem 154
  orthodox 62
  requirements of a true theory 150
  should study credit supply not
    money 221
Monetary Theory and Practice, by
  Professor Charles Goodhart 80
Money
  creation process 37
  definition of 8
  is debt 36
  is negotiable debt 222
  the credit theory of money 19
  two kinds of 220
Money and Banking in the UK: A History,
  by Michael Collins 43, 103
Money market 42-43, 72, 82, 154, 202
Money supply
  diminished by vertical integration
    149
  disaggregating 156
  measures of 80
  multiplier effect on 100
Monnaie faible 13-14
Monnaie forte 13
Monopoly
  of Bank of England 103
Mortgages
  endowment mortgages 147, 192-193
  high cost of servicing 62
  risk-weighting of 102
  subscription mortgages 147
Mortgagors 63
  many dispossessed 204
Multiplier effect 187, 201
  credit multiplier 38
  from investment 11
  investment multiplier 184

of bank reserves 86
of new lending 220
when is there one? 185
National Plan 215
National Savings 80, 132
National Westminster Bank 79, 108, 199
Nazism 13
Nestle v. National Westminster Bank 1984
important law case 163
Net interest margin
of Lloyds Bank 95
New Paradigm in Macroeconomics by Richard A. Werner 156
New Zealand, Reserve Bank of
remit on inflation 112
Newton, Sir Isaac
sets a value on gold 120
Overfunding 30, 94, 96, 98-99
Palmer, J. Horsley 51-53, 55
Palmer's Rule 56
Paper currencies 16
Parys Mountain Company 7-8
Pay claims
effect of 136
Peacock, Professor Alan 154
Pension funds 167, 171, 191
German 107
overfunding 171
Ponzi effect of 189
viability of 190
Personal sector
net seller of company securities 200
Pink Book, the 232
Planned economy 25, 138, 210
faults of 214
notorious for shortages 214
requirements for success 214
six propositions about 216
Planning 138, 212
bad planning the norm 139
planning system 34
state planning 25
will fail 211
Planning permission 34
Ponzi scams 189
Portfolio investment 178, 189
Post-Keynesians 136

Powell, J. Enoch 26-27, 141
Precious metals 17
use of 5
Princes of the Yen by Richard A. Werner 156
Productive investment
promotion of 181
Profit planning by banks 95
Profits
pay pensions 191
Propensity to borrow 50
Protection of Depositors Act 1963 73
Radcliffe Report 39, 72, 267
Ramey, Valerie A. 61
Real capital formation 176, 178
Recession 181, 188
caused by repaying borrowing 206, 220
Regulation Q 64
Regulators
of financial services 171
Religion
affects creditary structures vii
Repos 18, 42, 90
Reserve assets 60, 71, 73-74, 79, 86, 119
movements in 81
Reserve Bank of New Zealand 61
Retail Prices Index 49
Ricardo, David
opposition to revaluation 115
Risk-weighting 95-96
of government debt 100
Roosevelt, Franklin D.
devalues US dollar 130
Russia
its success 233
Sandilands Report on Accounting for Inflation xi
Savings 47, 143, 175, 177, 179, 184, 186, 190
banks as savings institutions 202
definition of 177
does not always finance real investment 174
illusions about 190
in Japan 107
savings industry 203
structures for 188
Savings and Loan Associations 64

Say, Jean Baptiste 9
  Say's Law 9, 180
Schacht, Hjalmar H. G. 131
Schmandt-Bessarat, Professor Denise 3
Schumpeter, Joseph A. 52, 56
Schwarz, Dr. Anna J. 85, 145
Seigniorage 121
Seleucids, 5
Selgin, Professor George 2
Sharp, Sir Bernard 77
Shekel
  ancient weight 4
Sheltered industries 130
Silver 4-6, 20
Silversmiths 22
Small business
  relationship with banks 207
Smith, Adam 2, 6, 13-16, 19, 25, 121, 211
  coinage versus bullion 121
Social Credit 128
Socialism 218
  the great experiment 137
Special Deposits 73-74, 76, 88-90, 93
  a cause of inflation? 92
  avoidance tactics 89
  supplementary special deposits 91
Specialisation 2
Speculation
  virtue of 166
The State Theory of Money 13, 19
Stagflation 93
  aetiology of 127
Standard Life Assurance 171
Statistical techniques
  validity questioned 146
Stock Market 45, 84, 167, 170, 193, 202
  1929 crash 190
  not a source of long-term loans to small businesses 164
Take-overs 198
Tamkarum (Babylonian merchant) 6
Tax avoidance 166
Tax havens 232
Taxation 186
  local 32
Taxes
  effect of Japanese taxes 110
Thatcher, Margaret 28

  ideology of her government 218
Thatcherism 25
The Treasury
  Sir Richard Hopkins as head 125
Tokens 3-4, 6, 8
  all coins are 19
Tolpuddle Martyrs
  cause of their grief 115
Tooke, Henry 56
  An Inquiry into the Currency Principle 122
Towards True Monetarism xii
Towards True Monetarism, by G. W. Gardiner xii
Townshend, Charles 14
Trade credit
  no control of 84
Trade cycle 206
  caused by varying credit supply 221
  ironing out 228
Trade deficit
  creates employment 184
  of United Kingdom 232
  of United States 233
Trade union 24-25
  attitudes cause unemployment 126
  Post-war power of 136
Trade unions 28, 85
  demand too much 41
  militancy 125
Trades Union Congress
  seeks more capital taxation 182
  wants foreign investment repatriated 184
Treasuries
  US government stocks 132
The Treasury 39, 58, 79
Treasury Bills 30, 39, 42-43, 71-72, 80, 122
The Treatise on Money, by J. M. Keynes 58-59, 105, 127, 135, 138, 174, 176, 221
Trust banks
  needed in Britain 227
Trust Banks, Japanese 107
Underfunding
  what effect? 99
Unemployment
  caused by monetarism 27

United Kingdom
  general election 24
  local taxation in 33
  UK lending 204
United States 17-18, 28, 43-44, 46, 87
  debts of 17
  local taxation in 33
  trade deficit 127
United States Federal Reserve Board
  105
United States Government
  attitude to risk-weighting 105
United States Social Security Scheme
  193
Unplanned economy
  not the same as a market economy
  211
Usury
  concealing 21
  condemned by religions 155

Usury Laws 51
Value Added Tax 157
Velocity of circulation 142
Walters, Professor Sir Alan 26, 36, 145,
  148, 161
Washington, George
  economic consequences of 17
The Wealth of Nations, by Adam Smith
  2, 14, 211
Wealth
  disparity of 213
  distribution of 204
  switch from young to old 205
Wealth Tax 182
Werner, Professor Richard A. 156
Wilson Committee 66
Wincott Foundation 141
Wincott Memorial Lecture 36, 154
Wincott, Harold 26, 67, 140
Wray, Professor L. Randall xi, 82, 86